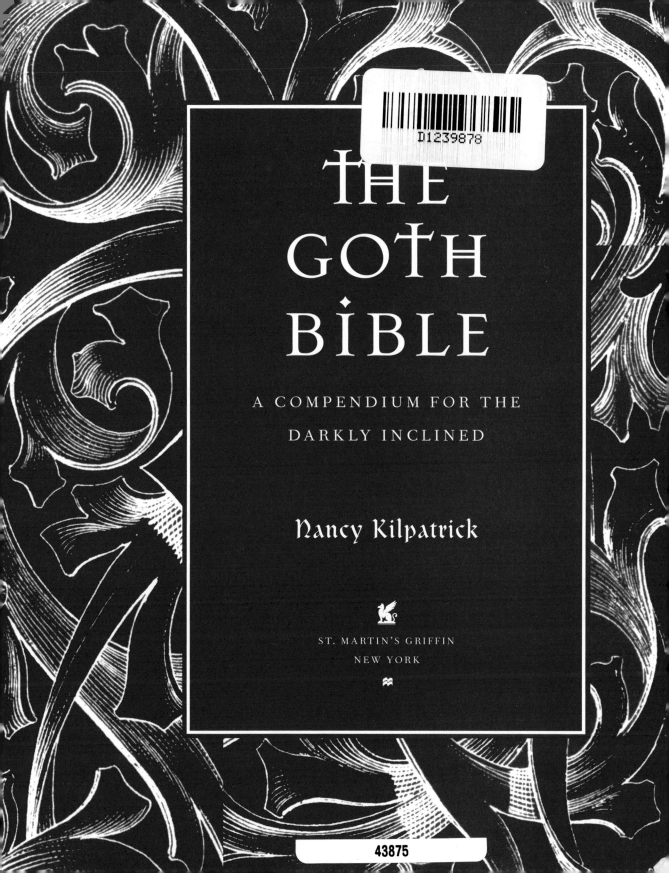

THE
GOTH
BIBLE

A COMPENDIUM FOR THE
DARKLY INCLINED

Nancy Kilpatrick

ST. MARTIN'S GRIFFIN
NEW YORK

www.stmartins.com

Book design by Michelle McMillian

Photographs on pages xx, 10, 28, 44, 76, 100, 120, 132, 156, 178, 206, 238, and 262 are courtesy of Fred Berger

ISBN 0-312-30696-2
EAN 978-0312-30696-0

First Edition: October 2004

10 9 8 7 6 5 4 3 2 1

THE
GOTH
BIBLE

This book is dedicated to
every goth roving the planet,
and to everyone who respects darkness.
Know this: your existence is precious.
The darkness you love loves you back.
Your value has and always will lie
in the courage of your being.

Contents

11. Subscribing to the Dark Arts *207*

Art of the gothic ✦ Languid literature ✦ Modern gothic writers on their art ✦
Bards ✦ Piercing periodicals ✦ Exquisite art ✦ The Pre-Raphaelites
✦ Modern gothic art ✦ TV with bite ✦ Sinister cinema ✦
High- and lowbrow art

12. The Preternatural is Calling *239*

Psychic phenomenon ✦ Dracula and friends ✦ Vampires unlimited ✦
The blood countess ✦ La comtesse du sang de France ✦ Peter Kürsten,
the vampire of Düsseldorf ✦ The Vampire of Foster, Rhode Island ✦
Frankenstein, or the modern Prometheus ✦ Lycanthrophy ✦ Ghouls
✦ Zombies ✦ Tools of the supernatural trade ✦ Talking boards

13. Esoterica *263*

Nourishing the wounded soul ✦ Remembering the Inquisition ✦
A relationship with the Grim Reaper

The X chapter: future tense *271*

Acknowledgments

A book of this magnitude is not possible without the help, love, encouragement, and generosity of a great number of people, some friends, others former strangers. I doubt I could mention one name without mentioning all—which would be a huge list—so I'll generally be vague, but you know who you are! Those without specific mention in this book, and who have no URL of their own, or people who have contributed information and help to an extraordinary degree are: Julie Bradford, editor of *All About Beer* magazine; Benjamin Bagby of *Sequentia;* Fred H. Berger of *Propaganda* magazine; Arsenio Giron; Michael Marchant; Mick Mercer; Marty Riccardo; and Pee Wee Vignold of *Sonic Seducer* magazine.

Those I am close to in my life cut me quite a bit of slack over the nine months of researching and writing this manuscript, and the additional months of revising it. As is my style, I often overworked and was preoccupied, making me not the best friend I might have been, but you understood. The one who suffered most is *mon compagnon,* whose love, understanding, and patience I greatly value, and who makes my life better. All my friends came through with suggestions and ideas that helped create what I hope is a unique look at the goth culture. Thanks for the loving and realistic input!

I interviewed a number of well-knowns for this volume, from a variety of fields—music, writing, photography, film, and those with businesses that cater in some way to goths. I certainly appreciate the time that each of you took away from your passion to respond so thoroughly to my questions. I regret that the lack of space and the limitation of time kept me from including many other individuals, groups, and companies that make a difference to the goth world.

The ninety-five not-famous goths I interviewed were the kindest and most giving of beings, opening their hearts and revealing their thoughts. Your responses gave me the courage to use the g word. I couldn't have done this without you. The nature of this book is such that selections must be made about the content, which means I was not able to include more of your fascinating comments. To that end, I've set up a Web site accessible from my home page, where you all get to say more, in detail. I did this because I felt your views deserve to be heard, and should not have ended up on the cutting room floor.

I must especially thank Lori Perkins, who asked me if I would write this book. Brad Wood, my original editor at St. Martin's Press, who "got it" right from the start and was savvy enough to see that darkness calls to a lot of people. And Rebecca Heller, the editor who took over the book on Brad's departure and added her unique input.

E-mail addresses change at the speed of light, and that alone is why a number of people contacted fell through the cracks when I could no longer reach them. Consequently, their material or images did not see publication. It's one of the pitfalls when cyberspace and publishing merge. Nevertheless, know that your responses were appreciated.

Lastly, I have to say that I'm grateful to the invisible yet potent powers that guide the universe for allowing me an outlet for my own dark interests. Every moment of this book was fun and exciting. More than once I was stunned to silence and reduced to tears by the graciousness and kindness of strangers from around the world who gave of their time and energy, and who traveled beyond ego gratification and moved to the recognition that something larger is at stake, and unveiled a part of their soul. This volume is a joint effort.

In the end, this work is dedicated to every goth roaming the planet, and to everyone who respects darkness. Know this: your existence is precious.

The darkness you love loves you back. Your value has and always will lie in the courage of your being.

—Nancy Kilpatrick
Montreal 2003

(*Disclaimer:* Pointing you to my Web site does not mean that my publisher endorses anything that might be said there. Also, bear in mind that the listing of any Web sites and/or other material as potential sources of information does not mean that either my publisher or I endorse anything that might be said there.)

FOREWORD
HOW TO READ YOUR BIBLE

in the beginning . . .

When my agent, Lori Perkins, said a publisher was interested in me writing a book about the gothic culture I thought, Hey, that's cool! I'm a writer, with twenty-six published books under my black leather and chain belt. And I'm goth. As several of my friends said, "Who better?"

I spoke with an editor who told me he wanted a book that would "talk to parents of goths, reassure them," because he had a toddler, and was worried about exposure to Marilyn Manson. I fell back against my Victorian settee, deflated. I wondered if I could possibly concoct such a book, keep it plausible, and still retain a shred of integrity. Fortunately for me, a bidding war ensued among several publishers. The book I *wanted* to write was for Brad Wood of St. Martin's Press, a guy with creative ideas, who went to clubs, knew the bands, and was not interested in a book where I'd have to say anything paranoiac about goth. "You're a goth," he said. "Write a book *to* goths, one you would like to read." I can hardly express how happy I was when St. Martin's won the war!

Brad moved on to another, better job. Fortunately, Rebecca Heller rescued the orphaned manuscript and helped improve it, for which I owe her much thanks.

For each ecstatic instant
We must an anguish pay
In keen and quivering ratio
To the ecstasy.

— Emily Dickinson's
poem #125

To write this book I decided to ask goths what they thought. I could have saved myself a lot of time and trouble by just asking my goth friends, but I was not convinced that the opinions of our grim little congregation reflected more than our own bleak world view.

. . . this goth begat that goth, and so on . . .

I sent questions out into the void. In this case the void is virtual and has a name: the Internet. I announced my intentions to every goth newsgroup and chatroom I could find, sent word to upcoming conventions and Web sites, requesting that anybody who wanted to talk to me about being goth, well, I'd listen. One thing that was important to me was to try to find goths from around the world, not just North America and England. So, with the help of friends and friends of friends, and Internet translation programs, as many goths as I could find from all age ranges, and from as many countries as I could gather climbed onboard for this voyage of the damned.

Ninety-five anonymous goths ended up in the Dark Ark. I presented each with a terrifying 125 questions. Four of them are using their real first names, everybody else goes by a scene name, or an Internet handle. In addition, I interviewed goth bands, publishers of goth magazines, owners of some of the major goth shops, and companies that cater to this community, writers, artists, and other creative types, as well as a plethora of random souls who in some manner like to danse macabre. They're all in here, testifying on their own behalf.

revelations!

I began to think affectionately of those ninety-five goths as *The † Section*. Consequently, that's what they're called. I managed to seduce vital stats out of most of them, and nearly half sent in photos. You can look at their pictures, check out their personal information on my Web site, and read their words as they discuss what it means to be goth. For more detailed responses to my questions, log onto my Web site, www.nancykilpatrick.com, and click on THE GOTH BIBLE. It is their views and opinions that guided me in the direction this book has taken. All of the interviews herein were done by me, except as noted. Praise goes to the contributors. Damnation can be hurled in my direction.

if you're a believer . . .

You'll figure it out.

if you're not . . .

WARNING!!! This book is *not* statistically correct! *The † Section* and everybody else speak for him or herself, and if you want to draw conclusions about a movement from that, so be it.

But instead of forcing that exhausted left side of your brain to organize yet more data and come to A Conclusion!, why not just sit back and permit the inherent gothiness of what lies between these pages to swirl through your right brain. Indulge in the forbidden pleasures of what it means to wallow in artistic and erotic darkness. Honestly, you won't die from it—at least I don't think so.

THE
GOTH
BIBLE

DEATH IN DOC MARTENS

Why do we love the tragedy and the dreams? My dear, you need only look into your silent existence to find out. Anon net goth

goth with a small "g"?

Defining goth is like defining God—we make efforts that always fall short of the reality. To call goth merely a subculture does not do it justice. And while goths are for the most part darkly artistic by nature, pigeonholing goth as an artistic movement only skims the surface.

Nobody knows the totality of what modern goth is about, but the simplest truth about goth is this: goth is a state of mind. And while most people who identify themselves as goth or gothic dress the part, a lot of people who do not wear fishnet and velvet are goth inside. Goth is a way of being that embraces what the normal world shuns, a lean toward and an obsession with all subjects dark and grim, a view of life that incorporates the world of night as well as the world of day. The gothically inclined make room for the *noir* in a global culture that favors white and prefers its darkness sanitized.

But saying goths are lonely and morbid is misleading. The mainstream views goth through a distorted mirror that sees only dreary music coupled with Morticia Addams fashions. Most goths and kindred souls dispute that shallow reflection. Romance is at the heart of what it means to be goth, and consequently tragedy is always a sigh away. In the modern gothic world, as in few other realms, the outward trappings of similarity belie fierce individ-

GOTH ACCORDING TO THE † SECTION

VampirMike

"Most people in the gothic scene want to distinguish themselves from the world of the average, where there is not a lot of place for imagination and deviation from the norm. goth is an imaginative world, a dark romantic place into which we attempt to flee."

The Crow

"...a peacefully dark work in which one can escape the masses and uniformity. The deep bliss this world brings gives the power and strength needed to experience life and love in an extreme way, intensely."

✢

Nimue "It is liking what other people find hideous, or disgusting. It is loving things that other people couldn't love. goths have ancient souls, ones that never really died."

✢

Krockmitaine "[It is] the research of estheticism, art, romantism in a modern society devoid of magic, hope, and humanity."

Reynaldo

"I like the dark music and gothic thinking, but I don't want to chang the world. I just want to keep my world full of real feelings."

uality. Every goth is an individual first and foremost, adamantly defending that position. Yet lurking within such independence is the intense need for community, which is glaringly obvious to anyone who cares to look.

Being goth is going on what cultural mythologist Joseph Campbell called the Hero's journey, exploring what psychologist Carl Jung dubbed the shadowy side of life. It is a path Robert Frost wrote about in his poem "The Road Not Taken," but in this case, goths promenade down that dark, unknown road that most of the population veers away from. Emily Dickinson wrote about what gives life its juice, "a moment of noon," when something happens. This is what goth is about.

Despite the dark current that carries goths along, and maybe because of it, goth is also about fun. About extremes. About edginess. About flapping your latex bat wings in the face of convention and secretly giggling at the notion that your very existence upsets the mainstream. If goth is anything definable, it is a living, throbbing entity composed of rabid individualists, a veiled underground realm where encompassing what the light of day fears or rejects is considered fascinating, compelling, and, at times, awfully amusing.

Does a black trenchcoat a goth make?

One of the most common misconceptions about goth is that it is some sort of devil-worshiping cult. A number of The † Section are Wiccan (see Chapter 13), and variations thereof. But only two identified their religion as "Satanist." *Sire Cédric* says, "I do not worship any sort of horned god. It's just that in the Bible and in Romantic literature, I identify with the Satan character. Also, God is the ultimate representation of misogynistic stupid males. I stand for the Goddess of Night, and the pleasures of the flesh."

Still, the mainstream will glare at goths and in their collective eyes you can read the letters C-U-L-T. Maybe it's the cadaverous makeup, or the ready-for-mourning-at-any-time-of-the-day attire, but nothing could be further from the truth.

Cults need leaders. Goth has always been and always will be leaderless. Goth, since it slouched out of the amorphic ooze of Punk in the 1970s, has never had a leader. The closest would be the bands, and none have assumed that role. Nor would goths permit it for a second—what a great way to ensure that goths no longer buy your CDs!

It's difficult for the average mortal pounding concrete to realize the worldwide scope of goth, and to believe that nobody started this. In that way, goth is much like the Internet—it emerged seemingly out of nowhere, and flourishes, yet nobody can figure out Who Is in Charge Here!!! At least when goths crash, they only effect themselves.

Andrew Eldritch, the currently blond genius behind legendary band Sisters of Mercy, is one of goth's best-known singers. His hauntingly spiritual lyrics combined with wicked instrumentals have rippled through darklings around the world for well over two decades. Eldritch has always divorced himself from goth, although goths are his biggest fans. Sisters were invited to do an autographing in 2002 at the *Sonic Seducer* music magazine booth at Germany's huge annual M'Era Luna Festival (see Chapter 5). The band's manager warned, "If the booth looks like a goth shop, they might just walk away." Maybe it did; Sisters canceled the signing. And while they continue to adore his music, goths have never been anywhere close to letting Andrew Eldritch take charge, even if he had wanted to be *Leader of the goth Movement*!

Goths resist being controlled—it's at the core of why most goths are goth. Goth is one of the premier artistic movements of the late twentieth and early twenty-first centuries, and true artists are, by nature, unique, and unpredictable.

When goth, with eroticized grace, first lifted its pale flesh out of a murky pool composed of a complex blend of music, literature, and philosophy combined with outré fashion sense, it did so on its own. Despite a world hell-bent on finding "the person to blame," or in this case, The One Who Started It All, in gothland, there is no such dark animal.

Amazing, then, that goth exists all over the world. This nonmovement movement can be found not just in the United States, Canada, and in most European countries, but also the Ukraine, the Far East, South America . . . Somehow—and the Internet is a major contributor to goth communication—people of like mind have built velvet bridges using music, fashion, art, literature, and philosophy to find soulkin. It's a given that goths can spot one another in a crowd.

One reason that goth has remained whole, as it were, unto itself, protected, still relatively pure, is that while through fashion and music it has been visible, individual goths are still elusive creatures. What goth *really* encompasses is the silver they keep hidden. And goths do not necessarily

Paola

"It's a slightly less optimistic outlook on life than other people's, and a lifestyle that becomes second nature and is absolutely impossible to shake off. It's got nothing to do with looks or culture."

Vena Cava

"It is dark, quiet, and magick. It is shadow and the night and all dwellers within; cemetery peace and the safety of solitude. An owl's cry at midnight, the soft whoosh of a bat's wing, the tolling of chapel bells. It is candle and whisper, incantation and prayer."

Lestat de Lioncourt "One thing I am sure goth is not–and this I can say because most goths I know are not–and that's judgmental. They can accept anyone for who they are, regardless of how deviant or egotistical."

want to be high-profile. Goth is an underground movement—that's the beauty of it—and it has existed largely apart from the mainstream. This is what has kept it alive, despite bits and pieces of debris hurled into the darkness.

Saturday Night Live started one of the most widespread goth usurpations with a spoof in the late nineties called *Goth Talk*. The occasional skits were introduced with Bauhaus's "Bela Lugosi's Dead," one song that can be clearly identified by all goths as goth music. "Goth" hosts Azrael Abyss and Circe Nightshade managed to savage every aspect of goth one can see by observing high school goths—who are the most self-conscious and least able to defend themselves.

It's a mixed bag of good and ill when goths poke their ringed noses into the mainstream, or the mainstream grabs an image to exploit. There have been academic papers written on goth—more and more of them, it seems. TV newscasts and articles in popular magazines and daily newspapers have profiled goths, not always in a favorable light. In the mid-1990s, Cher put out several issues of the catalog *Sanctuary*, packed with delicious goth decor. Goth artists have been featured in interviews, and there have been fashion models, like Donna Ricci, Lenora Claire, and *Sky Claudette* (of *The † Section*), and plenty of famous runway clotheshorses doing the

Ravenheart

"goth look." Haute couture designers have brought goth aesthetics to the forefront, for example, designers Rick Owens of Los Angeles ("Not one for color."—*Vogue*, Feb. 13, 2002), and Olivier Theyskens, who incorporates goth decadence into his fashions. All of the major design houses have ventured into goth style at one time or another in the last couple of decades. Calvin Klein's print ads, and Levi's commercials have used goth clones, and Italy's Fiorucci filled the catwalk with faux-goth clothes. Cosmetic and hair-color companies got goth a few years ago, for example, MAC, and L'Oreal, which has a line of dark makeup. World famous Bloomingdale's in New York featured goth garb in at least one of their catalogs. TV shows such as *Buffy the Vampire Slayer*, *Angel*, and *Dark Angel*, among many others, use goth actors, and films, including *8MM* and *Underworld*, hire goth extras when they require a gang of perverse and seedy clubbers. Whoopi Goldberg hosted the Oscars in 2001 and dressed goth, and many Hollywood movie stars do goth from time to time.

Britney Spears's HBO special featured goth-imitation dancers in the opening number. Everywhere you look, it seems, the mainstream is mimicking goth.

It's a given that the mainstream, seeking to entertain, excite, and expand itself, will always uncover and eat the edge. It happens with every subcultural phenomenon. Oddly enough, the collective culture thinks it understands what goth is all about. It does not. But every goth can see the middle of the road for what it is. After all, goths may have been born goth inside their skin, but they have usually grown up in "normal" families, gone to school, been raised in a conventional religion, shopped at the local mall, maybe even married a regular person and had children, just like everybody else. It is probably this knowledge through experience that will save goth from assimilation. The status quo has not yet thought of a way to seriously capitalize on goth, although the chain Hot Topic manages to bring goth fashion to the masses—presumably as long as it is profitable. But the minute exploitation takes hold in a big way, goth as we know it will be no more. The essence of goth is to be an individual, one who revels in the darkness that society usually fears and rejects. Perhaps that nasty, earthy, sensual quality of goth that lingers in the realm of entropy and dissolution will never appeal to the average citizen. We can only hope!

Photo courtesy of Sanctuary Magazine

But will the increasing focus on goth spell the beginning of the end? Can we expect the fast-food restaurants at the mall to soon be serving goth cuisine, like black pasta? Will Wal-Mart be littered with poseurs? Are bag ladies going to be wearing discarded fishnet and hauling chipped gargoyles around in their shopping carts? Even if these dire occurrences come to pass, they will, as well, pass. And goth will remain, lurking in the shadows, waiting for the light to fade so it can come out and party in the cemetery. Goths have always existed. They just call themselves "goth" these days because it's amusing!

the dark side of dark

Unfortunately, from time to time goth hits the mainstream in a way that encourages a perception of it as evil. Sometimes it's laughable. In November 2000, Mayor Carolyn Risher of Inglis, Florida (population 1,400),

Vena Cava "Alienated, miserable, vengeful teenagers have existed as long as there have been high schools, but it was harder to slay more than one or two of your enemies before you could get Uzis."

Nevermore "They were two confused children. They claimed to be Nazis, yet one was Jewish, so what could be thought of any claims they might make on being goth?"

Billy Mod "They may or may not have been involved in certain aspects of the goth scene, but this factor is irrelevant, only coincidental at best, and definitely not a cause-effect relationship."

Sky Claudette

Photo courtesy of Sebastian Seal

"So they listened to Metallica, big deal! It's the media that wants you to believe they were something they were not."

Individuation "Honestly, if those kids had been older and truly part of the goth scene, they might not have snapped."

nailed copies of her official proclamation onto posts at four entrance points to the city, declaring her town to be a "Satan-free zone." Risher claims she was targeting DUI drivers, child molesters, and "kids dressing goth."

Also in the fall of 2000, the U.S. Congress gave the town of Blue Springs, Missouri (population under 50,000), $273,000 for a Youth Orchestra Outreach Unit to "combat goth culture." Would that be the town's four peaceful and law-abiding high school goths, who hang out in the mall's parking lot?

But at least one event propelled goth into the headlines worldwide, unfairly, and with troubling ramifications. That horrifying incident happened at Columbine High School in Littleton, Colorado, on April 20, 1999. Eric Harris and Dylan Klebold, two deeply troubled students, opened fire at the school, killing thirteen and wounding twenty-three. Harris and Klebold wore black trench coats, claiming they were members of a small group of alienated students who had formed the Trenchcoat Mafia at Columbine. After the shooting, one traumatized student incorrectly identified the two murderers as "goths."

As has been the case throughout history, and now more so with the media that Marshall McLuhan assured us create a "global village," first impressions may be wrong, but they stick. The U.K. newspaper the *Guardian*'s article "Black Tuesday" is similar to other news reports around the world: Both boys—one the son of a military man—had a strong interest in Nazism. It claimed they described themselves as Nazis, white supremacists, fans of heavy metal, and interested in the occult. The *Guardian* stressed the point that Nazi dictator and mass murderer Adolf Hitler had been born on the same day 110 years earlier, and obviously that date had significance for the two. The *Guardian* also specifically identified the Columbine killers as goths, although neither Harris nor Klebold defined themselves that way. The paper stressed that the boys listened to the transplanted-from-Germany-to-Seattle industrial rock band KMFDM—the band's logo was on the baseball cap of one of the killers; the two quoted the lyrics of U.S. shock rock group Marilyn Manson; they listened to the German industrial band Rammstein. The paper also quoted several "authorities" on goths, including Sergeant Cynthia Burgin, a Texas police detective who lectures nationally in the U.S. on cults, and who talked about splinter groups that embrace both goth culture and neo-Nazism.

"They are using mystical violence and mystical illusion as a way of intimidating other members in their groups."

The paper also mentioned that Harris was addicted to the computer game *Doom*, and "The U.S. Marines used *Doom II* to train on." Oddly enough, the article did not blame the makers of *Doom II,* the U.S. Marines, the makers of baseball caps with band logos, or Army surplus stores for contributing to the killings! But the *Guardian* did blame goth. And theirs was far from the only media report that did.

The killers were not goth. But in the midst of the initial shock and fear generated by such a violent event, and the desire to understand the reasons behind it and find someone or something to blame, the world labeled the boys as *goth*. With time, and new information, that assessment altered considerably. But chasing down reality has never been a strong point when newspapers are going for circulation and television stations are fighting for ratings. Retractions and corrections do not make good news.

Many goths, particularly on the Internet, have taken a stand on Columbine, and tried to do damage control. One goth band, SEVEN 13 of Massachusetts, wrote the song "Outcasts" specifically about Columbine. Most goths would agree with Emily Brontë: "There's nothing poetic or beautiful about murder." And empathize with Calhoun: "I am goth, and the thought of harming anyone in that manner sickens me."

Unfortunately, it is not just in the United States where goths are unfairly blamed for crimes they did not commit, and Germany, for example, has had several killings where, because the murderers wore black, they were considered "goth" by the media.

All anyone can say, really, is what *Samael* repeats for all of us: "They were not goth!"

goths were children, too . . .

To be goth, or gothic, or gothically inclined has always meant this in terms of the larger world: You are outside the norm. Misunderstood. Sometimes abused. Goths are keenly aware of this.

Most goths are goth because of a refined sensitivity to life, and an ability to view and tolerate the shadowy elements that much of society is busy ignoring, like death. "Goth," says *White Raven*, "is in the shadows of the real world." Goths know that death is a sad business. As *Azazelle* put it,

rinaedin "So what if they were [goth]? I'm sure lots of murderers are Christians."

Miss Lynx

"There were so many horror stories about the evils of gothdom, accounts of schools sending kids who wore too much black off to counseling or suspending them, opportunistic politicians making inane statements like 'We need goth control not gun control,' and despite all the years I'd spent insisting I wasn't 'one of those,' I knew on an instinctive level that people like me were being targeted. I found myself getting so angry at the reactionary responses I was seeing that it kind of overcame the resistance I'd had to being labeled in that way."

50 Ft. Queenie "goth provides the mainstream with a handy scapegoat and whipping boy whenever something like Columbine happens."

VampirMike recalls another recent murder in Germany, wherein a couple who dressed in black and identified themselves as Satanists stabbed their friend to death with sixty-five knife wounds in order to use the blood in a vampire-like ritual. "TV here in Germany made it a big story. They claimed we have thirty-thousand Satanists in the country! People began to think that goths are Satanists because they don't know the difference between a goth and a Satanist. When I would drive into town in my goth attire, people began giving me the finger and crying, 'There! There's a Satanist!' It's so silly."

Zerstoerte

"Just because you wear black trench-coats and listen to Marilyn Manson does not make you goth. Those kids were ignorant crybabies who blamed society for their own problems, and were too stupid to seek help. Each one of us has been bullied at some point in our lives—if anyone thinks they were justified, then millions of people would be justified in doing the same."

Nadia "It strikes me as a curious twist of logic that, when trying to explain these murders, some people overlook free access to firearms in favor of those boys' (supposed) taste in clothes and music."

Tristan "...years of interactions with their parents and education systems had a lot more impact on them than what, in all probability, was an attempt to get someone to notice how deeply troubled they were. I don't see that as goth, I just see it as incredibly sad."

"Goth to me is an attitude that seeks to make death and pain aesthetic. In so doing, perhaps one can accept these unacceptable things."

When anyone takes on the grim business of shouldering the shadow for those who refuse to bear their own portion of the darker part of life, it's no wonder the pain of such an endeavor can feel unbearable at times. Personifying the elements that much of the mainstream is trying to avoid means rejection.

But are all goths selfless? Is every goth conscious of this monumental task of carrying the burden of despair on his or her velvet-draped shoulders like Atlas holding *up the world*? Are all goths paragons of virtue? Of course not. As *cypher* says, "There are idiots everywhere!"

But overall, goth is part of the struggle for true independence within the homogenized collective psyche, and individuals are always at odds with the conventional.

dismal by nature?

Life viewed in these terms is distressing. And while almost all *The †Section* would agree with the sentiments, most of them do not consider themselves dismal. Goths, in fact, are some of the most vibrantly alive beings walking the planet, largely because they are not afraid to face personal and collective demons.

Apart from growing up in circumstances that often encourage depression, sensitive young people universally have a hard time coping with their teenage years, with the intense emotions that can nearly overwhelm them, and with the depression that often surfaces due to the feeling of being misunderstood on a deep level. Goths for the most part direct their anger and turmoil inward, and it's not surprising that half of *The †Section* reported self-destructive behavior, usually in their teens, frequently involving cutting or other self-attacking actions.

About 90 percent of *The †Section* have seriously contemplated suicide. But contemplation is not action, and *Lestat de Lioncourt* speaks for many of them: "Although I love the allure of death, I love life more. I am too much in love with life, and would give anything for immortality."

Close to 25 percent indicated they have tried to end their own life on one or more occasions. For the overwhelming majority of those, their attempts were in the distant past and had to do with specific situations, or with ongoing bouts of depression that have dissipated with time. Almost everyone who has made a serious attempt at suicide has altered his or her behavior and thinking, and being goth seems to have made a positive difference in most of their lives.

URLs

gothic survey
www.nightmachines.com/gs

How to be Goth in Less than 1 hr
www.gothic.net/gothnicity/

Encyclopedia Gothica—history of goth
www.waningmoon.com/gothica/

Lenora Clair
www.lenoraclaire.com/

Sky Claudette
www.skyvlad.com/

SEVEN 13
www.seven13band.com

DARKLINGS WITH ATTITUDE

Old goths don't die, they just wear less makeup!

long ago but not so far away . . .

No sane person can hear the word "goth" and fail to envision another time and place, even if they don't know exactly what time and place that is. Words have power and, while on the face of it, goths of the new millennium have nothing to do with barbarians who lived over a thousand years ago, still, there might be a few similarities worth checking out.

The original Goths (capital "G") were Germanic tribes who, between the second and sixth centuries A.D. managed to do a lot of marauding. They loved to fight—apparently it was the ultimate experience—and, because somebody in Europe invented the stirrup around the second century, it gave one of those original Goths an idea: Horses could make not just an effective mode of transport and a larger-than-life pet, but the noble steed might be an excellent partner in battle when the terrain demanded something more than human feet, such as the plains of Eastern Europe and Russia. The Goths had speed but not numbers, and consequently were generally a nomadic people out of necessity.

These first Goths seemed to fall into two main groups, the Visigoths (visi = wisi = to the west) and the Ostrogoths (ostro = austro = to the east). The Visigoths took on the Roman Empire, fighting, losing, fighting, winning bits and pieces, and finally collaborating with the Romans against

The History of the Word goth/ Gothic by goth author Caitlín Kiernan

visigoths: The ones who go out to clubs and spend the evening looking at themselves in mirrors while they dance.

ostrogoths: The ones who stay home and take Valium

Gargoyles, Notre Dame Cathedral, Paris, France.
Photo by Hugues Leblanc

the Huns. Eventually those Visigoths roamed to France and Spain and tried to dig roots there until the French kicked them out of their country. A bit more war and Islamic rule became the norm for a while in Spain, but ultimately the survival-oriented Visigoths headed for the hills.

Meanwhile, the Ostrogoths, with probably fewer options, aligned with the Huns under the infamous Attila. The Huns, too, battled the Romans and lost, and the Ostrogoths ended up in Italy by way of the Balkans. They managed pretty well there until the end of the sixth century, when the Roman emperor Justinian started an internal war based on a kind of centralized-power doctrine that destroyed Italy and saw the demise of the Ostrogoths.

Beyond all this, from designs of jewelry and weapons and other things, it's clear that the original Goths had a connection to the Celts, but what and how seem to be mostly lost in the mists of time.

Generally, the word "Goth" with a capital "G" was used in the past as a pejorative. It meant a person of no refinement. They *were* barbarians, at least to the then civilized world.

Which leads to the Gothic style of architecture that originated in France around the middle of the twelfth century. Some of the most sophisticated and elaborate Gothic cathedrals were designed and built there and are still standing. Carrying on for about two hundred more years, the style was eventually picked up in Germany and England.

Gothic architecture came about because the French were tired of Romanesque and Norman buildings—square structures with a couple of columns and a bit of design work on a peaked roof. Gothic architecture took the inside of the building and put it on the outside. It's like taking the skeleton—the structure that holds us up—and placing it on the outside of the body. Gothic architecture turned the normal inside out.

Curving arched doorways with deep embrasures, floral-design windows, ribbed vaulted ceilings: the effect is openness, airy and light, spiritual. Gothic cathedrals draw the eye upward, allowing ordinary people to leave the mundane world and visit the realm of the soul in a free-flow communication. Flying buttresses permitted taller interiors, which provided great acoustics for choirs and organ music; exquisitely ornamental gables, crockets and foils added panache; those astonishing cross-species gargoyles—a perfect metaphor bridging the sacred and the profane (well, profane might be a bit extreme, since gargoyles were, after all, cute waterspouts acting as eaves troughs)—hovered at the edge of roves, ready-to-pounce guardians of the spiritual. These cathedrals were all fine woodwork and stonework and took centuries to construct.

Gothic architecture begat Gothic furniture, since the more practical people of the day realized it would be nice to sit down once you got inside one of those palaces. Cathedrals had no seating back then. Palaces and institutions needed furnishings, so there was a ready market. Today you can still run across Gothic and faux-Gothic pieces, beautifully carved of fine old hardwoods, often with the classic Gothic arch. They sell at steep prices. The furniture, like the buildings it originally inhabited, speaks of the powerful kings and church leaders who imitated a powerful God who ruled through omnipotence.

Present-day goths with a small "g" appear at first to have nothing to do with those rampaging Goths of old, nor with Gothic architecture. The nomadic Goths of history more resembled modern-day Punks, at least to the collective eye—wild, crude, tribal. But today's goth *did* crawl grimly out of the punk realm in the mid-1970s. The exquisite architecture known as Gothic (named for those barbarian hordes because it was considered crude by mainstream standards of the day) did discretely emerge in the 1170s. There has to be a connection.

Goths form a lose-knit tribe, functioning, both visibly and invisibly, within the status quo. And while goths are not warriors, nor nomadic for the most part, no one can deny that goth is removed from the larger society in which it exists. Goths are often feared and shunned, usually viewed as sinister, unwholesome, something . . . well, crude by the polished plastic standards of the status quo. Today's goths dwell in their own realm out of necessity, much like the original Goths. Goths existed and goths exist by implied rules of order, values, and a language that sets them apart from the rest of the world.

The beautiful Gothic style of architecture appeals to goths because it is the world of the interior. The gothic soul is drawn to these exoskeletons. What is inside is revealed outside, creating a synchronicity of the inner and outer world—mystery and romance, set in a realm of shadows. Smacks of goth to me!

And like the original Goths, modern goth is under siege, constantly threatened with annihilation through absorption into the mainstream. The mainstream has a history of devouring what's edgy, co-opting the wild

You Might Be a goth hick if...

- Your casket is on cinder blocks in your driveway.
- You name your child after your dog, and they're both named "Enigma."
- You think Dolly Parton should be the lead singer for Switchblade Symphony.
- Your coffin is lined with a velvet Confederate flag.
- You smoke cloves in a corncob pipe.
- You dye your sheep black.
- Your bull's nose is pierced six times.
- Even your teeth are black.
- Your rooster crows at moonrise.
- You have spent your life perfecting black corn.
- Your coffin has a side-mounted spitoon.
- Your granny crochets your fishnets.
- Your favorite comic is Johnny the Homicidal Tractor.
- You have an Elvira pinup in your outhouse.
- You get up at 4 A.M. every morning to collect eggs from the raven coop.
- You and your pit bull share the spiked collar.

goth resurrecting.
Photo by Hugues Leblanc

and innovative then corrupting it through dilution in order to nourish itself. It's an animal thing, basic survival à la Darwin, and goth is a tribe struggling like an endangered species against extinction.

Goth has endured for three decades; it took three centuries to construct many cathedrals. It has not yet been overtaken as the Ostrogoths were by the ruling society chanting "You will be assimilated." Goth draws inspiration from those clever Visigoths: maintain a low profile, and keep the intangible treasures hidden.

One of the interesting things about the Gothic period of architecture is that out of it, women began to gain a better position in society. This was the age when minstrels crooned of courtly love, when a code of chivalry was formed, when wooing a lady became a skill and a man who played the flute was looked on as desirable. Even the Virgin Mary ascended to the fourth position in the former triumvirate of the Church. Ultimately this led, however slowly, to a consciousness on the part of society that women are indeed human and equal, and deserve to be treated as such. Over the last centuries—in fits and starts, but clearly ongoing at least since the Romantic poets—this way of thinking has been extended to apply not just to women, but to the *feminine,* energy and values that include the often suppressed feminine side of men, qualities most goth men are proud to own up to and will gladly nourish within themselves.

During the Gothic period, European cities became more settled. The roaming tribes wanted a home. Universities formed, and study led to such questions as: Just what sex *is* an angel? After all, Gothic artists had to depict them in cathedral windows, so the point became important. A period of stability and peace in the world led to the blossoming of the opportunity to create art and beauty and move humanity up a notch on the evolutionary scale.

Modern goths, being the enlightened visionaries they are, manage to reflect in every aspect of their lifestyle, from ideals through fashion, a blend of all human history: tribal, the beautiful Enlightenment, and the disaster of the Dark Ages. It is amazing, and often frightening to those outside trying to decipher goth, to see this melange of romance and death represented by individuals so poetically. Goth reflects the turmoil of human history, the injustices, the knowledge of our impending demise. To be goth is to be rejected by the mainstream, to be outside the collective. To be goth is to constantly be paranoid of being consumed by the culture at large.

The mainstream does not understand goth, and it never will. At best it is envious. At worst, it tries to destroy what is unknowable. And yet goth remains, and grows.

gother than thou

Morpheus, one of the former co-owners of the long-time Toronto goth shop Siren, once said in a television interview: "We goths are a gentle people." True. But even the dark side has a shadow.

Anyone born in a competitive society is bound to be competitive—some more, some less. There are goths—not all of whom are faux goths—who have a large stake in being as goth as they can be. To these übergoths, the way others perceive them matters greatly. Thinking about it, it makes sense. While goths tend to be individualistic and feel rejected by the mainstream, at the same time the urgency to belong to a tribe and stave off suicidal alienation means that trying to "fit" can take precedence over other drives.

Courtesy of Fred Berger

Being gother than thou is usually an activity reserved for the young. Around the age of thirty years, an uncanny transformation seems to take place in the psyche. Not for nothing did the hippies warn, "Don't trust anyone over thirty!" Every decade of existence brings new changes, new directions. By the time someone reaches the beginning of the middle segment of their life on this planet, they have hopefully gotten over a few of the basic insecurities that plagued them in their youth, often exacerbated by a family and community that reflected values not wholly their own.

Not every goth wears black. Not every goth can be identified visually as goth. Goth is an amorphic grouping with only the most obvious identification markers distinguishable to those who are not goth, e.g., fashion and music. But as in every grouping, loose or tightly knit, there are always a few fragile souls who have an enormous stake in being the most, the best, top of the pile, to the detriment of others. Sometimes they are unsure of their status. Other times it's ambition and a desire for total attention. And for some, it's a confusion because they can't quite see what being goth is about, and they desire so much to belong but aren't exactly sure they do.

In gothland, that gother-than-thou attitude is not uncommon. In fact, it's so prevalent that the online magazine/forum *gothic.net* offered rolls of

How To Be
Gother Than Thou
The Most Pretentious Card Game Ever Made

(The Rules)

Absinthe Minded...

$+ \heartsuit 3 + \heartsuit 2$

Discard one card from the Fate pile you play this card into. If there are no cards in that Fate pile, discard this card.

Dire Fashion Blunder

$\frac{\varphi}{} 6$

Goth Points one could buy, little stickers to be given out to friends and strangers—the more you got, the gother you became. *The Corruption* is an online role-playing game where players win Goth Points. Who says goths don't have a sense of humor?!

R. Hunter Gough, owner of Savant Garde Entertainment, concocted the card game *Gother Than Thou*. "The whole idea of 'goth points' and being 'Gother Than Thou,'" he says, "had been around for years before I decided to make the card game, and I'd done some tinkering with card games before, so I decided that the three most important factors in 'living *la vida* gothic' were goth points, money, and keeping oneself right on the brink of being horribly ill. When I got evicted [from my apartment] because my übergoth roommate at the time had been spending the five months' worth of rent money I'd been giving him at Hot Topic and who knows where else, I decided that one of the primary sources of money in a *Gother Than Thou* card game would have to be a 'Gullible Roommate,' and the idea grew from there."

Gother Than Thou is a satire of the gothic lifestyle. To win, a player must accumulate twenty goth points while giving his or her opponents cards that subtract points. For instance, the "Genital Piercing" card gives the player who holds it six goth points, but takes away six money points. That card also gives the player two sickness points—not good! If a player gets five sickness points, he or she swoons, and must discard their Fate deck (as in "what Fate has in store for you"). The images are photographs of goths enacting the "Crying Yourself to Sleep" card, or the "Dire Fashion Blunder" card, or images of nongoths, for example the "Visit From Mom" card.

As with most small business ventures, *Gother Than Thou* was developed with help. "My ex-girlfriend took many of the early pictures, including the cover image, the card back image, and [the card] 'Fun With Eyeliner.' My roommate at the time, Megan Jones, was out of a job, so I put her to work boxing up 2,000 decks of *Gother* while she sat and watched daytime TV and tapes of *Fraggle Rock*. She still hasn't quite recovered."

Although the man behind the game declares he was never goth beyond a phase in college, "About sixty-five percent of our customers are goths. The game has equal appeal with goths, wannabe goths, former goths, and goth haters. *Gother Than Thou* owes some of its success to [the live-action role-playing game] *Vampire: the Masquerade*, which got a huge number of goths into games, and an even larger number of gamers into being goth."

R. Hunter sees *Gother Than Thou* as something to help goths "pass lonely nights in coffee shops. It's also a good stocking stuffer. And for the incredibly desperate, I suppose it could act as a checklist: boots good, eyeliner good, *Crow* makeup plus *Cat in the Hat* hat equals bad."

attitude

Propaganda is probably the only subculture publication known to just about every goth on the planet. This long-running—since 1982 and counting—stylish, visual chronology of subcultures, particularly goth and fetish, is the child of New York photographer Fred H. Berger, who has had a long love affair with the punk/goth/fetish look. "*Propaganda*," Fred says, "has always been first and foremost an aesthetic publication with a special emphasis on photography. This is what sets it apart from other magazines of the genre, which have focused primarily on music, the scene, and literature. *Propaganda* never neglected any of these aspects of the gothic experience, and actually enhanced their importance by dealing with them in a highly visual manner, favoring imagery over information in a way which was more compelling than mere verbiage."

Fred believes that the magazine's popularity with goths stems from "their overriding need to escape mundane reality, so they retreat into the shadows and night, body modification, masochism, magic and mysticism, vampiric role-playing, and fetishism. Let's face it, we live in a cultural wasteland where romanticism is considered cornball, imagination is laughable, and anything other than the hetero missionary position is considered pathological. I could tell you more than a couple of stories of kids dropping out of school, attempting suicide, and ending up in psych wards because the world could not accept that they were different. Goths came to see *Propaganda* as a sanctuary and a source of inspiration in a cruel and heartless world."

Such a cutting-edge visual publication evokes many responses from readers, particularly, Fred says, " 'Where do you find your models?' Well, for starters, there is no agency that offers anything resembling the exquisitely beautiful androgynes found on the glossy pages of *Propaganda* mag-

Gother Than Thou cards.
Copyright R. Hunter Gough and Savant Garde Entertainment.

Deacon Syth

"I used to drink other kids' blood when they hurt themselves in public school. Sometimes during sex I have tasted that of my lover. It is quite invigorating."

Jennie

"It's an aspect of my sexuality, blood drinking being more something I've done to excite other people's kinks, or a by-product of being a lesbian who isn't cowed by menstration."

azine." His most famous photo essay featured heroin-chic model Dmitri. "The reaction to 'Anarchy in Moscow,' the tale of a young junkie hustler in Moscow [No. 25, 1999], ranged from a group of club kids starting a fund to bring Dmitri to America, to a religious group attempting to bring charges against me for 'solicitation of a prostitute.' Controversy—it goes with the territory."

The past twenty-one years have altered Fred. "In a burst of idealistic naïveté, I started down this long, winding, and perilous path. *Propaganda* magazine has given me the opportunity to travel the globe in an attempt to escape the gravitational pull of bland reality, to seek out the exotic, the hidden, the depraved and otherworldly. But it has cost me my virtue, my vitality, and my hope for the future. I've essentially shot my bolt, having reached beyond where any man should ever reach, having seen what no man should ever see—beauty in extremis, writhing limbs and lapping tongues on crowded dance floors at the four corners of the earth, sex in cemeteries, nocturnal wanderings along streets littered with spent needles and condoms, drinking to the health of the Buddha, gasping for air in the belly of the beast. Perhaps the chaplain was right; perhaps I should have listened to my mother. 'For what shall it profit a man, if he shall gain the whole world, and lose his own soul.' [Mark 8:36]. All is vanity."

the classes of a classless subculture

It is mainly North American goths who tend to identify one another by category. It's the same with music. In Europe, goths are more enlightened in many respects, but then this is the home of goth. In other places in the world, like the Philippines, Peru, or the Ukraine, goths are an island unto themselves, floating in a mainstream not so accustomed to subcultures, and those goths must focus on similarities, not differences in their ranks.

One Web site, *A Study of Gothic Subculture: An Inside Look for Outsiders* (see Chapter 2 URLs), provides a list of goth terms, including categories that goths are often dropped into.

There are many common-denominator categories ascribed to goths, by goths, and by non-goths who are making a statement about what they see. For example:

Blood Drinker. Some goths identify with vampires, but few drink blood on a regular basis. They might indulge in sadomasochistic erotic rituals, or simply be obsessed with vitae and all the symbolism it holds. About a quarter of *The † Section* have drunk blood, or had their blood drunk, usually during an erotic encounter, and sometimes with a close friend. Others have drunk blood for ritualistic purposes.

Cemetery goth. Most of *The † Section* prefer graveyards to backyards. Only a very few suffer an aversion to death and everything associated with it; most are intrigued by the concept of demise, and find cemeteries lovely. Death interests include being enamored with lovely gravestones and angel statuary, and fascinated with gravestone inscriptions. As *creepy* says: "I'm interested, but not in a morbid way. I find the older ones [cemeteries] to be especially intriguing because of the history and stories. They also have beautiful headstones, so I go more for the art." Nevermore, who considers himself a Cemetery/Macabre/Death goth, has a favorite funereal outfit: "Black dress pants, my 1930s priest's cassock, long-sleeve black shirts with the cuffs frayed, East German–issue combat boots, and occasionally a black *Clockwork Orange*–style derby."

China/Oriental/Baby Doll/Schoolgirl. The innocence of the underaged. Makeup creates prepubescent round or almond-shaped eyes, chopsticks worn in the hair, Suzie Wong dresses purchased at a vintage shop and worn with Doc Martens, Catholic schoolgirl tartan plaid skirts worn with a black PVC top and kneesocks. The Wednesday Addams institutionally gray dress with white Peter Pan collar fits here, too.

Christian goth. What it sounds like—goths with strong Christian beliefs. There are Jewish goths, and probably Muslim, Hindu, and Buddhist goths as well.

Corporate goth. Those who work for a living in the corporations that rule the world. (See Chapter 8)

Cranky and cynical goth. That is, *most* goths. In a world where values have gone to hell in a handbasket, a lot of people are cynical. Goths, who are used to deceit and narrow-mindedness directed their way from the general population, become jaded at an early age. "Trust no one" has been a popular slogan since before Fox Mulder was warned for the first time.

Madame X

"As nothing other than a passionate expression during lovemaking, I have been known to bite and draw my lover's blood from usually the neck or shoulder area, via transdermal permeation (through the skin without leaving marks). Even so, I do not 'feed' in this manner. I do not need or crave blood. I simply use the 'vampire's kiss' as a special sensual enhancer, and as yet another level of being one at the time of the most passionate embrace."

Being a full-time cynic is exhausting, and it makes one cranky. But the glorious thing about cynicism is the humor it breeds, and goths are some of the funniest people on the planet. It takes a wound to produce a belly laugh, and the sensitivity that is a prerequisite for being goth lays the groundwork for a twisted view of life. The Internet offers many goth humor Web sites.

Cyber. (See Chapter 3). Futuristic, hardwired, circuit-boarded goths, fingers melded with keyboards, alive with becoming, and doomed by a the-future-is-over attitude. Katwoman considers herself Cyber. "I have always been heavily into sci-fi, computers, graphic novels, futuristic scenes, the Internet, and general computer geek things." *Blade* in goth makeup, and outfits from *The Matrix*.

Dark Fairy. Fragile and wispy, these are ethereal boiz and gurrls, otherworldly waifs, on the verge of evaporating into thin air. The ones who give the word "languid" its deliciously consumptive meaning, and for whom fainting couches were invented. The pre-Raphaelites painted them, and fairies were big in Victorian paintings, which often depicted them naked. Queen Victoria herself was dubbed "The Faery" by England's Prime Minister Benjamin Disraeli. Popular goth photographer Stéphane Lord makes them a fetish.

Richard Wagner wrote *Die Feen* (*The Fairies*) in 1834, and Daniel Auber composed the Parisian grand opera *Le lac des fées* (*The Lake of Fairies*), which premiered in 1839. The movie *Photographing Fairies* is the story of cousins Elsie Wright and Frances Griffith from Yorkshire, who photographed fairies in 1917.

Fairies and Celtic mythology are inextricably intertwined like the knot designs on a Celtic cross. One popular belief is that angels ejected from Heaven fell short of Hell and ended up on Earth as fairy hosts. Ariel of William Shakespeare's *Tempest* is the most popular classical fairy, and Tinker Bell from *Peter Pan* is the contemporary notable.

Fairies can represent many things: buried sexual desire, a desperation to escape from daily routine, passion for the unknown (which includes the spiritual and/or occult), and a tribute to the power of feminine energy (in females and males) to charm and seduce. In the past it was thought that cocaine, and absinthe (which was nicknamed "the green fairy") enhanced the ability to see those flighty little beings. *Malinda* considers herself into the Dark Fairy look and prefers to wear "anything to make me look otherworldly." *White Raven* wears fairy boots that are "black, buckled and pointy." And like a lot of the black moths flitting through the night, she enjoys listening to Celtic songstress Loreena McKennitt.

Dark Wave/New Wave. Eighties-style music. Most of *The † Section* enjoy this music, which often includes all of the classic synth bands, like the ones Slavel favors: "Depeche Mode, Pet Shop Boys, New Order, PiL, OMD, INXS, Bauhaus, Frontline Assembly, Skinny Puppy, Legendary Pink Dots, Coil."

Melinda by Jeff Olsen

Diva. An oval Victorian photograph depicting a large and lovely female draped in lace and satin and velvet, obviously feeling beautiful and unashamedly flaunting her sexuality.

Most denizens of the first world have learned from the media that all goths are cadaverously thin. Many are. Many are not. Goth is a wonderful door through which larger women, and older women, who often are the first rejected—which makes them cranky and cynical—can wander freely without fear of any more rejection than most women suffer, and quite a bit of tender gentlemanly response coming their way. Plus-size and senior goth gurrls—and boiz!—can wear romantic outfits made of satin, velvet, and lace, dye their hair black as night, and empty a bottle of eyeliner onto their lids and not feel like a freak. Of course, getting *to* a club for these divas of despair is another story, but once inside, most goths are not so judgmental about divas, and the world becomes refreshingly celebratory.

Jola photo by Dan Locke

Elder goth. The originals. Third gen. These are goths who are now over forty, who were there around the mid-seventies when goth first wafted up out of the chaotic mire of punk and took on a darkness all its own. Some of *The † Section* who have been goth over 20 years are Elder goths. Vena Cava is "relieved I am not the only [older] one. When I see younger ones I am delighted—the fewer preppy clones the better. But I also realize for many of them it's just a fad." *Ravenheart* says, "I think the 'vampire youth' can be narrow-minded where older people are concerned, like they are the only cool goths and being older equals being uncool. I just laugh, and tell them I have shoes older than them."

Egyptian. Quite a few goths experience a synchronistic attraction to all things from ancient Egypt. This is a world of ankhs, lush quietude and the fragrance of patchouli oil, right from the tombs of ancient Egypt to you! Mummification and ancient funereal customs play a part in this realm, and the inscrutability of ancient symbols. It helps to like cats!

Fetish (See Chapter 8). Those who break out the PVC, chains, and whips. Goth lends itself nicely to fetish. For years, Amelia G and Forrest Blak have run *Blue Blood* magazine, an artful blend of goth and fetish, full of stylish and sexy photographs and sassy slut-goth fiction. The magazine has been in living-dead mode for sometime, but it's not yet suffered the true death. Amelia G says, "We will continue to publish *Blue Blood*, but we will do it at a schedule and pace where we can maintain the quality it is known for without suffering to put it out the way we once did. A recording artist who puts out a great album every year or so would be thought to be doing well, and I'd rather do something really good once in a while than do something only sorta good regularly."

Mistress Hades is, among other things, a fetishist. She will carry a black leather riding crop, and her two favorites in footwear are her "thigh-high patent leather boots, and my black leather Oxfords with a 5-inch heel." *Shekinah* likes her "spiked collars, rubber bracelets, and Betty Page style shoes."

Gay goth. Being both gay and goth can't be easy. Goths on the whole are not fearful of same-sex love, the love "that dare not speak its name." Many of *The † Section* identify themselves as bisexual, even if they are currently practicing heterosexuals.

Gothabilly. When Elvis meets Elvira! The Cramps first used the term in the late 1970s. The music blends twangy classic country with somber goth rhythms. Bands like Fields of the Nephilism are adored by those into Gothabilly. The fashion playfully blends goth styles and fabrics with country-and-western outfits. These goths will wear goth attire and cowboy boots, and line-dance when nobody is looking. They are the goths who helped make animal prints fashionable, and whose decor isn't complete without a tacky Elvis bust!

Graver. Goths who rave. Usually goths under thirty who like to go to raves and dance to techno all night. They wear gothish black Spandex, modified makeup, and maybe a silver-lamé tank top. It's the darkness that differentiates them from fellow ravers: of costume, of attitude.

Industrial (See Chapter 3). Industrial goths bond around Industrial music. They wear basic black, not complex attire, and adornment sometimes involves leather and chains, with or without a fetish edge. This style nudges the biker look. They are ready for physical action, and it's not surprising when an industrial goth ends up buying a motorcycle. These solid worker-bees believe in muscle. They are the guys and girls hired as security at goth clubs, and can come at goth with more action than contemplation. *Morbius* likes Industrial, and her favorite outfit is "my black oh-crap shirt, black tight pants, black purse with silver, combat boots." *Reynaldo* is industrial and simply wears "Black T-shirt, black pants." *Lisiblac* says one of her favorite clothing items is her "black leather biker jacket." She recalls: "Neil Gaiman (see Chapter 9) [who usually appears in public in a black leather jacket] said to me at a signing once, 'It's not a jacket, it's an environment!' Spot on!"

Kindergoth. Aka Baby goth. These are the sixteen-and-under goths, illegal still, and pressured from every direction—parents, school, religion, community—not to be goth, but to conform and be "normal." These are the gothlings mimicked on *Saturday Night Live*'s "Goth Talk." It's easy to poke fun at younger people, especially junior goths, who are struggling to test out everything in a world where all is new and fresh. Yet they are dependent, often stuck in an environment that does not encourage dark exploration. Many Kindergoths are huge fans of Marilyn Manson (see chapter 5) because Manson seems to speak to them. *Vile* is sixteen and a kindergoth. She likes to wear "a large black velvet Mad Hatter hat, black ballet shoes, black fishnet is a must, any cute morbid T-shirt, Jack Skellington jewelry, and black and white Spice Girl sneakers with striped tights." She listens to

GOTHIC39
Photo by Jim Skipper Productions

50 Ft. Queenie "My Net name is taken from the title of the PJ Harvey song, about a woman who dreams of being 'the king of the world.' "

Arantèle "It's an old French word out of use now. It means the web of a spider and I liked the sound. And it rhymes with the French word dentelle, which means lace."

Daoine o' "It's pronounced THEE-na, not the hard th but a drawn-out sighing sort of sound. The o with apostrophe means nothing, it just flowed well with the name. Daoine is Celtic. I liked the way it looks juxtaposed with how it's pronounced. It's a good way to judge if someone actually knows me, if they can pronounce it properly."

Lisiblac "It's the name of a thirteenth-century Welsh witch."

D.J. Caluna

"It's a mixture of my real name and my affection for the moon."

a lot of "Old School music, and Sneaky Bat Machine, the Cruxshadows, and the Misfits."

Medieval/Renaissance. Those enamored with knights and their ladies, the world of Camelot, and courtly love. *XjUsTcRuCifyX* loves her "Medieval dress, flowing witch skirt, and my arm warmers, which I made." *The Crow* prefers to "dress Medieval from head to toe for parties." *Arantèle* likes her "Medieval-style belt made by Black Widow Designs."

Net.goth. Goths who virtually live on the Internet (See Chapter 9).

Perky goth. Terminally happy creatures of the night, these are often the goths who get things done. They are enthusiastic about goth and about life, and such happiness can irk other goths who see an abundance of joy as the annoying opposite of sorrow. Perky goth usually carries a negative connotation, but not always. *Micah* considers herself perky. She likes to wear "Poofy and swingy transparent skirts, and corsets."

Poseur. Goth wannabes, usually young kids going through a goth phase who do not hold to goth sensibilities but want to be part of the goth crowd for one reason or another. In a year or two you can hear them whine dismissively: "I was goth when I was younger but I grew out of it." *Daoine o'* has trouble with these " 'Batbabies' whose clothing is no doubt bought at Hot Topic with Mommy and Daddy's money!"

For most goths, a goth is a goth for life. As Neil Gaiman says, true goths are "born to it."

Punky goth. Delightful relics no matter their age, these throwbacks provide a taste of the post-Punk era when punk and goth were joined at the hip like dark and darker. A typical look is a T-shirt with the sleeves ripped out, army fatigue pants, and a fauxhawk. *Prosthetic God* likes the punk look, and wears "my mesh top and white fishnet stockings. A Celtic ring my mother bought me, my studded bondage/dog collar, my Medieval necklace, also bought by my mum. *20 eye Docs* but I still lust over a pair of kneehigh Rocks." *RaVeN* also loves the punky goth look: "My spike necklace and my huge wallet chain, really tall platforms from Hot Topic, my black glitter bondage pants, and my black beater with an anarchy sign on it. My hair is blond with bloodred tips, dyed with Manic Panic."

Slut aka Femme Fatale aka Vamp. Gurrls and boiz you might not trust around your significant other. The term *slut* when used in the goth world also means a sexy, sometimes sleazy look that has its own appeal. Trouble comes when the slut acts out that sleaziness, making life messy for everyone too close for comfort.

Tribal aka Pagan. Those with the maximum number of tattoos, piercings, and gothified dreadlocks, and a plethora of chains. Equally responsible with Gothabillies for animal prints. *Taoist* wears a "Black Spank top with silver tribal motif and exposed midriff, and Australian cowboy boots with two-inch heels." He also has "seven wicked tattoos."

Übergoth. Way over the top. The goths who dress to the nines to run out and buy milk.

Vampire. Those in love with the image and lifestyle of the undead. Vampires are mysterious, charming when they want to be, sexy. They almost always get their way, are eternally gorgeous, and do not suffer fools at all. *Nimue* describes herself as into the Vampire look. She favors "Morticia-sleeved shirts." *VampirMike* adores "my lovely bat necklace." *Vena Cava* is an eclectic vampire. "I'm a Vampoccalyte, someone who believes in the apocalypse and is a bit bloodthirsty about it. And an Envirogoth, a banshee crying the earth is dying, stop killing it."

Victorian. (see Chapter 3). Goths enamored with gentle spectacle, the subtlety of romance and courtly love. Victorian goths adore the languid lifestyle. They emulate those ladies and gentlemen who gave a serious nod to manners and decorum—hand-kissing is de rigueur—all while wearing lush attire that can border on the baroque. The New York boutique Religious Sex is one well-known purveyor of goth Victorian attire for all genders. *Moonglum* loves the Victorian period. A special article of clothing he values is "a hand-made black velvet cloak with purple satin lining made by my wife for our wedding." *Paola* wears "long skirts, tailored jackets, long

Madame X "I was given the name Xavier, and I really like the name. It's often mispronounced, as is my first name. One of my all-time favorite paintings is Madame X by Sargent, (a notorious yet regal Victorian lady wearing a then-thought-to-be-scandalous black dress falling off her shoulders.) I resisted taking on the name in my younger days. Today, being a rather well-known elder goth, who fancies the arts and boasts of her Victorian sensibilities, I have accepted the scene name proudly. Besides, I really can't keep the strap on my shoulder."

Vena Cava "I changed my birth (dull) name to this in 2000—new name for a new millennium. Loosely translated, it is Latin for Nightvein, because I consider myself a true creature of the night (night runs through my veins), and it sounds deliciously vampiric, as the vena cava is the big vein in your heart."

Rois

"Pronounced rose. It's the name of the main character in one of my favorite novels. Also because it was easier to spell than Brociliande (which got me called Broccoli for a few years)."

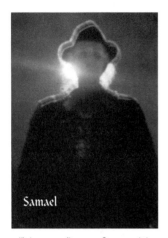

Samael

"It is an angelic name. Some say it is one of Lucifer's names, Lilith's consort, one of the watch angels who fell in love with mortal women, the angel of destruction, or just some generic fallen angel."

Photo courtesy of Phil Anderson

Shekinah

"My name is biblical, <u>light of god</u>. Ironic, huh?"

Sky Claudette "I have been told before my mind takes off so much in thought that I am always in the Sky, dreaming..."

WantonBlood "I use the term <u>wanton</u> affectionately for myself in the same way that I'd tease a good friend.

tailored coats, Victorian costumes with corsets and flowing skirts. I wear a lace scarf that belonged to my grandmother, carry small black bags and a tiny Furla rucksack. I adore silver Victorian rings." *Ravenheart* favors "black lacy long dresses, tight black pants, steel-boned corsets worn over clothing, frock coats, long black dusters, antique rosaries, and cool chokers and necklaces made by my friend Emily."

Wiccan/Pagan goth. (See Chapter 13). This is one of the many spiritual paths of the gothic world. Goths value a return to a more nature-based re-ligious belief. rinaedin says about her pentacle necklace, "I never leave home without it."

goth Names. Contrary to media propaganda, day to day, most goths use no special name. When they do, it's a nickname, or an Internet handle by which they like to be identified. Goth names, naturally, almost always evoke the bleaker side of life. Goths do not choose a name lightly. But sometimes, they choose with humor. And frequently a name chooses them!

URLs

Jewelry and designs of the original Goths
www.hp.uab.edu/image−archive/ujg/ujgp.html

Notre Dame de Paris−Paris, France
www.bluffton.edu/~sullivanm/ndame/ndame.html

Cologne Cathedral−Köln, Germany
www.coam.net/~ct/fourth/sld063.htm

Chartres Cathedral−Chartres, France
www.medieval.pdx.edu/chartres/default.htm

Salisbury Cathedral−Salisbury, England
www.salisburycathedral.org.uk/

Glastonbury Abbey−Somerset, England
www.glastonburyabbey.com/

St. Bavon Cathedraal−Ghent, Belgium
The Lamb of God
www.sunsite.dk/cgfa/eyck/ghent/

This Corruption online role-playing game
www.sfgoth.com/~raveneye/GtheC/index.html

Gother Than Thou card game
www.savant-garde.com

Propaganda magazine
www.propagandamagazine.net

A Study of Gothic Subculture: An Inside Look for Outsiders
www.gothics.org/subculture/

Hugues Leblanc—cemetery photographer
www.tapholov.com

Christian goth site
www.christiangoth.com/

Gothabilly
www.gothabilly.net/

Insta Goth Kit
www.sykospark.net/goth/

How to be Goth in Less than an Hour
www.gothic.net/gothnicity/

gaygoth.net
www.gaygoth.net/

Perky goth manifesto
www.odk.com/wilson/goth/manifesto.html

Posers—take selection of list at
www.members.tripod.com/gotherthengoth/poser.htm

Religious Sex
www.religioussex.com/

I added <u>blood</u> because it's an interesting and proactive topic on its own, and gives it a touch of vampiric menace and allure. Not to mention that it tends to ward off illiterates who aren't sure what <u>wanton</u> means. I hate it when they ask me if I'm Asian (thinking I mean wonton, as in soup)."

XjUsTcRuCifyX "I was looking for a new ID to use online, and I could absolutely not think of one, so I went to some gothic message board and asked for help. Several people came up with some nice ideas, but this is the one that stood out as unique and...perfectly me!"

Zerstoerte "It is German for <u>destroyed</u>, and it is one of my many online names. I chose this one because it is part of a title to one of my favorite Einstürzende Neubauten songs ("Zerstoerte Zelle"). It's visually appealing, and I love names with letters that aren't often used, i.e., <u>x, z, q</u>."

EVER UNCHANGING FASHION

I'm just wearing black until I can find something darker!

demise as a fashion statement

Goth fashions have a range. You can wear black, or you can wear black. All goths love black—it goes with the territory.

Much of the world holds to the tradition of black as a color reflecting morbidity and mourning, if not death. Kali, that multi-armed Hindu goddess of vast destruction, is all black. And so is the infamous Black Madonna, as depicted in statues and paintings in Poland. Poland and other European Christian countries—the one who is less ethereal and more physical. But black is also sexy, mysterious, dangerous. Coco Chanel knew this when she designed her "little black dress," still considered by many women the world over to be the ultimate in chic. Ozzy and Sharon Osbourne have brought everyday black out of the closet and into the hearts and minds of TV viewers.

Goths utilize all of the above reverberations when they dress. Or dress to kill, as the saying goes. Dressing goth usually requires a lot of thought to achieve an effect. This is *not* a low-maintenance lifestyle, and leaving a black widow/vampire count impression takes time.

One of the oldest remaining goth shops in the world is Toronto's Siren, opened in 1988 by Groovella Blak, who says "I loved the aesthetic and at that time there was not a gothic shop in Toronto. I traveled to England

- **Black jeans/leggings.**

- **Long black skirt** (and this can hold true for the boys as well as the girls). Again, style and fabric are your choice: velvet, silk, wool; straight, flowy, poufy...

- **Black boots.** Pointy-toed boots with lots of buckles and Doc Martens are goth favorites, but you're by no means limited to those.

- **Black coat.** Once again, choose what you like: leather biker jacket, wool overcoat, oversized blazer. It should give you a silhouette somewhat larger than normal, and if you can get that "billowing-in-the-wind" effect so much the better.

- **Interesting black T-shirt.** Shirts for goth bands are obviously common, but this is a place where you can really exercise your own style. Look for something not everyone has.

- **Sunglasses.**

and, seeing the potential over there—the goth craze was huge in London—I came back inspired and with a suitcase full of black clothing to bring gothic fashions to this city."

Siren is an upscale goth shop, given to high-quality fashions and exuding Victorian romance. Groovella—who herself personifies goth romanticism—sells her own designs as well as a wide range of items by other designers. "The change rooms are decorated in lush brocaded fabrics, with a turn-of-the-century couch to recline on. I wanted the entire shop to be warm and inviting and of another era . . . an environment to lose oneself in."

Groovella, who was goth before opening her shop, says, "I may not dress as elaborately and dramatically as I used to, but goth is more about the inner expression which manifests into the outer expression. It is a lifestyle. I remember in the early days an older woman saying to me, 'Oh, I love this store, it makes me feel so very young!' I felt this was a wonderful compliment. If I can create such a feeling in people then I consider that I have done a great job."

Ipso Facto is another long-time shop, opened in 1989 in Fullerton, California. Terri Kennedy began creating her own fashions at the tender age of seven. She loves dark literature, and went from punk to goth "later." After working for eight years in the fashion industry, Terri opened Ipso Facto, and now carries the most popular underground designers, as well as a wacky and wild assortment of items like handcrafted wreaths with animal skulls.

Terry says one element of Ipso Facto makes it stand out. "We pride ourselves on being able to offer a place where like-minded people can browse items of interest and feel at home, particularly when it comes to recommending new music to customers, and we allow them to preview CDs before they buy." They also cater to Divas with "Rubenesque clothing, for the generously proportioned."

Shop-till-you-drop . . . dead—clothing, food, music, furnishings—is a perennial goth pastime. Apart from the thousands of shops catering to goths around the world, eBay is a goth buyer's and seller's paradise. Type in "goth" or "gothic" on eBay and it's not unusual for 20,000 items to be listed for sale, everything from fishnet and industrial spiked collars to ninetenth-century French Gothic reliquaries.

Goths—especially those not living in major urban centers—learn from magazines about the latest fashions, particularly the latest cyber-wear, the haute couture of the goth world. This fashion of the future, cybernetic in design, is what H.R. Giger might create, if he decided to do clothing instead of art.

Meltdown magazine has been publishing out of the UK since 1999. Founder Natasha Scharf focused on the goth scene for a radio documentary she submitted as part of her journalism degree, and the print publication grew out of that. "I thought that if the scene had a more 'serious' and professional-looking magazine, people outside would take goth more seriously, and see that it wasn't just a sad, outdated musical/fashion genre. Also, it is a response to mainstream negative press goth was receiving, mixing it up with blood-drinkers, Satanists, and Marilyn Manson. I wanted to show what goth is really about."

Besides cutting-edge goth fashions, *Meltdown* covers beauty, culture, music, film, literature, everything goth, particularly from a British slant. Natasha believes "it's a good idea for goths around the world to find out what's happening in other countries. There's some great stuff out there one wouldn't necessarily hear about."

Copyright Meltdown Magazine.
Photo by Stephané Lord, model Marianne

Another high-profile goth fashion magazine is *Gothic Beauty*, which comes out of Portland, Oregon. Steven Holiday started the glossy with the idea of bringing the goth community a quality fashion mag. "It began as a Yahoo! club," he says, "then went to print in 2000." He sees the role of *Gothic Beauty* as "bringing together all these wonderful designers and giving them an outlet to an audience they might not have had access to. Besides working with talented goths in the US, I get to work with goths from across Europe, which has enriched me."

Copyright Goth Beauty Magazine.
Photo by Tyler Ondine Whitmao

the Queen is IN

Victorian is the standard to which many goths aspire. Lots of long dresses made of velvet and lace and satin, adorned with beadwork, crochet, even tatting. These are the gowns with hems and sometimes sleeves that sweep the floor, that, whether worn on the lithe, languid frame or the Diva's voluptuous form, cut quite a figure as a goth gurrl makes an entrance. Vamp and vampiress and Morticia Addams hosting the Royal Tour! Goth boiz of a Victorian turn favor mock greatcoats

Victorian Mourning Customs and Rituals

- People died at home.

- Large copper pennies were placed on the eyelids to hold them shut until rigor mortis began.

- Family and friends were notified of the death by notes written on black-edged stationery, envelopes sealed with black wax.

- Postmortem photographs of the deceased were taken in the coffin. Children were sometimes posed in lifelike positions.

- Mourners wore solid black: dresses, coats, trousers, gloves (kid not permitted), hats and veils, black-edged handkerchiefs, walking canes.

- Black-plumed horses pulled black carriages and the hearse.

- Specified length of wearing black for mourning: Widows–two years of deep mourning: first year solid black; second year black tempered with gray, white or deep purple. Mourning a parent or offspring–one year. Mourning a brother, sister, grandparent–six months. Mourning aunts and uncles, nieces, nephews, and cousins–three months.

- Driveway strewn with straw to dampen sound of carriage wheels and horses hooves.

- Crepe draped over doors and windows and black wreath on front door, black antimacassars on backs of chairs.

- Mirrors covered, blinds drawn, lilies displayed in vases.

of heavy brocaded fabric, the frill of a ruffled shirt peeking out of the sleeve, tight laced-up-the-side pants and high boots, fingers full of silver rings to the second knuckle. These are dandies: elegant, romantic, courtly, with understated (by comparison) eroticism and a lavish presentation.

The Victorian era emerged out of the sixty-four-year reign of Queen Victoria (1819–1901)—the longest reigning queen of England. She has been deemed one of the true prudes of history, and yet there is evidence to the contrary.

Alexandrina Victoria was born in 1819. An only child, she ascended the throne to be Queen of England in 1837. Surviving journals and candid letters make it clear that Victoria was romantic, impulsive, and emotional when she met and became betrothed to her first cousin, German Prince Albert of Saxe-Coburg-Gotha. They married in 1840.

Victoria loved Albert for the entire seventeen years of their marriage. She depended on him utterly for clarity of judgment and companionship, as well as the erotic encounters that are recorded in her private papers with the utmost of discretion. His death left her devastated.

From the moment of Albert's demise, Victoria dressed for forty years in what were known as "widow's weeds." The Queen withdrew from public life, so much so that politicians became extremely worried about the impact on her subjects. Never one to hide her grief, Victoria slept nightly with Albert's freshly washed and ironed nightshirts. Images of Queen Victoria attired from head to toe in mourning black abound.

Victoria stayed in deep mourning, making a fashion of mourning outfits until she departed this mortal coil in January of 1901. During her eighty-two years of life, Victoria presided over a style of manners, decorum and subtlety hardly known today outside the goth world. In the twenty-first century, we are more than used to the overt. While the Victorians covered the legs of their chairs with skirts for the sake of modesty, today it is not unusual to see fully naked strangers in every area of the media.

According to Linda S. Lichter, the Victorians had what our modern no-holds-barred world does not. In the introduction to her book *The Benevolence of Manners: Recapturing the Lost Art of Gracious Victorian Living*, Lichter says, "We devour the remnants of Victoriana in magazines and period movies because they evoke far more than wistful images of safe, civilized streets, good manners and stable families. We also hunger for an era when people lived with dignity. . . ."

The best Victorian look tends to emulate actual Victorian styles, bustle and all, and then takes them a step further, mixing up fabrics and shades that would have left the Queen herself nonplussed. One imagines Victoria never considered wearing a corset *over* her dress, although generations before her in Spain they did just that!

Victorian Gothic Couture in Victoria, Australia, has been selling such gothwear since 1999. Louise Favetto runs what she describes as a "dark glamour" shop, awash in burgundy, black velvet, gold fringing, and tassels. She designs all the clothing, including exquisite Victorian-style dresses, and coats and jackets for both genders.

In her spare time Louise, who DJs at local goth clubs, has this advice for anyone wanting to open a goth shop: "Do a lot of research, work ridiculous hours, and be prepared to give up your social life! And all for minimum wage. It's definitely a job you do for love, not for money."

Gallery Serpentine, another Australian shop, in Sydney, excels at Victorian-style coats, capes, and corsets—over- and underbust. Their Web site even features a dog corset! Annette Magus has been running the fashions-made-to-measure shop for six years, and 95 percent of the designs are her own. She works with brocades, velvets, and PVC—for a modern spin on classic styles. Annette has been goth for about sixteen years, and opened the store because it "fitted in with my lifestyle, and I sort of felt driven to do it." And she finds her customers refreshing. "One came to the door one day and said, 'The rabbit ate my corset, could you fix it for me?'" Her designs can turn outré easily. "I guess a Victorian bustle made from PVC isn't the most common thing. And then there's the transparent plastic hoop skirt with varnished toast visible inside."

Goths try to live with dignity. They aim to respect one another, to respect all life on the planet. The Victorian goth is a genteel character, mourning that environment which nurtured sensitivity and venerated consideration.

proletarian by night

The Industrial/Military look is a more in-your-face approach to goth living. Black, as basic as it gets. The fabrics are leather, black denim, cotton, sometimes vinyl. Women wear low-cut tops and miniskirts of shiny latex or cowhide, men prefer tight black jeans, plain or with side eyelets and lacing, or paratrooper pants, and a simple black T-shirt, often with the

- Jewelry made and given to mourners as a keepsake, sometimes including strands of hair of the deceased.

- Emergence of park cemeteries and the building of elaborate family mausoleums.

logo of a favorite industrial band. Of course, like all goth boiz, they can also wear a skirt!

Accessories reflect a tough industrial element: black leather, metal rings and chains, spiked jewelry. These are the fabrics of the 1930s through the 1950s. Durable materials that last. No matter how plain the clothing, the boots give it away—military, rugged, full of hardware. Like the soldiers this look emulates, and the industrial workers the disciplined attitude honors, industrial/military goth style says this: I am self-sufficient. I am prepared to tackle concrete reality head-on. Try not to get in my way. This is the edge of punk.

Industry and military mean getting the job done. It's a direct approach to life. In much the same way that soldiers deal with the reality in front of their faces, goths who favor such fashion tend to be practical and pragmatic. More males than females choose the full-blown style, but there are plenty of women who dress this way as well.

Industrial/military often embraces a German-soldier quality, and a style with even a vague hint of Nazi Germany can frighten nongoths. A shaved head accentuates this connection. It is the power inherent in industry and the military that matters, not the politics. This is a pure aesthetic—goth at its simplest and most masculine, salt-of-the-earth, no-nonsense. What you see is what you get.

Lip Service, one of Southern California's premier designers, is one place designer Industrial fashions can be hunted down. Many goth shops carry Lip Service clothing. Rocker Drew Bernstein is founder, and self-described rivethead Ebony Joseph (aka Webkatt) president of the Internet division of this legend, which shut its real-time shop in 1992 and now runs retail exclusively off the net and sells wholesale to shops throughout the world. Ebony says they sell only their own designs. Besides Industrial, goths can find glam and fetish fashions, like their Stretch F**k'n Jeans.

Lip Service makes "only a hundred pieces of each style," Ebony says, "and they are rare and hard to come by, collector's items in a way. We don't mass produce unimaginative pieces for the masses." One of the drawbacks of limited editions is weird customers coming out of the woodwork. "I have had crazed fans of bands write to me demanding the same clothing we supplied their icons for their tour." On the other hand, "Mostly I have customers who appreciate the customer service we give them, and love the quality of our merchandise."

cyborgs among us

Cyberwear splices futuristic fabrics like PVC and latex and sometimes good old-fashioned rubber with odd-shaped designs that replicate the mysterious workings of circuit boards and hard-writing, of scars and surgical sutures, of beings of cybertronic and cybernetic origin. The Cyber look implies the wearer is connected to a vast network behind the scenes, a technological wonderland where anything goes and all is possible. The look is flamboyant, and can bring out the feminine in men, and the surreal in both men and women. Insect-pod backpacks, "moth eaten" PVC dresses, vinyl corsets for men that run from waist to knees, "zombie-boy" shredded shirts with PVC spiderweb overlays. These are costumes, and they are costly, and consequently are not for everyone. A full-body suit tight as a second skin, slick as black oil, or the muted black of rubber, with odd, disjointed, asymmetrical lines, and angular appliqués running through the fabric and implying layers of hidden sultry power, can skyrocket to a thousand dollars US. Most goths who love Cyberwear mix it with other styles, for instance, a PVC and stainless steel corset over a Victorian long velvet dress. The look is modern, passively defiant, futuristic, androidal space dweller full of mystery and possibilities. David Bowie is father of modern Cyberwear. He ushered in the look back in the 1970s, and goths have run with it since.

Diabolik of Montréal, Québec, is one shop that specializes in cyberwear and goth tribalwear. In 1996 Sonia B., who moved to North America from France fifteen years ago, opened this, the second of her goth stores (previously she co-owned Cyclops Underground, also in Montréal). Sonia adores working with latex and PVC. She creates most of her slick, sexy, macabre fashions in the back room of her dark little shop and is famous for odd designs. "My boutique continues the passion of my lifestyle," she says. Her Web site features several video excerpts from fashion shows, one accompanied by the band Cryterium and another from Le Bal en Noir fashion show featuring the goth band Western Dream.

Cybergoths owe a lot to Fritz Lang. In 1927 he released the eerie silent film *Metropolis,* which gave us the prototype for the classic cybertronic look. In the mid-1920s, between two world wars, German film technically surpassed that of all other countries. Lang's futuristic vision coincided with the industrial movement that had overtaken the world in the late 1800s. The filmmaker saw the working class as being eaten alive by indus-

THE † SECTION ON WEARING THE COLOR BLACK

DJ Caluna "Everyone asks me, what does it mean, all that black that I wear on my body. It's the suffering that eats away at me, the honesty which is missed, the hatred of human creativeness, the ignorance, lies and false promises, that is all black on me. Greed, and the shortsighted view, religion that breaks people, morals that kill, hypocrisy that everybody knows, all that is black to me. The sense that nothing will change, stupidity that reproduces itself... Black is my view. Black conscience. Black resignation. Black isolation."

Katwoman "It hides things—your weight, your finances, how long it's been since you've been to the dry cleaners."

Ravenheart has an unusual history with black. "I actually started wearing black because of my work. Before everything was done on computers, we used rapidograph technical pens full of India ink, and when the tips would clog, we would drag it across our pant leg and it would clear. Rather than ruin any jeans, I began to wear black ones that the ink would not show on, and I liked the look on me."

The Crow "[Black]...gives me power and self-confidence, and this beautiful dark feeling."

DJ Caluna "Black protects me and caresses my soul. It creates a certain

try, a continuous-motion machine that subjugated all for the enhancement of technology. This idea was not specific to Germany. It was the era when powerful labor unions blossomed around the industrialized world, out of necessity. The goth Industrial/Military look stems from this era.

Germany of the 1930s was also the epitome of transgender and bisexual decadence, a world of fiery excess with a cool emotional veneer. Cyberwear replicates that otherworldliness: I am here, but how did I get here? And where is *here* again?

Cyberpunk is the term used to describe the groundbreaking novel *Neuromancer*, by William Gibson (and other works) focused around punk sensibilities and human-machine interfacing. Goth emerged full-blown from punk. Cybergoth formed out of firing neurons and sizzling electrodes that married man and technology to birth grim cyborgs. Cybergoths are hardwired to technology. They are frequently net.goths (see Chapter 9) who appear in real time dressed like the Borg from *Star Trek*. Johnny Mnemonic happily living in the Matrix.

Today, technology threatens to overtake humanity. Machines will drive one another, we are told, so we mere mortals could become superfluous. Even the great techno thinkers like scientist Bill Joy (who designed the Berkeley UNIX system, the backbone of the Internet) predict a bad end for Homo sapiens. Our culture is already littered with the notion of bionic body parts, of machines implanted into the flesh that will ostensibly heal us and possibly grant us something close to immortality, at the price of sacrificing our autonomy. Joy warns us that future machines will replicate themselves, and will be able to outthink human beings. The future will see bodies implanted from birth with identification chips. What we once considered sacred has already nearly vanished. Individuality, if not the human race, may be becoming obsolete. Cybergoths are rabid individualists who replicate this dark evolutionary prediction.

fashion politik

Some goths dress a cybertronic future misery—fashion as premourning in advance the loss of the human race, when machines will rule, and the only way to beat them will be to emulate them. Other goths are aligned with workers caught up in the cogs of an unfulfilling nine-to-five job, victims of a routine that deadens the soul. And still others long for a gentler time, where subtlety and discretion prevailed, and a glimpse of an ankle meant something.

But goth is not just about despair. Goths have a sense of humor too, and many enjoy the joke that fashion plays, and that only other goths understand. Fashion reflects at least the attitude if not the psyche of the wearer. But it can also show irony. Goths choose to live with paradox, and taking your look seriously while laughing at yourself is just one of the many dualities they manage to balance. A favorite pastime at clubs is watching to see who has put what together to create something original and special while still under the Grim Reaper's all-encompassing goth black-lace mourning umbrella. Victorian goths draped in industrial chains. Industrial goths with Cyber hair spikes. Cyberwear that is ruffled latex, reminiscent of an exotic fish in a Victorian fish tank. Goths are nothing if not creative dressers. Fashion as living artform. Fashion as body politic.

when colors collide

Goth looks can range from lingering death to finally dead to eternally undead, but black is the one constant, the color of choice.

Goths love black for any number of reasons. Black is the night, that time when all might be as it is in daylight but the lack of light ensures mystery—what goths crave. Those who long to be hidden can hide. When everyone is in black, other senses besides sight are required, and that forces experimentation—maybe even relying on that sixth sense, or second sight, which many goths seem to possess.

All fashion roads in gothland lead to this supreme darkness. Goths use black to express what they think and feel. To the world, that statement is dismal. But almost all of *The † Section* said they do not consider themselves dismal. Most believe that exploring darkness allows one to appreciate light. This is a sophisticated attitude, a Jungian concept, one that requires thinking in dichotomy—you cannot know day without night, so bring on the shadows!

Why do goths, whatever their predilection, dress in black? One of the most common responses was as *angelus* says: "It just looks good on me, and it matches everything I own."

The wearing of black can, by the world at large, easily be perceived as an act of rebellion, or a scream for attention—after all, most people will

space between me and the normally dressed, which I need to feel comfortable. Black means understatement."

Calhoun "Wearing black takes on a spiritual aspect. Black absorbs light. Metaphorically that means I am 'absorbing' all that surrounds me. Taking in everything."

C.B.

"Black makes you look thinner (and paler!), and is very dramatic! The only problem is that black fades and it is hard to match sometimes—believe it or not, there really <u>can</u> be thirty shades of black!"

Nevermore "It better reflects my naturally gloomy personality."

moonglum

Photo by Bill Knispel

[wears black because] "I know I am going to die."

wear black occasionally, but not everything in their wardrobe is the color of a raven.

Black has a solid history as a color. Besides the mourning Victorians, and the Chanel elegance, some of Morocco's desert-dwelling Bedouin tribes wear black caftans—as any goth will tell you, if a person is *not* moving, black clothing blocks out sun and heat and keeps the body cooler. Theda Bara, the originator of the word *vamp*, popularized black on the black-and-white silver screen, as did Rudolph Valentino—when he wasn't wearing a sheik's robe! Black was the uniform of the supercool, existentialist Beatniks of the 1950s. Bikers favor traditional Harley black garb and hogs. And black continues to remain the preferred color for chic evening wear, largely because it does evoke a tremendous sense of mystery and danger infused with eroticism.

While black is the predominant color in gothwear, including hair, lip and nail color, as well as liner and eyebrow pencil, many will employ other colors to accessorize. Silver, the more vibrant sister of grey, the element of the moon, of Venus (along with copper, the metallic element of blood), a soft feminine metal, one that reflects back like a mirror, is de rigueur for accessorizing. Medieval superstition Barbara G. Walker tells us in her *Women's Dictionary of Symbols and Sacred Objects*, held that women would not get a good hearing by going directly to the patriarchal God (represented by the sun). They'd do better praying to their own feminine deity, using a piece of silver and calling on the moon. The fact that goths wear an abundance of this traditionally feminine metal suggests a lot about the essential core of goth, that it is generally nonpatriarchal. It is a subculture where the feminine is loved—feminine as in a universal nurturing quality and receptivity to emotional possibilities—by both men and women. A life-oriented quality that allows personal freedom and change and encourages experimentation and creativity.

Some goths will wear fabrics that come in silver, like silk, or PVC, or mesh fabric with metallic threads. Makeup can be silver. Most accessories tend to be black and/or silver, with leather and metal being favored materials, and perhaps the odd touch of bloodred creeping in. Nothing is as startling as a drop of red. The late artist Edward Gorey (see Chapter 11) made effective use of this. In one of his many marvelous black and white sketches, a vampire carries off his victim, with just one small red drop appearing at her slender throat. The power of that dot conveys how the sparing use of color can nearly overwhelm an image. And it speaks volumes about the gothic use of red.

When goths wear an out-and-out colorful outfit, the most popular choice of color is red, its various shades reflecting hemoglobin, life, vitality, the direct connection to the vampire, who must steal the blood of the living to survive.

Powerful, mainly unconscious symbolism surrounding blood pulls on the fears of all human beings, like the universal terror of losing it. Goths who are drawn to the seam between life and death have an especially strong fascination with blood. If we exsanguinate, we expire.

It is from the Judeo-Christian Bible that Dracula quotes when he reminds us, "For the blood is the life." The ancient Mayan priests cut out the hearts of human sacrifices as an offering to the gods, then placed the bloody organ into the bowl the Choc Mool holds on its stomach for later consumption. The Hindu goddess Kali, who symbolizes the dark side of creation, destruction—the natural dissolution we all face—sips the blood of those she slays. The Christian religion believes that Christ shed his blood to intercede for mankind with his Father, and atone for the sins of the world. The holy Eucharist, that mysterious process of transubstantiation employed during communion, turns bread into the body of Christ, and wine into his blood, to be drunk by the priests and the congregation. The Jews, under the domination of the ancient Egyptians, were instructed by God to paint the blood of sacrificial lambs above their doorways so the Angel of Death would pass them by.

In the past, Gypsies—tribes rooted in ancient India—upheld a wedding tradition wherein the couple ate bread with a drop of the other's blood to ensure they became one flesh. Sometimes they mixed the blood of the blissful couple from wound to wound. The blood bond has been part of many cultures through the ages. Goth couples who undertake Wiccan Handfasting ceremonies frequently incorporate variations on this tradition.

Ancient cultures believed that a woman stopped menstruating in order to retain her monthly blood, which then coagulated and formed a baby. For the nine months of our prenatal life, and during the excruciating trauma of our birth, we are surrounded by blood, intuitively sensing the power of its flow. goths involved with Wicca (see Chapter 13) as well as most women are keenly aware that the monthly menses, which continue to menopause, are a powerful reminder of both birth and mortality.

Today we are bombarded with the knowledge that blood can carry HIV, hepatitis, and a variety of other illnesses. Goths, who travel the darkest roads, have a perpetual fascination with blood, and many of *The † Section* have cut themselves, particularly as teenagers. The wearing of red holds all this symbolism and more, especially as it screams to be heard, in sharp contrast to black.

Purple is the other end of the spectrum from red and goth Divas love it for its dramatic effect. *Daevina* says, "Very very rarely I'll wear burgundy-colored velvet skirts, or a plum-colored shirt with black pants. But there is always one article of clothing that is black." The color is a favorite with Medieval goths. In Shakespeare's time, blood was called "purple." Traditionally, it has been the color of royalty in many lands. Ancient Roman emperors wore a deep wine red (derived from the Murex mollusk, found only in Mogador). In Latin, *purpureus* means extremely holy.

Gray lies somewhere between black and silver. The *gris gris* (gray gray) of vodoun (voodoo) blends herbs, seeds, hair, and other elements into an amulet that is worn in order to work magic spells, both white and black magic. Gray is the institutionally drab dress Wednesday Addams prefers, an outfit sought after by goth gurrls. Gray is the color of the shadow, the part of the soul the ancients believed was detachable. It is the twilight and predawn, when the birds do not yet sing, and the squirrels sit stunned in the trees. The time when the spirits can slip unseen between realms. For many cultures, the hair turning gray signifies wisdom.

Gray is also an acceptable color when one is required to blend with the mainstream. As *Paola* says: "I can only tolerate a sharp gray suit if I am meeting a client or discussing our mortgage at the bank. I may be goth, but I'm also practical: In the really important occasions of life you do have to look conservative. Hindering your career or being refused a mortgage because of your looks is *not* worth it."

Many goths like shades of blue to contrast with the black in clothing, for a nice bruised look. *Thyssen* wears "Dark blue and dark green clothing sometimes . . . I like to combine them with neat suits."

Occasionally a goth will venture into green, shades ranging from new mold to the pea soup that Megan from *The Exorcist* regurgitated. It's a problematic color for many goths, since it often brings out a sallow quality of the skin, a bit of jaundice, and for many that seems unbecoming.

Those who tackle green usually prefer the darkest shades, like forest green, which *museumbitch* prefers.

For some of *The † Section*, like *Elusis*, color has to do with the day. "I don't dress in black all the time. I almost always have something black on, but it's more typical for me to wear black and red, black and burgundy, black and green, black and purple, black and white. On the days when I am in monochrome, it's usually just because it's easier."

Colors you almost never see on a goth include gold, the color of the sun god, of daylight, of ostentatious wealth. Goths, being nocturnal creatures, are drawn to darkness, to what is hidden. The reflection of the silvery moon offers a chance to use the imagination, to romanticize. Sunlight causes melanoma, or simply hurts the eyes, especially coming out of a club at dawn! Still, gold trim on a Medieval gown is not unheard of, and more than one goth has painted a wall black, or deep red, and used a gold leaf trim.

You rarely see a goth in brown. Somehow brown, the color of mud, seems a poor substitute for black. But brown has a tradition in the Victorian, Edwardian, medieval, and Renaissance eras, and with the Greek and Roman styles, and goths love costumes.

Outside of period costumes, goths rarely appear in yellow or orange, unless they are headed to a rave, in which case you might see those colors in the strands of their hair. *TankBoy* takes a sensual approach to color and mixes wine red and purple with black, or will wear "a simple white shirt. You can mix and match not only colors but textures and sensations."

rinaedin doesn't believe goths need to dress in all black to be goth. "I dress in whatever suits my mood, mainly dark colors."

But leaving black behind is not easy. *Daoine o'* admits, "I've been tempted to buy something colored, so I do, but I end up never wearing it, and I get rid of it."

For *Sally*, all black "is a habit. Sometimes I want to change but the black's always back."

And finding clothing other than black to wear can be a major headache. *Ariana* says, "Going to a 'normal' friend's wedding is a bitch!"

Regardless of color or lack thereof, goth fashions are not usually cheap. But goths ferret out alternatives, like Morticia's Attic, an online shop run by Karina, which for four years has sold recycled clothing. And Shadow

Tank Boy

Clad, an online goth flea market owned by Dragonbach for two years. There is also competition for eBay with GothAuctions, where goths can auction off previously loved items. The technically inclined can sew their own. Many goth fashion patterns are available on eBay.

if I wear black, can I be goth?

From time to time, goth fashions hit the mainstream. Angelina Jolie, among other film stars, wore goth black to the Oscars. Fashion models can look gothish, and musicians who play nothing close to goth or related music can assume the look.

It's a paradox in a way. A person can be goth and dress nongoth, but can a nongoth dress goth and be goth? Likely not.

Goth is far more than fashion. For most goths, fashion reflects an aesthetic that permeates their entire existence. It is a thought process. A reality base. A way of life that includes what you wear as an expression of a deeper realm, embraced on a soul level. Tossing on a black velvet dress does not a goth make any more than wearing a training suit means the wearer is an athlete. But it might be the first step to unearthing the goth within, that dark being lingering by the crypt door, waiting patiently for it to be flung wide. Opening up the possibility for a flight one evening into the darkly moonlit night.

URLs

alt.goth.fashion
www.ice-princess.net/gothfash/faw.html

Academia Gothica
www.ice-princess.net/academia.html

Siren
www.sirenweb.com/index1024.html

Ipso Facto
www.ipsofacto.fateback.com/

Fashion Nation = Vixens & Angels
www.vixensandangels.com=

Victorian Gothic Couture
www.vicgothic.com/

Gallery Serpentine
www.galleryserpentine.com.au/

Lip Service
www.lip-service.com/

Vixens and Angels
www.vixensandangels.com

Diabolik
www.diabolik.ca/

Cryterium
www.cryterium.org=

Western Dream (via Golem Records)
www.golemrecords.com

Meltdown magazine
www.meltdownmagazine.com/

Gothic Beauty magazine
www.GothicBeauty.com

Morticia's Attic
MorticiasAttic@aol.com

Shadow Clad Flea Market
www.shadowclad.com

GothAuctions
www.gothauctions.com/auction/XcAuctionPro.asp

Gothic Fashion Sewing
www.josienutter.com

Gothic Cyber Fashions—how to make them
www.sc.essortment.com/fashioncybergo_rfdx.htm

Darkthreads: The Bay Area Gothic Sewing Circle
www.sfgoth.com

THE ACCOUTREMENTS OF GOTH

You know you're goth when you joyfully undergo cosmetic dental surgery!

high maintenance

Goth is definitely a high-maintenance lifestyle. The process of dyeing hair alone is time-consuming, and when the color is black, it requires constant touchups. Dramatic makeup takes much longer to apply than the natural look. And anyone who has regularly laced up a pair of twenty-eyelet boots really understands the phrase, "He died with his boots on."

Goths, unless they favor the Industrial look—basic black T-shirt, pants and boots, and a few good chains—face amazing and unique clothing problems as they promenade through life. Torn fishnet might have been inherited from punks, but goths have adopted it as a necessary style. Both fishnet and lace snag on just about anything, especially chains, crosses, and full-finger snake skeleton rings with spiky points along the spine. Brocade is easily stained and requires dry cleaning, as do silk shirts. Candle wax seems to find its way onto velvet dresses at an alarming rate. (A trick for getting wax out of most fabrics is to place waxed paper on the wax, turn the fabric over, and press the inside of the fabric using a low-heat iron. The wax will go onto the paper.) Latex rips easily, and once it does, this cousin of the plastic garbage bag can't be stitched back together. (Duct tape on the inside of the fabric can hold it together for an emergency wearing.)

hair, dyed, and the wool

In 1977 the Bellomo sisters, Tish and Snooky, opened a punk boutique in New York. It was their mom who termed their activities Manic Panic, so we can only guess at their energy level! The sisters were performers in their own right, and their shop catered to early punk bands like Blondie. Tish admits, "I always leaned towards the morbid punk Morticia Addams look—we even share the same name!" Snooky adds, "Tish always loved the Vampirella look, but punk came first!"

The energetic sister act felt driven to open a shop, and it survived by word-of-mouth. "The underground community needed something like us!" Snooky says. "No store existed till ours, and since people always imitated our style, we thought we might be able to sell it. Goth as we know it today did not exist back then, but we always loved the vampire look and sensibility." Tish adds, "We were creatures of the night! The goth look was beginning to emerge back then, but there was no name for it."

Manic Panic's Tish and Snooky
*Courtesy of Sic F*cks*

Today, their clientele includes Marilyn Manson; Davey Havok (of AFI); Kembra Pfahler (from the Voluptuous Horror of Karen Black); the Cramps; the Damned; and their own punk band, the Sic F*cks. The little shop is gone, and they now work out of a huge warehouse in Long Island City, where the offices and showroom are a goth/punk blend. Snooky describes the "black curtains with cats, skulls, a (fake) fireplace with cherubs, candelabra, dead roses around the doorway." Tish adds, "And our five-thousand-foot storage closet resembles *The Addams Family* basement!"

Trish goes on to confide, "We had a lovely goth girl working her way through mortuary school in our sales department. She dyed her hair green, her skin was milk white (naturally), and she listened to goth music nonstop. It took her a long time to get a job because no one would believe she was strong enough to lift a dead body. Happily, she is now a successful mortician!"

Many Goths dye their hair at home and use those little Manic Panic jars of cream-color shades like Deadly Nightshade, Black and Blue, After Midnight Blue, Raven, and, especially Vampire Red. Manic Panic also does cosmetics, with lipsticks and claw colors in Tramp and Venom, Belladonna Child, and Nightmare, among others.

Snooky describes their oddest product: "Vampyre's Veil tattoo defender and pallor protector, an SPF 45 sunscreen cream for the face, inspired by people like us, who run from the sun, crave that white pallor, and also want to prevent our tattoos from fading. We picked this gorgeous little black bottle that looked so 'witchy.' Tish designed the logo out of lilies and dripping vampire letters. We packaged it in a coffin-shaped silver box with black gothic writing. The counter-top display was a huge black coffin with a bat and black lace covering it. It was the coolest product ever!" And Tish adds, "I can't live without it."

Wigs, braids, and other fake hairpieces also continue to be popular in the goth world. Initially, goths would dye streaks (usually dark red, or blue), and sometimes weave in synthetic hair to contrast with the main color for a tribal effect. Now, wool is often woven into real hair for goth-style "big hair," full of color. Brands have blossomed to take advantage of this fashion trend—at a recent Convergence, Hair Police didn't have a minute to spare making woolen dreads and adding synthetic hair wisps to goth heads.

Sonia Peterson opened Hair Police in Minneapolis in 1986, and a branch in Amsterdam in 1993. The company has been online since 1997. Now they do "dread tours," where they take the show on the road.

"A few years ago," Sonia says, "I realized that goth clients had great style and great clothes but bad hair. I thought our hair extensions would be a good alternative for goth-inspired styling, both human hair extensions/synth extensions and all kinds of dreadlocks. We started serving the San Fran community in the mid-nineties."

Hair Police specializes in extensions and dreads made from human hair and synthetics, and in dread perms, which they developed in 1986. One NYC goth DJ had them "create a single dread cone on her head, with tendrils of her own hair coming out the top of the cone like a volcano." About one quarter of their clientele is goth, and the styles the company is famous for hinge on the Industrial, Tribal, and Cyber goth look. Sonia sees her own look as "spaceship captain."

The future of goth hair styles as Hair Police envisions it tends toward a Cyber look and involves "more unique ways to attach hair, with plastic clips that can be installed like hair extensions, and then the hair can be changed. I call them ports and plugins." Sonia went as far as Hong Kong to find some!

otherworldly eyes

The Eye of Horus (600–400 B.C.), a popular ancient Egyptian symbol, was frequently invoked during funerary rites. In ancient Egypt and Rome, eye beads were employed to ward off evil. But it took the Late Georgians to make eye jewelry a fashionable fetish.

One variation of mourning jewelry was the painted eye, sometimes with an eyebrow of real hair, or a teardrop either painted on or simulated by a small diamond, made into rings, brooches, and memento boxes. Charles I, when he was Prince of Wales, gave a locket with a painting of his right eye on it to his morganatic wife. Many people have been fascinated by eyes and eye jewelry, including film director Alfred Hitchcock, who often used images of eyes in his films.

The first reported surgery involving removal of a human eye was described with text and illustrations by the French surgeon Ambroise Paré in the sixteenth century. At that time, there were three different types of artificial eyes available: eyes worn over the eyelid and fixed with a steel spring attached around the head; enameled oval-shaped gold and silver bowls; and oval-shaped glass eyes partially coated with lead—which, of course, ultimately proved harmful to human health. By the seventeenth century, Paris became the fashionable center of glass eye manufacturing. The first German artificial eye made of glass was developed by Ludwig Müller-Uri in 1835. Cryolite glass, still used today, was invented in 1870. Over the centuries, almost every material known to man has been used as an orbital implant: gold, silver, ivory, glass, silicone, cartilage, bone, fat, wool, rubber, catgut, acrylics, magnets, asbestos, peat, agar, paraffin, sponge, rubber, cork, titanium mesh, polyethylene, and hydroxyapatite. A variety of shapes have also been tried, including a sphere with small knobs projecting from the surface. The British Optical Association Museum has a collection of 160 glass eyes.

The Eyeglass Museum in Cadore, Italy, displays an extensive collection of all types of eyewear, including pince-nez, lorgnettes, and monocles. Also on display are walking sticks with compartments, snuffboxes, and fans (all popular concealments for spyglasses and monocles). Cadore, the place the spectacle industry was reborn in 1878, is home to 312 of the 650 companies in Belluno, Italy, where 80 percent of today's eyeglasses are produced.

Sunglasses, that staple of daytime gothwear, were invented in 1752. Those first prescription lenses, made of blue or green glass, did not shield the eyes from UV rays. Sam Foster (Foster Grant Company) in 1919 created the first protective sunglasses, and by 1929 was selling them in Woolworth's on the boardwalk of Atlantic City.

Combined, all of the innovations in eyewear cannot hold a beeswax candle to the leap made when contact lenses were developed. 9mm SFX is a company with a large theatrical and goth clientele that makes unusual custom contact lenses, which can be ordered (with a doctor's prescription and measurements) over the Internet. They have created a variety of vampire lens styles, including: Vampyre Lestat (eerie blue), Vampyre Louis (eerie green), Vampyre Armand (otherworldly brown), Vampyre Lilith (black pupil, red iris, black rim), Alien Vampyre (out-of-this-world purple), Lost Boys (creepy yellow), and Forever Knight (distorted yellow), as well as many other types of cool and weird lenses, such as Spider (the pupil is a black spider over a pale blue iris), Spiderweb (ditto with a web), Manson (white iris, black rim, black pupil), Blind Eye (all white), Dark Angel (black pupil, blue iris, black eyeball), and even glow-in-the-dark lenses. Goth-specific lenses can be found everywhere now, for example with tiny black Celtic crosses imitating the eye's pupil.

Dental accessories of the damned

Vampire fangs come in a variety of forms, everything from candy fangs and the cheap plastic variety bought around Halloween, to filed incisors that create the hungry undead look. Many goths go the dental cap route for permanent, no-muss, no-fuss teeth.

Serrated Smiles is an online company in Maryland run by Michael Bray. "I was offended at the prices of some of my competitors. Out of spite I decided to create a fang company that offered high quality fangs at a reasonable price."

Michael makes the fangs in a studio that "looks a lot like an empty classroom—a few desks, a fume vent, and small windows."

About 75 percent of his customers are of "the gothic/vampire persuasion, or way of life." Michael doesn't consider himself goth, "although I don't own a piece of clothing that isn't black."

Serrated Smiles fangs are hand sculpted from high quality dental acrylic, and they focus on blending the bridge with the natural teeth. Fangs come in long, medium and short lengths, and besides natural shades, in gold, silver and a variety of colors. Styles can span Dracula, Nosferatu, vampire queen, parasite, werewolf, etc.

Michael's customers often take on a vampire persona, so he's used to that. One, though, rattled him: "I received a letter from a thirteen-year-old boy who'd written that he was at his wits' end trying to convince his parents he was a vampire; he didn't have the money to buy our fangs. He wanted us to send him a pair on the house, and for this, he would be eternally grateful. I was a little shaken by the letter, to say the least. I fully embrace the gothic/vampire lifestyle and I blame no one for the problems this little boy was going through, but I found it hard to enable this kind of behavior. In the end I told him I'd send him a free pair of fangs if he would convince me he *wasn't* a vampire."

a genderless lipstick called bruise

Goths, the visual drama queens that they are, wear a lot of makeup. It comes with the territory. It takes time and the skill of an artist to apply enough black eyeliner and lipstick to replicate the Morticia Addams look.

"Does pink make you puke?" is Urban Decay's slogan. Launched in January of 1996, the company began with "two friends, searching for a shade of purple nail polish to satisfy their alternative makeup tastes." Those friends, Sandy Lerner and Wende Zomnir, began marketing makeup, lipstick and Lip Gunk (lip gloss) in street-savvy shades called Bruise, Frostbite, Roach, Gash, Axphixia, Burnout, Paranoid, and S&M, with matching nail polishes to paint fashionable acrylic Vampira-like claws.

Few goths do not wear makeup. Those over thirty-five generally wear much less than they used to, but will still make the effort for alabaster skin when clubbing. Black is a great color to help the young look mature. It is a disastrous color for Elder goths, because it tends to make them look . . . elderly! Elder goths use shades like dark browns and reds for hair and lips, which provide an effect similar to black without being unforgiving. *The †*
Section overwhelmingly prefers black lipstick and polish, usually buying "the cheap stuff," as several said. The chain Hot Topic has been a godsend to nonurban Goths, who used to have to wait for Halloween to, like *TankBoy*, "stock up on purple and black then." *Rois* says, "I prefer cheap

makeup, since I melt everything off in a matter of minutes. The cheap stuff stains, so it'll stay when everything else has sweated off." They also wear red, dark red, or browns that are very dark. Vena Cava uses "dark-brown dried-blood color. Metallic, shiny, wet red or copper."

Some goths like a bit of color on their lips and nails and over their eyes. Blue in hair or on lips and nails, especially pale shades, results in an asphyxiated look. This is cyanosis at its sexiest, O_2 depletion, a delightfully cadaverous pallor. Mold, slime and the gooey corpse look aren't the most popular, but some goths tackle green in makeup.

Green lipstick is not new. Called "magic" lipstick because it is green in color but turns red on the lips, this artifice has been popular for centuries with women from Morocco. This is the country that gave us that green shrub grown in the Draa Valley that, when ground into a powder and mixed with water, turns into a paste the color and texture of pea soup, called henna. David Bowie in his Ziggy Stardust phase twigged us to the coppery delights of henna as a hair dye. It can also be applied with a fine brush or pointed stick to the skin as it is in many countries, like Morocco, and India, to create tattoo-like patterns called *mehndi* that will fade with washing . . . eventually.

ðead for centuries

Goth and pallor is pretty much a media invention. Kindergoths often go for the shocking corpse-white skin with the help of foundations like Manic Panic's Goth White, but generally as goths age, less and less makeup is used, and the first to go tends to be white foundation.

Many goths prefer night, which means they avoid daylight as much as possible. This has the added benefit of lowering the risk of melanoma (skin cancer). And energy somehow increases after sunset for subcultural types, probably because what is inspiring is found in the darkness. While a lack of Vitamin D can cause ricketts, thanks to multivitamins, goths can remain out of sunlight. Lack of sunlight keeps the skin paler. Of course, not all goths are WASPs (white Anglo-Saxon Protestants), but goths of color like paler skin too—it seems to be in the goth gene.

For those who want a paler look without resorting to makeup, Gawth-Pallor has an entire Web page of tan remover and skin lightener recipes (see Chapter 4 URLs).

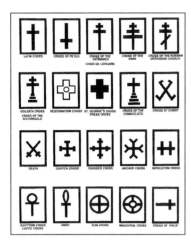

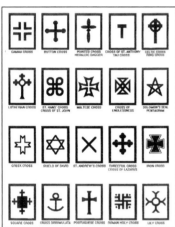

Courtesy of Hugues Leblanc

Contrary to popular belief, the symbol of the cross was not incorporated as a Christian symbol until about the seventh century A.D. Prior to that, Christ was represented by a lamb, or a shepherd—the good shepherd.

Crosses are ancient symbols, used in many cultures and religions. Some have fallen out of favor, like the Iron Cross, which came to represent Nazis' insanely driven belief in genetic purity that resulted in mass murder.

But for the Latin Cross and its variations, the obvious symbolism is that two (or more) elements are intersecting—for instance, life and death. A cross to bear means carrying a burden, as did Christ. When Christianity adopted it, the cross took on a power it had not found before. A vampire or a suicide should be buried at a crossroads, the idea being that the cross representing Christ will keep both unholy spirits from rising again. The metaphor is clearly one of power, transformation of the physical to the spiritual and vice versa. Being buried at a crossroad also confuses the returning spirit—which way should I go?

Psychologist Carl Jung saw the cross as a symbol for the creative process, and most goths are artistic. The creative process usually leads to a crossroads, a place where the artist can go this way or that and a decision must be reached. In both the artistic process and in the process of creative living, that decision requires contemplation and soul-searching. There are always two obvious choices. But following "process," as most goths do, often involves *not* choosing, but holding on, waiting out the tension of indecision. Process is about being patient until a third, unforeseen, unanticipated alternative spontaneously emerges. Human life itself is the best example of process: an ovum and a sperm join, out of which, when the time is right, comes a third thing, neither the one nor the other, a magical blending of the two—new life.

In 1998 AntiSally of Washington State went to a party. "I noticed people wearing traditional rosaries and thought they would look much gother if they had skulls on them."

The Goth Rosary was born. AntiSally makes every rosary by hand in a production area of her home where "there are beads in boxes that stack up to my knees and completed items hanging from every possible hook, pin head, lamp, or nail. Around my computer are yellow Christmas lights and five tiny Day of the Dead figurines."

Her rosaries on first glance resemble traditional ones. She does custom orders, but her four basic styles are: Type O, Type A, Type AB and Type AB Negative, with a choice of beads which include pewter Our Father skulls, connectors that can be, among other things, a Madonna, a pentagram, or a spiderweb, and a talisman to dangle at the bottom, ranging from a traditional crucifix to a skeleton, raven, gargoyle, or red devil's head. She also sells clergy shirts and last-rites crucifixes. Besides goths, her satisfied customers include: "Catholics, Satanists, Pagans, Wiccans, vampires, SCA [Society for Creative Anachronism] members, Grateful Dead followers, rockers and people wanting me to copy an item of jewelry worn by a hip-hop singer. I am always pleased that they find me, and I really enjoy the whole process of making their items become a reality."

AntiSally excels in packaging too—the rosaries arrive in little plastic coffins that include candies. The secrets of her success: "Subvert the dominant paradigm, and keep prices low and service high!"

One of the most startling pieces of information from *The † Section* is that a third of them own no crosses—which, of course, goes against stereotype. In some cases, they are not now nor have they ever have been a part of the Christian faith, so wearing a cross doesn't feel right. For others, who *were* part of the Christian faith, hostility toward a religion they feel has oppressed them lingers. The nearly two-thirds of *The † Section* who do like crosses own over 800 of them. Roughly 75 percent of those crosses are for jewelry, and the rest are used in home decor—this includes a few ankhs.

In Egyptian hieroglyphics, the ankh can mean both "life" and "hand mirror." The ankh represented the great Goddess—a narrow triangle, surrounded by crossbar arms and an oval head (similar shapes come from Africa and represent fertility goddesses). In ancient Egypt it became known as a symbol of sexual union, as well as of immortality for the gods, which they might confer upon their priests and priestesses. The loop of the design was often painted red, to indicate that this gift came through the blood—the menstrual blood—of the goddess. Most Egyptian deities are depicted wearing or holding an ankh.

the grave revisited

AntiSally of The Goth Rosary fame has also developed a series of scents that goths can relate to. She says, "Due to the lack of truly interesting fragrances on the market, I have taken it upon myself to fill the void. I have formulated and produced a line of uncommon scents for uncommon people. The line includes Graveyard—the smell of rich loamy soil, fresh green grass with a note of flora; Nocturnal—black clothing; Dark Streets—the smell of clove mixed with patchouli and *nag champa;* and Gothic Rose—bloodred Roses, the smell of unfurled deep crimson petals."

jewelry to weep over

The people of the seventeenth through nineteenth centuries took Death seriously. Two hundred years of plagues barely left a family that had not lost someone to disease. No parties were thrown to celebrate the life of the deceased. Death was a grim reality.

During this time, cemeteries, which had formerly been grounds for mass burials, became organized cities for the dead. Mourning evolved into ritual where fairly strict protocol was followed. Charms and amulets to ward off death have been used by human beings since antiquity. But it became fashionable between the 1600s and World War I (1914–1918), especially in Britain, but also elsewhere in Europe and in North America, to wear jewelry to commemorate the death of a loved one.

The trend seems to have begun with King Charles I of England in 1649. After his execution, loyalists wore his portrait in miniature set in the bezels of rings, with a lock of his much-treasured hair hidden behind the picture. On the ring the words were inscribed: "The glory of England has departed," accompanied by a skull and a crown.

In the late 1600s, memorial rings were made and given to family and friends as keepsakes after a funeral. In the early 1700s, the French introduced a light-hearted rococo element, including ornate lettering, to mourning jewelry. And in the early 1800s, the fashion in Germany and elsewhere was Berlin iron and cut-steel mourning jewelry, lacquered black.

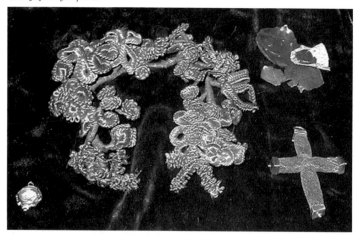

Hair Mourning Jewelry
Courtesy of Nancy Kilpatrick

Initially memorial rings featured death's-head motifs—a skull, or a skull and crossed bones—against a background of silk, ivory, or perhaps hair, all under heavy rock crystal. Then bracelets, brooches, lockets, stickpins and earrings joined the rings. Mementos were formed out of gold and silver, decorated with pearls and enamel, carved in ivory, bone, Whitby jet (lightweight coal), vulcanite, bog oak, horn, French jet (black glass), or gutta-percha (tree sap), or cut out of steel or iron.

Skulls fell out of fashion, replaced by motifs that included clasped hands, funereal urns, carved silhouettes, Gothic archways, hearts entwined, roses, painted eyes, and the lovely image of a woman weeping over a tombstone with foliage like a weeping willow as a backdrop. The words "Memento Mori" (Remember that you must die), and "Mizpah" (from Genesis 31:49: "And Mizpah: for he said, The Lord watch between me and thee, when we are absent, one from another.") were often used, or the more impersonal "In Memory of."

The most intriguing material incorporated into mourning jewelry was human hair. The earliest jewelry from the 1600s sometimes included a lock of hair. But by the early 1800s, hair became a basic material in its own right. Usually the hair was braided on a braiding table, to form shapes like fleurettes for earrings, or crosses for a necklace, but was mainly just plaited, with gold clasps for the bracelet or watch fob. Some of the more interesting pieces were hairs flattened against a background and swirled into lovely curlicues held together with a strip of gold.

As *Godey's Lady's Book* of May 1855 said: "Hair is at once the most delicate and lasting of our materials, and survives us, like love. It is so light, so gentle, so escaping from the idea of death, that with a lock of hair belonging to a child or friend, we may almost look up to heaven and compare notes with the angelic nature—may almost say, 'I have a piece of thee here, not unworthy of thy being now.' "

The range of mourning hair jewelry runs from the cheap knockoffs of the day—with complaints that professional weavers substituted horsehair for the hair of the departed—to the work of fashionable award-winning hair weavers such as Antoni Forrer, hairworker by appointment to Queen Victoria, and Lemmonier et Cie of Paris, who embellished pieces with turquoise and gems. Today, Victorian mourning hair jewelry is expensive, and highly collectible.

Another interesting facet of Victorian funereal custom is the hair mourning wreath. Anywhere from four to twenty inches in length, it is made entirely out of woven human hair, sometimes added to over genera-

In visions of the dark night
I have dreamed of joy departed
But a walking dream of life and light
Hath left me broken-hearted.
Ah! What is not a dream by day
To him whose eyes are cast
On things around him with a ray
Turned back upon the past?

—Edgar Allan Poe

Logo by Alchemy Gothic England

tions, often displayed in a deep shadow box. These wreaths are rare, delicate, and astonishing artwork.

Poe's Attic is an on-line Victorian mourning jewelry resource. The dearth of information about mourning items makes this site special. Images and articles predominate, accompanied by written descriptions.

Rachell Frazian, who set up the site, says most of the people who visit are "women who have an interest in mourning items." One type of mourning memento she displays on her site is casket plaques from the 1800s which were attached to the coffin but removed before burial and kept by the family as a keepsake. Occasionally, visitors have a more direct connection to the items they see. "An American man wrote regarding an English funeral receipt I'd displayed. The receipt, dated 1878, was from a 'Carpenter & Furnishing Undertaker' for a coffin and other funeral items. The undertaker was an English ancestor of this man. He wanted to include it in his collection of family artifacts, which he did."

Rachell believes, "The Victorians addressed the pain of loss with a prescribed social structure of custom, dress, and jewelry. This gave the bereaved a way to channel their grief, providing comfort and direction at an emotionally devastating time. Mourning jewelry gives an insight into how one group of people coped with the inevitable conclusion that all of us face."

the grandpapas of goth jewelry

In 1977, Geoff (Deth) Kayson and Trevor Phillipson, two out-of-work English youths, were making metal jewelry for punks and rock bands. Their interest in history and art contributed to their unusual designs, and they earned a modest living, enough that by 1980 they could start a company. Today the name Alchemy is legend, and about half of their customers are goths.

What is the mysterious Alchemy workshop like? "Despite having ambitions and pretensions to owning and working out of the attic of a remote Medieval castle in forested Central Europe," Geoff says, "the reality of business dictates that we confine ourselves to a practical, fully regulated environment convenient to our zealous, Renfield-like, but mortally dependent staff. The place is still, however, infested with coffins, skulls, altar-crosses, church benches, nooses, black makeup mirrors and countless other sinister reminders testifying to the temporary insanity of our darkly deranged staff."

Alchemy designs and produces a variety of products, including T-shirts, furniture, even crystal balls! But it is their high-quality jewelry and accessories for which they are renowned, particularly items like necklaces, armor rings and poison rings. Their classy Medieval, Renaissance and Victorian motifs incorporate vampires, crosses, dragons, and pentagrams, in silver, pewter, and other good metals. Because they are designers, they like to do one-of-a-kind items when they can. Geoff describes "The High-gate," a remotely controlled, six-foot-long, hand-carved, solid oak "coffin on a tomb" gothic cocktail bar—standing seven feet high when opened, with a built-in fridge, stereo system, lights, and a full eighty-plus-piece set of hand-cut leaded crystal."

The company moved gracefully from punk to goth. "The goth community has a need for its own highly specialized, dark strain of aesthetic individualism," Geoff says. "This, however, as far as fashion and lifestyle is concerned, needs to be achieved with taste, and within the confines of an unspoken but intellectually understood protocol. Variety, quality, and authenticity are essential ingredients of such eccentric self-expression." Twice yearly, they travel to the Whitby Goth Weekend, an event "where we meet and cavort with thousands of the best, most outrageous and fun characters in England in a bizarre three-day orgy of darkness and noise."

Twenty-five years of catering to goth tastes requires devotion, Geoff agrees. "You have to live it and feel it to understand it, and to earn the respect of your potential clientele. The experience we have gained and put back into our chosen discipline makes Alchemy, probably, the most comprehensively skilled and practiced creative craftsmen in the genre anywhere since the mid-nineteenth century."

Pre-Raphaelite arts and crafts design workshop founder William Morris would have been proud.

femme fatale jewelry

The word "abiosis" means "absence of life." Collections d'Abiose from Québec is anything but lifeless. The antique-silver plated line incorporates the delicacy of historical jewelry design with modern materials.

Eight years ago Ann d'Abiose appeared out of the mists with an old Victorian suitcase lined in red satin, a Rococo mirror and a couple of candlesticks, displaying her exquisite creations at goth events. Her original hand-made designs have been sold at and worn in fashion shows at several Convergence conventions. She sells to only a few shops around the world. "I'm picky about the people I deal with. I want to have fun, and also to deal with nice people. If someone treats me as if I'm a big manufacturer and does not want to understand the person that I am, that's too bad, because I won't deal with him or her. I don't care about the dollars I will lose."

Collections d'Abiose consists of four types of jewelry, with various motifs possible, for example: delicate vampire necklaces, dainty Versailles metal headbands, ornate Baroque finger tips, Gothic gloves of metal and rubber that hook over one finger. Ann loves to sell directly to individuals via the Internet. Three quarters of her customers are goth, and it's common for her to receive much-deserved "sweet comments on my work."

Her collection is available directly from her Web site for North Americans, and for those in Europe and the Far East from the distributor in Italy, Lacrime Degli Dei.

widow's weeds and other graveyard trendsetters

The epitome of goth fashion is the widow, dressed in black from head to toe, the skirt kissing the soil beneath her granny boots, the black lace-trimmed handkerchief applied delicately to her nose hidden by the multi-layered mourning veil.

The wearing of black around a corpse is an ancient practice. There has always lingered within the human psyche a fear of the dead. Spirits of ill will can hover near the lifeless body, and when the living wear black, they are less conspicuous, especially during those long nighttime vigils beside the coffin.

Queen Victoria is our role model for mourning, thank you. After all, she did manage to mourn her dead husband for forty years. Quite a feat.

Victorian mourning veils were multilayered, so that a shorter or a longer veil could cover the face, while another part draped down the back. The fabric, often crepe, ensured that the bereaved's face was well hidden with but the vaguest sense of features behind, keeping tear-stained cheeks a private matter. One difficulty with original mourning veils is that the fabric was frequently colored with indigo dye, which contains sulphur and arsenic, both of which are poisonous when inhaled. This could explain why more than one Victorian widow fainted at the graveside.

Azrael's Accomplice Designs is an online store run out of Texas for the last seven years by Batty, who is well-known to the net-goth community. She offers, among many other items, black veils. The shop also has a nice line of men's clothing, from ruffled neck cravats to PVC coats. "Being part of the gothic subculture for many years, my designs naturally reflect my love of that style of dress. A lot of stores try too hard to be 'goth' . . . sticking to some sort of 'must look spooky' mantra. I just try to make things that appeal to my tastes, and are well made. Perhaps I want to help expand the gothic fashion horizons. I'd say about 60 percent of my customers are goth."

Batty designs all the items herself, save a few collars created by her boyfriend. "I don't want to be one of those stores that has the same old stuff by the same old designers." Her veils come in a variety of lengths: single, double, or multi-layered, and are either clip-on or anchored to a mini-hat or cluster of flowers. The styles range from classic to fairy. Something for every mournful occasion.

angel, devil, fairy wings

Imagine a room full of corpses, skeletons, and coffins propped against the walls, wings hanging above them as if about to take disembodied flight. This is home to Deviance Designs, a two-person Las Vegas company, owned by Subrina Khan (who goes by the name of Ange) and Mike Dunn.

Wings are extremely popular fashion accessories for dark moths. All types of wings, from delicate and fragile gossamer fairy feathers to hard, stainless-steel, metallic, demon-from-Hell wings. Deviance Designs is the first company to specialize in making latex wings. "A lot of people in underground subcultures have a deep love of latex. Some like it because it looks nice, some because the feel excites them, some for other reasons. People like our wings because they have a realistic look and feel to them. When we make our evil butterfly wings, we offer them with scales, for an ultra-real look." Their best-selling wings are rounded, lace-style.

Deviance Designs also creates . . . corpses. "We're one of the few companies that makes full-body corpses over a skeleton. Many companies we've seen make only the head and hands, and construct the bodies from cotton and dowel rods! We give a lot of attention to realism." Always important to fill that empty chair and even out a dinner party!

idle hands; or, working for the devil!

It was when Louis XVI ruled France that brides took to giving their personal fans to their bridesmaids as wedding presents. The fans were hand-painted, the theme usually mythological figures; they were works of art.

Purses in Victorian England ranged from fabric drawstring bags known as reticules to tiny silver or metallic mesh purses. Victorian goths still carry replicas, and original items if they can find them. House of Ill Repute makes a satin reticule with fringe trim at the bottom and the funeral letters IHS embroidered across the front. Gwyn Strang has been running her shop in Toronto since 1994. "Goth was my lifestyle. I couldn't have opened any other type of store." Most of her products are of her own design. One of her hottest-selling items is her bat-shaped purse.

Other goth purses in vogue range from industrial hardware like workers' stainless steel lunch pails and old military ammunition cases painted black over their camouflage, to coffin-shaped purses in a variety of fabrics, and cyber insect-pod backpacks.

Goth took to gloves instantly. Wasn't it Boy George who started the trend of the fingerless glove, one he picked up from the Victorian upper and lower classes? The upper class wore gloves—kid, silk, satin, lace—with and without fingers, the latter for doing embroidery and needlework. The Cockneys cut out the fingers of their woolen gloves to separate items like the Dickensian matchsticks. Ladies of the night clipped the fingers from their net gloves to count the money.

Ever ingenious, goths took gloves a step further. They stabbed a hole in the wrist seam of a fishnet or mesh long-sleeved shirt and hooked their thumb into the opening, creating an insta-fingerless glove.

Kambriel, the owner of Kambriel (formerly the well-known Salem, Massachusetts, goth shop Atrocities), says, "When we began in 1994, we used to offer handmade tombstone- and bat-shaped candies, which we made little velvet pouches for. We also used to offer tiny hooded velvet cowls for 'children of the night'!" Now their line includes an array of clothing, and accessories like gloves, hats, handkerchiefs, black Victorian bloomers for women, and opiate (smoking) jackets for men. They also make hand-sewn black mourning veils, both floor-length and blusher-length (covering the face).

Kambriel says their work environment is important. "We tend to surround ourselves with images to inspire our creativity and stimulate our imagination. This can help when we're drafting new designs. Some examples would be pre-Raphaelite vignettes, vintage photographs, Art Nouveau illustrations, and photographs of awe-inspiring architecture. We create a lovely and exotic environment to work in since we are there so much, and can't help but think some of that beauty and influence rubs off on the items we produce!"

She also says about her partner, Curse, and herself, "We consider ourselves to be gothic in our own sense. We would likely fall into a Romantic gothic realm, with a sense of mystery, drama, and the fantastical. We do adore those classic gothic elements such as soaring cathedrals, eerie and powerful classical music, the romanticized interpretations of past eras. Majestic environments lit by moonlight and the like all hold an allure for us."

the curse of sunshine

Canes and parasols became fashionable with goths in the nineties. Early goths were too close to punk to carry such apparatus, even if the cane handle was carved ivory, and the stick pulled apart to reveal a knife or sword hidden within. Canes, of course, smack of the dandy. They also double as a fetish toy.

For a long time, the only frilly umbrellas available to goths—unless they made their own—were from China. White lace umbrellas with pale wooden handles might or might not dye black. Another option was Chinese paper umbrellas, with Oriental designs in bright colors for the China Girl look.

Tenebrae (meaning "shadows") is a seven-year-old gothic parasol company, run by Mirabai Vayne, who says, "Tenebrae is the culmination of a lifelong love of history, spurred on by a dissatisfaction with our present era and a desire to bring back an aesthetic of beauty, elegance, and mystery that has been absent from our society for far too long."

Goths, she believes, need parasols, for practical purposes, and for aesthetic reasons—for example, "to preserve their lovely pallor. Our sun-loving culture has all but forgotten this once-essential accessory. While in recent years many have become aware of the damaging effects of sun exposure and have taken steps to choose a daily lotion with SPF, the cult of tanning one's skin as a symbol of health and leisure (particularly in America) still holds strong. People continue to bake until well done, regardless of consequences. At one time, history told quite a different story. For thousands of years a porcelain complexion was the much-heralded mark of elegance and refinement."

Tenebrae's debut line features an elaborate hand-carved and lacquered hardwood handle meticulously reproduced from an 1870s original. "We have improved upon the past by offering new and elegant fabrics such as velvet and PVC, and a more dramatic canopy shape. Our parasols match the quality found in fine antiques. Our customers do not want a mere parasol, they want a Tenebrae."

Mirabai feels strongly about recapturing elegance. "Sadly, for those of us who embrace this culture as self-defining—our very souls—the worldly perception of 'What is gothic?' as propagated by our media-obsessed culture is disheartening. What has been forgotten and/or for the most part ignored is that what was once commonly termed 'Gothic' gained its roots from Romanticism, dating from roughly 1760–1830. This era was best known for Shelley, Keats, Byron, Coleridge, Emerson, Goethe, and countless other brilliant minds whose works put an emphasis on the sublimity of individualism, a retreat from the artificiality of the world and its conventions, the belief that imagination is superior to reason, a devotion to beauty, love of and worship of nature, and a fascination with the past. The Gothic genre originated in novels of this time—mid-eighteenth century; the catalyst being Horace Walpole's *The Castle of Otranto* (1764), as Romanticism's natural counterpart. Its focus: exploration into the subterranean shadow realms of the human psyche, offering up a predilection for the macabre, the mysterious, the supernatural, and the terrifying, particularly in the pleasure of terror. It is in this history that I live, breathe, and find my very defining element and inspiration."

hardware

Goths like to wear leather. And chains. And if they are vegetarians, they like to wear veggie-leather (usually vinyl) and chains. Because black and silver are basic goth colors, these accessories work well with most outfits. Leather and metal combined bring out the seriously sexy of the Industrial look. They also hint at, and sometimes overtly identify the wearer as someone who has an interest in fetish or S-M.

Like many purveyors of gothic leather accessories, Hugues Leblanc of Montréal's Tapholov "made my first items out of necessity, since I couldn't find anything in the shops. Then I made things for friends, and they convinced me to start putting my products in stores. It became a nice way to make the acquaintance of goth shop owners and others in the goth community. I'd say 100 percent of my customers are goth, and they wear my armbands and wrist cuffs for several reasons. For some, it's strictly fashion; others are a bit kinky and indulge in erotic sports. I've always felt there's a huge crossover between goth and fetish."

Hugues has been making his items for five years, and "I still work out of my apartment, on the floor mostly, as they do in Asia." His goods are high quality, using two layers of leather, stitched as well as glued, adorned with studs, spikes, and rivets that form designs. Every piece, he advertises, is "made one by one." His top-selling items vary, since fashion changes a bit from year to year, but some perennial favorites are vampire gauntlets, boot extensions, and Oriental hair cones, which come with four black lacquer chopsticks or four stainless steel chopsticks. He admits that "Success won't pay your rent unless you order everything from a Taiwanese manufacturer. I do it my way, the slow old-fashioned way, because I like the work, and I like to make people happy. Sometimes my customers even buy me a beer!"

the agony and the ecstasy

Despite Napoleon's dire warning that "The corset is the murderer of the human race," these fashion accessories have had a long and illustrious history.

The women and men of Minoan society—1500 B.C.—loved their sports, including bull-jumping, which required support for waist and back. Both genders wore corsets as overgarments, and goddess figurines that have survived display them prominently as outerwear. Tiryns and Theban frescoes show corsets over the waist and hips, the framework seemingly made of metal plates. The ancient Greeks wore leather bands to slim the waist and flatten the hips. Gowns from 1170 suggest manipulation underneath clothing, and although Chaucer referred to corsets, fashion being the fickle creature it is, not much was heard of them again until the 1400s.

About that time, the Spanish dictated fashion. They favored the tiny waist and flattened chest. The corset, with the help of the farthingale (like a hoop skirt), would allow a long slender waist to end in a point. These corsets, worn by both genders, imprisoned the body, forcing an upright posture and a "dignified" walk.

HOW TO LACE A CORSET

1. Loosen lacing before getting into the corset.

2. Crisscross the corset lacing from top to bottom.

3. Tie a knot in the two free ends at the bottom.

4. The lacing now is a continuous loop with no free ends.

5. At the waist, pull out the loops on each side.

6. Begin tightening lacing from top down to waist, then from bottom up to waist. Waist loops will become longer.

7. When corset is tight enough, pull the waist loops tightly, making sure to keep pressure even.

8. Tie the waist loops together. They can be knotted and hidden inside the back of the corset, or tied in a bow, or tied in the front of the corset. The Victorians allowed 1" per decade of a woman's life. Lace accordingly.

Somewhere in the 1500s the Italians created the *coche* or early busk, an object placed under the lacing, which allowed a smooth straight line. By the late 1500s, corsets had become hinged metal cages resembling armor, sometimes perforated with airholes. Catherine de Médicis, an Italian princess reigning in the French court, was responsible for the flexible steel framework innovation, making life a bit less painful. She also determined that waist size should correspond to a lady's position in the court. Men at this time also wore corsets of a similar style, although the female body was encased more rigidly.

It took until the middle of the 1600s for the French to propagate their titillating décolleté fashions, which revealed some bust. Corsets were stiffened with paste. A true busk was invented, made of wood, ivory, silver, and later whalebone, which could be removed and played with by a lady much as she would a fan. Some busks were shaped like daggers!

Corsets were worn at court, horseback riding, by pregnant women, and by children, who were corseted from the moment they could walk, to give them the coveted "upright carriage." They have been worn under clothing, over clothing, and as a bodice only. Lacing happened in the front, in the back, on the sides, or all of the above. Materials have ranged from silk, satin, cotton and linen to metal and rubber. The boning was usually whalebone, later supplemented by cane and metal strips.

By the 1700s, the textile industry adopted mechanical processes that made proliferation possible. Corsets fastened on either side by a "stomacher," a triangle that masked the bodice opening. For a while, the French Revolution put a crimp in corset sales in that country, because the garments were associated with the debauched nobility.

In the early 1800s the divorce corset came into vogue—not spouses but breasts being divorced (separated) one from the other. Another fashion was the pregnant stay, which covered the body from shoulders to below the hips. In 1848 metal eyelets were invented. Prior to this, lacing holes were sewn around with silk, and consequently corsets could not take extreme lacing without damage to the material. Tighter lacing became the trend, and the seventeen- to twenty-one-inch waist was the standard. Every girl's ambition, it seemed, was to have a waist measurement not exceeding her age. There is no real proof that women removed a rib bone for a tinier waist, but there are allusions to tightening a corset as a way of controlling behavior.

By the mid-1800s day corsets with shoulder straps were in vogue, and eight- to ten-inch demicorsets were worn for domestic work. Small straps and buckles adorned the front, and one model sported a spring latch that apparently popped open at the most inopportune times! Overpetticoats attached directly to the corset, and suspenders sewn onto the bottom hooked onto stockings, replacing garters. A brief attempt in 1851 to kill the corset and substitute trousers for women met with horror.

By the end of the century the long-waisted, sleek-silhouetted Gibson Girl look was all the rage. One Paris corsetiere created a specimen halfway to the knees, which probably made certain of nature's calls nearly impossible.

In the 1800s men did not usually wear corsets except for therapeutic reasons, although dandies had their tail coats waisted and corseted to create the hourglass shape. Ready-made corsets became available, and mid-1800s the first rubber corsets were sold, ostensibly for hygienic purposes.

By the initial decade of the 1900s the wasp waist was passé, and the "natural" waist fashionable. Corsets turned straight-line. Clock-spring steel covered with hard rubber or celluloid knocked out the whalebone industry. Nineteen-ten saw the elastic step-in corset, and the ventilated corset made of net or mesh. In 1930 latex panty girdles were mass produced. The foundation garment, a combo of corset and bra, appeared. In 1947 the waspie, or waist cincher, was born.

Corsets per se virtually vanished until the 1980s, when they again hit the big time as an overgarment, or in the fetish world, the *only* garment. The rest is history in the making.

Corsets worn on top of clothing are a staple in the goth wardrobe, for both genders. Dianna DiNoble has been designing and making corsets from different eras since 1993. "I quit college to turn Starkers! into a full-time business." The name is one of those delightful British idioms meaning "stark naked"!

Dianna's Toronto workshop is Victorian parlor meets computer geek. "On the other side of the fish tank is the apocalypse-land production area," says Dianna, who admits, "I'm not sure if I'm [still] goth. My fiancé describes me as the woman from *Terminator 2!*"

What makes Starkers! corsets unique is that Dianna heavily researches eras—Edwardian, Victorian, Georgian, among others—replicating original designs but using more comfortable modern materials. "I love roman-

Photo courtesy of AMF Korsets

tic style and historical clothing, as do most of my clients. Starkers! reflects my own tastes. We encourage goths to have their unique shape and sense of style incorporated into a corset, instead of being at the mercy of retail store size and style availability."

Her corsets are so popular she once made a black leather "Batty" corset for a woman in Sweden, "who went to a bar one night and ran into a woman who was wearing a white patent leather 'Batty' corset. They looked at each other and yelled, 'It's a Starkers! "Batty"!' They both e-mailed me with this story. Apparently it sparked a friendship."

Probably the most unusual corset shop in the goth world is the decade-old A-M-F Korsets (Aesthetic Meat Factory), of Germany. Louis Krebs started the company out of necessity. "I was running a bondage club in Berlin, and I needed to be able to create unique leather gear and bondage equipment. Over the years, interest has grown rapidly, and for the last five years, leatherwork has been my sole source of income." The name and the corset designs reflect Louis's philosophy: "Aesthetic Meat Factory is a division of *Aesthetic Meat Foundation*, an organization to spread the virus of apocalyptic art and culture and infect the consciousness of a vacant mass of soulless meat-machines."

Half of Louis's business comes from the goth-industrial crowd, and half from the S-M/fetish world, with a bit from the film industry as well. A-M-F Korsets creates wearable artwork, made of sculpted leather, painted in striking hues, and some designs seem to challenge gravity. "We turned an ancient style of armor into a line of comfortable corsetry and accessories so our customers can unleash their demonic beauty and elegantly enter the apocalypse. A-M-F supports the need of the individual to express him/herself."

Louis goes on to say, "It is A-M-F's philosophy to push the evolution of subcultures, and therefore shift the social focus away from a mass media–invented reality, and mutate the idea of self-awareness, creating a rupture in standards of reality, and dissociation from cultural and social boundaries."

Such an anti–established-order philosophy can lead to problems. "I received a death threat about a T-shirt I designed after Columbine; the shirt contained a statement on the back declaring that Violence is not a product of the entertainment industry, but rather, is a direct response to the suppression of the individual, a suppression that has its roots in a social neurosis that spreads fear of individual thought, change, and self-expression. I proudly present this death threat in the history section of my Web site, for the public's perusal."

In addition to corsets, A-M-F's original designs include fetish items like masks, chokers, cuffs, and wings. "The oddest piece in our line," Louis says, "is the Destroyer, a male chastity belt made with daunting spikes, as well as metal and chains that engulf and protect the male genitalia with six locks, assuring the wearer a vampire-proof, demon-withstanding night of abstinence!"

foot fetishists

Goths are not the only foot fetishists in the world, but they do love their boots. Doc Martens have been the favored black boot with goths, well, since the beginning of goth.

Klaus Maertens, from a town near Munich, injured his foot skiing in the Bavarian Alps. While convalescing, Maertens envisioned a super-comfortable shoe with lots of support. He teamed up with an old college friend and they produced the world's first heat-sealed air cushioned sole. Their success in Germany led to selling the rights to English footwear manufacturers R. Griggs & Co. Docs have been the boot of choice for many subcultures, beginning with the Mods, through the Skinheads, Punks, and onward. Doc Martens is way different than most mainstream companies—they actually embrace the various subcultures they sell to, including goth—which have in turn embraced them, and that's probably one of the reasons—the other being fashion—that Docs are a goth footwear staple. Most of *The † Section* own or have owned one or more pairs.

"Writhe and Shine" comic
Copyright by Robert Tritthardt

HEY SHINE, WHEN IS IT THAT THEY STOP BEING PLATFORMS AND START BEING STILTS?

HELL IF I KNOW, WRITHE. HEH, AT LEAST WE CAN SEE UP HER SKIRT!

Courtesy of X-tra-X

At the other end of the spectrum is Vancouver, Canada, designer John Fluevog. Fluevogs come in many styles, but the two that appeal to goths most are his Derby Swirl boots, with their "angel" soles that resist "alkali, water, acid, fatigue, and Satan," and the Ultra Vogs Grand National Boot, probably the only Satanic boot in existence, the heel being a cloven hoof.

Boots are so much a staple of gothing-out, most goths own quite a few pairs. *DJ Ladybee's* closet is stuffed with fifty pairs of boots and shoes.

Many shops sell boots, including Pennangalan Dreams, run by Doktor Joy in the United Kingdom. Their online store went live in 1998. Doktor Joy had an agenda in starting his virtual shop—about two-thirds of his customers are goth. "I wanted to make British goth boots available to the world, and to do it at reasonable prices. The markup on boots at retail stores is approaching 200 percent. I find this to be almost criminal."

Pennangalan Dreams sells many styles of boots, including "veggie" boots, which avoid animal hides in favor of man-made materials that imitate leather. Two of his best-selling items are Storm Commandos, and Gladiator boots.

Doktor Joy finds, well, joy in selling boots. "Something that we get fairly often, and that always makes me smile, is when a goth girl from some far corner of the world orders a pair of boots, and then her mum orders a pair shortly afterwards, telling us she likes her daughter's boots so much she has to get some as well. Just last week we had a mother call up after her ten-year-old goth son (how young can you start these days?!) had found our Web site—and she ordered a pair for him and a pair for herself."

X-tra-X is Germany's largest purveyor of underground fashions. They have been in business for thirteen years, operating both online and out of three shops. Alexa and Monaco are the owners, and they produce a 370-page catalog of everything gothic, from Victorian, Industrial, fetish and Cyber clothing to wings to decor objects. X-tra-X is one of the few goth shops with a section for children's goth clothing, from babies to mid-teens. One of their specialties is boots, like New Rock, made by a company in Spain that creates styles extremely popular with goths, especially those into Cyberwear, because of the futuristic look and metallic additions. As well as imports from all over the world, X-tra-X also sells their own line.

Each of the three X-tra-X shops is distinctive. Alexa describes them: "In Berlin, we have a big metallic-winged angel looking out for us; in Karlsruhe, the shop is decorated in vampire-comic style Purgatory with Lady Death; the Ulm shop looks like a voodoo-rocking hell for vampires, with lots of gargoyles, angels, and demons."

Alexa says she and Monaco have "both been interested in goth and vampires since we were fourteen. In Germany, there had been no way to buy clothes or accessories for gothic people, so we tried to offer everything. I love goths—we carry mystery and darkness. We're free and do what we want to do." X-tra-X is like a goth department store, offering more than 5,000 items to their customers, 80 percent of whom are goths. They also count a number of bands among their clientele: Das Ich, Clan of Xymox, 69 Eyes, Dimmu Gorgir, and Theatre of Tragedy.

X-tra-X enjoys feedback from their customers, "especially goth marriages, where they write thanking us for the beautiful clothes. It makes our day!" And while the shop has never had a bad experience with goths, they have had some frightening moments. "Whenever a sensational headline about goths and Satanic practices appears in the paper—like 'goths' killing cats and stupid untrue things like that—the normal people come in to yell at us that we're aggressive aliens, or serial killers!"

permanent vs. temporary, or, tats Я us

For the mainstream, tattoos evoke images of carnival sideshow acts, tribal cultures from exotic-sounding but primitive locales, and drunken sailors on shore leave sobbing as the word "Mom" is stenciled inside a heart and inked onto the skin over a biceps. (In reality, most tattoo artists refuse to work on an inebriated body, since excess bleeding due to alcohol-thinned blood means more danger of infection, plus the tat will not hold.)

It has been argued that tattooing goes back 12,000 years B.C. "Ützi," the so-called mummified Ice Man discovered in the Alps in the early 1990s, is 5,000 years old, and he sports tattoos. The Bog People, mummified remains found in the bogs of northwestern Europe, the oldest dating to 8000 B.C., show tattoos on their preserved skin. We have drawings of Egyptian priests and priestesses from 2000 B.C. with tattoos clearly visible. The ancient Incas, Mayans, and Aztecs loved to tattoo their bodies. The Vikings preferred to depict their family crest on their skin. The ancient Romans tattooed their slaves, and both the Romans and the Americans tattooed

---

Tattooing Recipe from 6 A.D. Rome

Courtesy Aetius, Roman physician

1 lb. Egyptian pine wood bark
2 ounces corroded bronze, ground with vinegar
2 ounces of gall (insect egg deposits)
1 ounce vitriol (iron sulphate)

Mix well and sift. Soak powder in 2 parts water and 1 park leek juice. Wash skin to be tattooed with leek juice. Prick design with needles until blood is drawn. Rub in the ink.

TATTOOS OF THE † SECTION

angel "A black tribal design back of my neck (to mark my first year of celibacy); a black dragon on my shoulder (victory dragon, for beating cancer); biohazard symbol on my lower back (reminder to keep body clean and disease-free)."

Medea

"My husband and I exchanged tattoos for wedding gifts."

Lord Madd "The Chinese pictogram meaning to make music. If I ever find someone to spend my life with, I will get two more—To make love and to make a Family."

Zerstoerte "I've lost count! I keep adding onto older tattoos, so they're becoming one big one! [laughing out loud]. I've probably been tattooed at least thirty-five separate times."

Deacon Syth "I have many tattoos but regret one of them. The NHL Colorado Avalanche logo on my left shoulder blade—it will be covered soon."

criminals. In the UK, army deserters were marked in this way. And the Nazis tattooed dehumanizing numbers on the wrists of those they interned in concentration camps.

The word we use for the process comes from the Tahitian word *tatau*, meaning "to mark something." Tattooing is simple: cut or prick the skin, insert pigment or coloring into the scratch. Anyone can do it, and some do their own. But not everyone is an artist and, because the pigment is under the skin, the color is permanent. Laser skin shaving and reinking with something close to a natural skin tone are the happiest ways of "removing" a tattoo, which still leaves a scar. Traditional implements for creating a tattoo were sharpened bones, thorns, knives, and needles. Modern practitioners use electric needles.

Tattooing not only goes back to antiquity, but has been found in most cultures, and often holds deep cultural and spiritual significance. The art has soared in popularity in the last few decades, especially among youth and members of subcultures, who reflect the modern primitive expression of what they value. Human beings will have ink and dye injected just under the skin for a variety of reasons. Ornamentation is a big one, ritual another, and emotions sometimes dictate decisions. But the deepest songs of the human heart and soul probably account for most designs.

The majority of *The † Section* have tattoos, often quite a few. Goths tend to prefer their tattoos, like most everything, black. And black with grey shading is popular. Black outlines colored in are rare on goths, although red is one favored hue. So-called tribal patterns and Celtic designs are popular. Some of *The † Section*, such as *Cemetery Crow*, *Ravenheart*, and *Micah*, designed their body ornamentation. But even for those goths who have had an artist create the image, tattoos are usually extremely personal. Sometimes, they are a way to mark life-altering experiences.

piercing reality

Every major city in the world now has a plethora of piercing shops, but not all piercers are experts. Many goths like to self-pierce, but most pro piercers say it's better to see a knowledgable professional who has studied anatomy and sterilization procedures, and has the best equipment for the job. "Piercing," says professional piercer Pierre Black, "whether for aesthetic or spiritual reasons, should be a good experience, even fun. Pain is subjective, but certainly it should not be an ordeal."

Jewelry needed for the body is different from the jewelry used for pierced ears. One requirement is that the piece be smooth and seamless. Implant-grade stainless steel is often recommended, or titanium, or gold no less than 14K.

Pierre says using topical or injected anesthetics for piercing isn't a good idea. "While they may slightly reduce the pain of the procedure, ultimately they can cause more pain, bleeding, and swelling later. And applying ice before the procedure will increase the pain, and may cause bruising."

The body does not often reject a piercing—a process wherein the pierced skin slowly dies and the jewelry is pushed out. Piercing of some parts of the flesh is more prone to rejection than of others. Skin, post-piercing, must be cared for properly. If infection does occur, Pierre says there are "dozens of products that should *not* be used, and could prove dangerous, including Polysporin, Vaseline, aspirin, vitamin E, rubbing alcohol, to name just a few. One safe treatment is salt water, made with one-fourth to one-half teaspoon sea salt in 250 milliliters of warm water." He points out that severe infection is extremely rare. Symptoms of serious problems are: Skin around the piercing turns green, purple, or black; skin swells beyond the capacity of the jewelry; extreme pain; numbness or hardening of the skin around the piercing; pus from an infection is dark green or mixed with blood; a lump, cyst, or abscess forms near the piercing. For such extreme symptoms, he suggests not removing the jewelry, but rushing to see your professional piercer, who can likely clear up the infection easily or, if need be, recommend that you see a doctor.

Body piercing probably goes back to the caves. Museums hold fragments of pottery that prove the long history, like the image from Iraq in the ninth century B.C. of a man with ear piercings. We know the ancient Egyptians pierced, even the ears and noses of their cats, and they also used ear cuffs. Piercing has been done for beauty, for religious or spiritual purposes, and as a rite of passage. The Tlingit of Alaska used piercings to indicate social status—the more, the wealthier. Multiple piercings are not new. Statues from Iran in 3500–2900 B.C. show people with dozens of ear piercings. Stretching of earlobes has been done in a variety of cultures, and modern ear plugs and spools resemble those of the ancient Mayans. Until the nineteenth century, the Eskimos of Alaska wore bone lip plugs, called labrets. Another universally popular place to pierce is the nose, on either side of the nostril, or through the septum (middle).

Sally admits "I have only a tiny little one. It was an allergy test for the ink, and I was allergic. It's a spiral."

But the most controversial piercings involve the genitals. The male version once again takes us back to Victorian England. The very same Prince Albert, husband of Queen Victoria, had his penis pierced, and in so doing bequeathed such piercings his name. In Victorian England a pierced penis was not uncommon, and the jewelry worn came to be known as a "dressing ring." The ring on the pierced penis head attached to a hook on the inside of the trousers so that the organ could be held firmly against the leg to minimize the bulge when wearing those tight britches that Beau Brummell made so fashionable. Tailors of the day would inquire if a gentleman dressed to the left or the right, and tailor the trousers accordingly. The royally approved rumor has it that Prince Albert wore his to hold back his foreskin in order to keep his genitals sweet-smelling for the Queen, but we know his piercing was done prior to his marriage. Since we also know that Victoria loved him passionately, that she bore nine children, and that she mourned his passing for nearly half a century, we can assume that the erotic advantages of this piercing did not escape Her Majesty's notice.

Genital piercing in females is often confused with female genital mutilation, aka female circumcision, which it is not. The latter is a serious and sometimes life-threatening procedure forcibly performed on girls between the ages of four and ten in Africa, and parts of the Middle East and Asia, the most severe types occurring in the Somalian and the Sudanese populations. This ritual act goes back to antiquity, and local healers and midwives still use knives, razor blades, broken glass, or scissors to remove, without anesthesia, the clitoris and/or all the skin surrounding it, including the labia minora, and in severe cases, the labia majora. To control the bleeding from the clitoral artery and raw tissue surfaces, crude stitches are made with catgut or thorns, and mud poultices are applied. The risks are great: hemorrhage, shock due to secondary blood loss or extreme pain, local infection that fails to heal, septicemia, tetanus, trauma to the adjacent structures, and urinary retention—not to mention the psychological effects from all of the above, as well as from being seized and forcibly held during the procedure. The results are lack of sexual pleasure during intercourse, and extreme difficulty during childbirth.

Genital piercings, which enlightened women may have performed on their clitoral hood and other parts of the female genitalia, are done intentionally by the person pierced, for various reasons, including aesthetics, a private ritual, and enhancement of sexual pleasure.

Multiple ear piercings are common among goths. Other areas of flesh *The † Section* have had pierced are eyebrow, frenum (fold of skin), lips, nipples, navels, noses, scrotums, throats, and tongues.

A few other types of body modification exist, like implants beneath the skin, which are exceptional. Intentional scarring through cutting is more common, and usually involves personal ritual. Branding is still extremely rare.

URLs

Dark Side of the Net
www.darklinks.com/

Gothic Resources
www.vamp.org/Gothic/Resources/Business/.?

Dark Sites
www.darksites.com/

The Velvet Garden
www.velvetgarden.net/

Dark Auctions
www.darkauctions.com/

Manic Panic
www.manicpanic.com/

Hair Police
www.hairpolice.com/

Head Razor
www.headrazor.il2.com/

Urban Decay
www.urbandecay.com/

Morgeve—a page on fashion, makeup, hair
www.morgeve.dk/guide/intro.html

Gawth Pallor
www.geocities.com/RainForest/Vines/2010/gawthpallor.html

Dark Wyccan's Gothic Guide to nail care
www.waningmoon.com/nails/

Gothic Scents from AntiSally
www.gothrosary.com

Serrated Smiles.Com
www.serratedsmiles.com

Eyeglass Museum—Pieve di Cadore, Italy
www.sunrise.it/musei/occhiale/.?

Web page of glass eyes at Augenprothesen
www.augenprothesen.info/html/bilder.html

9mm SFX
www.9mmsfx.com/

Poe's Attic
www.poesattic.com

Victorian Hairworks Society
www.hairwork.com/

Alchemy
www.alchemygothic.com/

Alchemy's Gothic Emporium
www.oldcuriosityshop.net

Collections d'Abiose
www.abiose.net

Lacrime Degli Dei:
www.lacrimedeglidei.com/

Kambriel (formerly Atrocities)
www.kambriel.com/

Azrael's Accomplice Designs
www.azacdesign.com

LdyGothic's Boutique
djbarbz@aol.com

Illustrations of mourning dresses
www.msu.edu/user/beltranm/mourning/mourning.htm

Tenebrae—Purveyors of Fine Parasols
www.tenebrae.com

Underbelly (parasols)
www.underbelly.net/home.html

Deviance Designs
www.velvet.net/~deviance/main.html

2Dye4
www.2dye4.net/

Starkers!
www.starkers.com

A-M-F Korsets
www.amfkorsets.com

Ritual Designs
www.ritualdesigns.com/

Tapholov
www.tapholov.com

Pennangalan Dreams
www.pennangalan.co.uk

X-tra-X
www.x-tra-x.de/

Art of Dark (Germany online clothing)
www.artofdark.de/de/index.shtml

Coemeterivm (Italy)
www.coemeterivm.nasha.com/

Tattoos.com
www.tattoos.com/jane/steve/toc.htm

Black Sun Piercing Studio
www.blacksunstudio.com/

Steelwerks
www.steelwerksjewelry.com
www.steelwerksextreme.com

MUSIC OF THE MACABRE:
IN THE BEGINNING . . .

Now are you feeling zombified?!

then:

Gregorian chants have floated down the corridors of time to land gently in the velvet-covered lap of goth. Goths adore such evocative sounds: a cappella voices that emulate the soul drifting from the body, that evoke images of funeral processions and angels hovering above tombstones. This is otherworldly stuff, transcendent material. That the human voice can beckon spirits is amazing—feathered angel wings for the ears.

It was Pope St. Gregory the Great of the sixth century for whom these chants are named, because he promoted the use of religious chanting. Chants are voices singing the same line of music together, without instrumental accompaniment, melody only, no harmony, the words Biblical. The lines of singing are based on breathing, which is the natural break point. Consequently, the lines could not be counted, which limited the presentation. The overall effect was termed "plainsong," hauntingly spiritual sounds most goths adore.

In 1098, a true visionary was born, and a particular goth favorite among the chanters. Hildegarde von Bingen appeared on this earth, tenth child of a knight, and at the tender age of eight entered the coed (for the day) Benedictine monastery Mount St. Disibode to be educated. This particular monastery was of the Celtic tradition, which must have influenced her later work. At eighteen Hildegarde became a nun, and twenty years later they named her Abbess of Rupertsberg, on the Rhine at Bingen, Germany.

Hildegarde was an amazing woman, far ahead of her time. Besides being a writer, and in her spare time enjoying religious visions, she cranked out some pretty wicked music, which she intended that the sisters at the convent would sing at liturgical and other functions. Known as "The Sibyl of the Rhine," she received rave reviews, including this excerpt of one from Master Odo of Paris in 1148: "It is said that you are raised to Heaven, that much is revealed to you, and that you bring both great writings, and discover new manners of song."

During that tricky Romanesque era (850–1150), great changes began to occur in all of the arts. Painting was developing the science of perspective. And in music there emerged a major stylistic change. Polyphony involves regular meters, which produce a steady beat that allows lines of musical notes to be counted, and music measured. For the first time, everybody counted the same measurements, enabling different voices employing more than one distinct melody to keep together so harmony could blossom. The music we enjoy today is only possible because of polyphony.

Between the thirteenth and fifteenth centuries, the music of northern Europe entered the Gothic phase. Such schools as Ars Antiqua, Ars Nova, and the Burgundian school emerged. Instead of chanting monks, choirs and organs began to fill those Gothic cathedrals the French were building. Individual composers took charge of compositions, and works became complex.

Goths love dark music. Those who enjoy Norse mythology appreciate Richard Wagner (1813–1883)—perhaps the most controversial of classical German composers. Wagner called himself "the most German of men," and "the German spirit." Wagner was considered an anarchist and socialist, as well as an anti-Semite and a proto-fascist. His reputation was not enhanced when his music was adopted by Austrian madman Adolf Hitler, who took over Germany in the 1930s, followed by much of Europe, and almost single-handedly led the world to a major war and helped pave the way for changes in weaponry that have brought us to the point where annihilation now looks promising. Hitler, a favorite with skinheads but shunned by goths, was responsible for the deaths of many millions of human beings, hating them if they were Jewish, gay, Gypsy, or simply non-German. His goal was that the planet would be populated with a pure Aryan race. The stigma of Hitler is attached to all Germans by those over fifty, and German goths must fight this stereotype. That country has produced much Industrial, techno, and electro music that makes many people instantly think military, then: Hitler. But German goths, like goths everywhere, are not looking to take over the world, militarily or in any other way.

Other classical composers speak to goths, especially Handel's ethereal tones.

now:

Goths also love many modern musicians who evoke other worlds, even if they are not goth-specific. Current goth favorites include the German group Enigma, whose meditative repetition of sound and lyrics strongly resembles Gregorian chants. Another goth favorite is Canadian songstress Loreena McKennitt, whose hauntingly beautiful sounds glow with Celtic myth and fantasy; a perennial goth music-to-dream-by is "The Lady of Shallot," based on the poem by nineteenth-century English poet Alfred, Lord Tennyson (see page at right).

Many other musicians who are not goth speak to goths, for instance, the late Johnny Cash, the original Man in Black, whose rendition of "I Walk the Line" could have infected Alien Sex Fiend's version. Leonard Cohen has always found the poetic words that convey goth emotions. Vintage Velvet Underground, Roxy Music, and David Bowie have also ridden the time continuum into the goth world.

and then there was goth music

Everyone seems to have a slant on where modern goth music originated. Most people concur that goth is a darker offspring of punk, and the bastard pansexual cousin of glam, emerging from the mists in England sometime in the mid-1970s.

Deacon Syth was born in England and now lives in Canada. He hosts a popular goth radio program, *The Embrace,* and is founder of an annual Vampire Ball in St. Catherines, Ontario. He also does guest DJing. He talks about the murky beginnings of goth in the UK, and the Big Four:

"In the late 1970s, England's social and political climate was one of drastic change—thanks greatly to the punk scene spearheaded by the social commentaries of groups like the Sex Pistols and the Clash, and aided by the theatrics of bands like the Damned, suddenly England's youth were

THE LADY OF SHALOTT
(EXCERPT)

Heard a carol, mournful holy,
Chanted loudly, chanted lowly,
Till her blood was frozen slowly,
And her eyes were darkened wholly,
    Turn'd to tower'd Camelot.
For ere she reach'd upon the tide
The first house by the water-side,
Singing in her song she died,
    The Lady of Shalott.

Under tower and balcony,
By garden-wall and gallery,
A gleaming shape she floated by,
Dead-pale between the houses high,
    Silent into Camelot.
Out upon the wharfs they came,
Knight and Burgher, Lord and Dame,
And round the prow they read her name,
    The Lady of Shalott.

Who is this? And what is here?
And in the lighted palace near
Died the sound of royal cheer;
And they crossed themselves for fear,
    All the Knights at Camelot;
But Lancelot mused a little space
He said, "She has a lovely face;
God in his mercy lend her grace,
    The Lady of Shalott."

— Alfred, Lord Tennyson (1832)

becoming more aware of their social surroundings, and wanted to stake a claim for themselves—they wanted to count as people, too.

"A new sound of music erupted from the post-punk holocaust of Britain. A sound that took punks' aggressive attitude and intellectually aware storytelling, but also drew on something else from England's past—that of the flamboyancy of the glam rock scene, specifically Ziggy Stardust himself, David Bowie. If this new subculture of youths wanted to be noticed, they wanted to be seen for their fashion and appearance as well as for their viewpoints and ideals.

"In fact, in an interview regarding his 1974 album *Diamond Dogs*, Bowie himself referred to it as 'gothic' in its styling. He gave no explanation, but the word was suddenly applied to music.

"The term popped up again five years later on September 15, 1979, when members of Joy Division where interviewed on the UK television program *Something Else*, and their music was referred to as 'gothic in comparison to the pop mainstream.' Joy Division's manager, Martin Hannett, later stated in a Factory Records press release that Joy Division's album *Closer* was 'dancing music with gothic overtones.' And in the same interview, Joy Division bassist Bernard Albrecht cemented the term in description when he compared their music to his love of the film classic *Nosferatu*. Albrecht stated that 'The atmosphere [was] really evil, but you feel comfortable in it.'

"But the largest initial impact on the scene arguably arose from the work of four musicians from Northampton, England, who united together as one musical project in 1978, when gangly David Bowie and T. Rex fanatic Peter Murphy joined the band The Craze (featuring Daniel Ash, David J, and Kevin Haskins) and the four renamed themselves Bauhaus 1919. They soon dropped the '1919' and became known simply as Bauhaus. These four created the blueprint, musically and visually, for a generation of gothic bands. 'Bela Lugosi's Dead,' their hit single released in 1979 on Small Wonder Records, was fueled by Peter Murphy and Daniel Ash's love of erotic vampire imagery. This song began the fascination and connection with the undead for the scene that would become goth.

"Two years prior to Bauhaus's inception, a former member of the Sex Pistols' entourage, Susan Dallion (known around the clubs as Siouxsie Sioux) formed her own band, Siouxsie and the Banshees. Her fashion sense was astonishing to behold, and her bizarre style of dress is still one of the most copied by female goths. *The Scream*, released in 1978, is officially the first full-length release in the genre of goth.

"Also in 1979 the Cure released *Three Imaginary Boys* (later released in North America as *Boys Don't Cry*). Robert Smith's tender sensitivity and melancholy romance—which contrasted with the stark sexuality of Peter Murphy—struck a chord with the disenchanted youth of the UK. If Peter Murphy wrote about the sexual exploits of Dracula, Smith told the story from Mina Harker's standpoint.

Amanda in the band SEVEN 13

"The last of the big four who initiated the UK scene is Joy Division. Ian Curtis, the band's troubled frontman, was a poster boy for all things goth would come to stand for (though largely in stereotypes). His morbid fascination with things gone wrong led to the conclusion that life was a losing game. Curtis committed suicide May eighteenth, 1980, becoming goth's first tragic folk hero. Although Joy Division's music was probably the least gothic of the four, they have had a lasting impact on the scene.

"It's ironic that the early big four of Bauhaus, the Cure, Siouxsie and the Banshees, and Joy Division never acknowledged that they were involved with what became the goth scene, despite their obvious influence, visually and musically. Peter Murphy and Daniel Ash always assumed Bauhaus was just another glam band, albeit a dark one. The Cure's Robert Smith always said his band was nothing more than a pop band. And Siouxsie and the Banshees and Joy Division believed they were more directly related to punk than to the foundation of a new goth movement.

"The goth scene in the UK has always gone in waves of severe winds of change to quiet lulls, but never completely disappears. The goth scene was essentially created through the drunken coupling of the punk and glam rock that ran rampant in Britain's streets throughout the 1970s. But this child became a powerful alternative for those who felt like outsiders in a largely spoon-fed bubble-gum-pop-and-manufactured-happiness musical cosmos."

Deacon Syth is also the front man for the Canadian band Angels of Addiction, and has this to say about the Canadian goth music scene:

"One arena you would expect more from is the Canadian goth music world. The reason such expectations would be so high is that Canada has had an immense impact on the Industrial scene, a scene with close ties to the goth community. Such heavyweights as Skinny Puppy and Front Line As-

Deine Lakaien
Project Pitchfork
Das Ich
Einstürzende Neubauten
the Fair Sex
Wolfsheim
Goethes Erben
Lacrimosa
Terminal Choice
KiEw
Murder at the Registry
New Days Delay
:wumpscut:

sembly created a monstrous impact on the grinding assault of the Industrial revolution, influencing such bands as Nine Inch Nails and Ministry. But as for the darker sister scene of goth, Canada has remained, unfortunately, more of a sideline player.

"That's not to say Canadians haven't had their share of musical contributions. One of the earliest would be the Toronto band Vital Sines. Their gloomy New Wave romanticism was often tied in with the burgeoning goth scenes of the world, due in part to the dreariness of their lyrics and their fashionable affinity for all things black. The foundation of two great Canadian industrial bands can be traced out of a neo-goth new wave band of the early 1980s called Images in Vogue—Kevin Crompton (aka cEVIN kEY of Skinny Puppy) and Don Gordon (of *Numb*) both started out in this Vancouver pop outfit. But, as with the UK's 'Big Four' (Bauhaus, the Cure, Siouxsie and the Banshees and Joy Division), these two bands may be hard pressed to admit to actually being members of this young scene. And one of the UK's earliest outfits, the Southern Death Cult (shortened later to the Cult), had a young transplanted Canadian named Ian Astbury as their founder and frontman (Astbury moved to the UK from Hamilton, Ontario, in his early teens).

"Through the decades many Canadian bands have helped out the cause, some with a great degree of success throughout the world, some merely content ruling their own cities' pantheons. Bands such as Rhea's Obsession, Mona Lisa Mescaline, Exovedate, Ariel, Masochistic Religion, Santeria, Sex Without Souls, Western Dream, and the gothability band Vampire Beach Babes have all made sizable contributions, just to name a few.

"But this seeming black hole has actually made Canadian goths an educated lot. By not having an overabundance of goth heroes to call their own, Canadians look to other countries' scenes for more music to tempt their dark palates. By embracing foreign scenes and blending them with the limited scene that Canadians have at home, they create an ideal potpourri of goth culture and have managed to create a unique 'gothic biosystem.'"

Besides the UK and Canada, Germany has had a tremendous impact on goth and especially goth-Industrial music. Much of what we know as Industrial has come out of Germany. Thomas Thyssen—a freelancer who writes for all three of Germany's major music magazines—*Zillo, Sonic Seducer,* and *Orkus*—and also DJs at Germany's oldest and most traditional goth club, *Zwischenfall,* is also one of *The † Section.* With his brother Ralf, he runs the ongoing Pagan Love Songs events, which bring in goth bands from around the world. He has this to say about goth music in Europe:

"It's hard to describe the evolution of goth music in Europe. Taking into consideration that the goth scene has been in existence for more than twenty-five years now, it is even harder to realize that it still doesn't get the recognition it deserves from either the mainstream media or mainstream audiences. I truly believe that the influence of goth on the overground has been totally underestimated.

"The first indicators of what would later become known as goth can be found in the year 1979. The music scene in the late seventies and early eighties was much more diverse than nowadays, more than today's music fans would ever believe. Besides lots of punk splinter groups, there was the Ska revival, the beginning of the Industrial era. Psychobilly was still hot and running, and the seeds for New Romantic were planted. Out of this bizarre mixture the early goth bands gradually emerged, but they weren't called 'goth' at the beginning, though their musical style was referred to as being gothic as early as 1979.

"One of the forerunners of this particular genre, and to my knowledge—besides Joy Division—one of the first bands ever to be termed 'goth' was the British positive-punk outfit U.K. Decay. This may surprise the vast majority of goths, who tend to believe that bands like Sisters of Mercy or Fields of the Nephilim invented goth. Those bands have to be considered as the second or even the third wave of bands inspired by Joy Division, Bauhaus, Siouxsie and the Banshees, and U.K. Decay. Compared to later goth-acts, early artists were much edgier, livelier and, yes, more punk rock, and they were pigeonholed as Positive-Punk.

"The debut albums of Siouxsie and the Banshees (*The Scream* 1978) and Joy Division (*Unknown Pleasures* 1979) should be treated as milestones for a genre that has lasted until today. Bauhaus's debut twelve-inch—the classic "Bela Lugosi's Dead"—also did its best to help categorize the band as a goth-act, due to its somber content, creepy rhythm, and Peter Murphy's haunting vocals.

"In 1980 and 1981 a second wave of bands emerged out of the shadows of the earlier influences. Acts like Play Dead, The Danse Society, Sisters of

"Writhe and Shine" music comic
Copyright by Robert Tritthardt

Mercy, and Robert Smith's Cure created their very own vision of gothic music, which is now far more popular then the original sounds of the first crop of bands. Andrew Eldritch's sinister deep vocals are as characteristic of goth as Robert Smith's painful and melancholic chants. It's a shame that high quality acts like Play Dead never got the attention they deserved, while Sisters and the Cure literally became pop stars over the next years.

"The crucial period in the development of goth into a full-fledged subculture was mid-1982 to mid-1983, particularly 1982, the year the new movement suddenly started receiving major media attention, with, for example, the grand opening of the now legendary Batcave club in London. It was that event which brought the attention of the mainstream press and media onto this new subcultural movement, which from then on spread widely throughout England.

"The evolution from punk into goth in Germany was in some ways identical but in other ways absolutely different from in the United Kingdom. The first very raw German punk bands, for example Male (headed by Juergen Engler, who later founded the famous Die Krupps) or KFC (headed by Tommi Stumpff, who later on became a prominent solo-artist) were as important for the goth movement as the first German New Wave and Industrial artists, like Einstürzende Neubauten, D.A.F. (German American Friendship), Malaria!, Abwaerts, and Fehlfarben. Small, independent record labels like Atatak and Zick Zack released tons of great avant-garde records, which are considered rare nowadays, and very expensive.

"October 1981 saw the release of the first seven-inch of X Mal Deutschland, called "Schwarze Welt" ("Black World"). Although the band never considered itself goth, this record can be seen as a real milestone in Germany's goth history. X Mal Deutschland went on to become Germany's most famous goth act worldwide during their stint with the legendary 4AD label in the '80s.

"What began in the late seventies as the German version of New Wave gained interest with the mainstream record companies as well, so that they began to bill the most popular acts from this era as "Neue Deutsche Welle" ("New German Wave"). The problem with this development was that soon the industry began churning out its own plastic pop bands, which had no artistic or dark aesthetic background—a necessity for goth. They were just there in order to make money, and therefore they were in complete contrast with what punk and new wave stood for.

"Ironically, goth did not get big in Germany in the eighties, although there were lots of great bands, like Asmodi Bizarr, II. Invasion, Unlimited Systems, Mask For, Moloko †, and Maerchenbraut, among others. It wasn't until the early nineties with the founding of *Zillo* magazine that goth underwent a huge renaissance in Germany. Backed by a new bunch of bands, for example, Deine Lakaien, Project Pitchfork, and Das Ich, *Zillo* magazine was responsible for the first nationwide networking of all the splinter groups that were still into that kind of music.

"Today all those acts are highly successful artists, regularly climbing into the Top Ten of the German media-controlled charts, with heavy rotations on the German music-TV stations.

"I have watched these developments, on one side happily, but from a highly skeptical perspective on the other. Due to the huge influence of techno and dance music on this scene—which still calls itself goth—I am not able to follow all the newest trends and musical evolutions. To me, incorporating sounds, styles, and ideas from something that isn't fresh anymore is not evolution. It would be better if people would stick to their roots, but that directly leads to another big problem in Germany.

"Most of the people who call themselves goth today do not really know where this term comes from and what it stands for. VNV Nation is *not* goth, and in my humble opinion it won't be long before this overblown thing which is now termed the goth scene will splinter into many different subdivisions. Tom Stach, singer of the underestimated German deathrock band Murder at the Registry, once told me that he dreams about something like a subsubculture, a new underground movement in which people redefine themselves without the pressure of the music industry. Hopefully this is where the road will lead us . . . maybe someday!"

European Industrial music information comes right from the source. Germany's *Sonic Seducer* editor Pee Wee Vignold tells us all about it.

"As we all learned from Quentin Tarantino's *Pulp Fiction*, there are slight differences between Europe and the United States that make all the difference in the end. Unfortunately, writing his notorious 'Quarter Pounder vs. Royale' speech must have gotten him so excited, he forgot to have Vincent Vega tell Jules how he went to a small record shop after his McDonald's visit, and that Industrial record he bought there didn't have any beats or guitars or bass lines on it, not even proper songs. Nothing but pure noise.

"Then again, it wouldn't have been as good a laugh as the burger tale, but the fact is still true: While nearly all commonly known musical genres—rock, pop, metal, etc.—define a certain style of music that follows the same or at least similar rules wherever in the world you look for it, Industrial barely has the same face in different places.

"In the United States the term was mostly defined by Nettwerk (Vancouver) and Waxtrax (Chicago), two independent record companies dedicated to hard-edged electronic music. Besides releasing North American-based acts like Skinny Puppy, Front Line Assembly, Ministry or KMFDM, Waxtrax soon started licensing European acts like Front 242 and Clock DVA and brought their 'Electronic Body Music' (as it was called in the old world) to the US audience and dance floors, where it soon got the 'Industrial' label.

"But when that day in the late seventies came, when cut-up terrorist Monte Cazazza stated his immortalizing 'Industrial music for industrial people' line, he gave a name to something that was actually intended to destroy dancing. What he meant had to do with the subversive sonic threats and audio-visual assaults of Throbbing Gristle and the 'information war' they declared on the free world. Armed with big stacks of electronic noise producers and lots of disturbing images and films to screen at their performances, Throbbing Gristle intended to be a wake-up call, and they did their best to flood their audiences' senses with something they couldn't ignore. They mostly succeeded, and their shock tactics, consisting of brutally loud anti-music that pushes to the limit as well as disturbing video projections that do the same, too soon became the basic formula of a whole next generation of Industrialists whose definition of Industrial already moved on to 'music as hard as the world we live in.' It wasn't only the untrained ears that realized it couldn't get much heavier. The peak reached its max very soon, and musicians found themselves at a dead end from which there was only one way out: going soft. Metaphorically, that is.

"As so often happens, it took Japanese help to crank it up some more. But even though the spirit of Throbbing Gristle, as well as their formal legacy, carried on in Japan and spawned the so-called 'Japan Noise' genre (ironically enough, the biggest difference between original industrial and Japan Noise are those very names), the western European definition of Industrial opened up to become more accessible, listenable, and later even danceable. Bands like Current 93, Coil, or Psychic TV took it to a spiritual level and made the music part of magick rituals while others discovered a different kind of heaviness involving distorted beats. Like Esplendor Ge-ométrico from Spain, whose rhythmic noise loops and monotonous beats are reminiscent of the sound of heavy machinery and influenced Dirk Ivens (singer of the Belgian minimal electronic pioneers the Klinik) to create Dive and later Sonar. Both are still some of the biggest names in modern-day Industrial, which meanwhile has almost lost all of its artsy aspect and become credible dance music with an attitude, or Power Noise. When Techno came along and reanimated the DIY spirit of Punk with new, cheap technology, Industrial in a way also became what Punk could never be—a vivid antithesis to pop that keeps changing its face fast. New influences show up, new subgenres clip off and form something new again, and even after twenty-five years it all happens unseen by the public eye. And once a year they all gather at the *Maschinenfest* in Aachen, Germany, which can be seen as the ongoing 'annual report' (as Throbbing Gristle's first album was named) of the Industrial movement. For three days and nights in a smoky bomb shelter, Industrial people from all over the world come together to see and hear the status quo of present day Industrial, ranging from ritual-style ambience to heavy power electronics, and all that lies between. Sub-mitting themselves to the next generation shock tactics, finding out they are actually alive, remembering to party, and to dance. It's a hard world, you know."

One other country that has made exceptional contributions to goth music is the United States. Joshua Gunn is a goth lover, and he is also pro-fessor of communication studies at Louisiana University. For many years he has run a site that discusses goth music. He is also author of the article "Dark Admissions: Gothic Subculture and the Ambivalence of Misogyny and Resistance" in the academic book *Goth: Undead Subculture,* edited by Michael Bibby and Lauren Goddlad (Duke University, 2002). And he has published several provocative academic papers on goth music, including "Marilyn Manson Is Not Goth: Memorial Struggle and the Rhetoric of Subcultural Identity." This is how he sees the evolution of goth music in the US:

"The trouble with genres, especially music genres, is that they are la-bels that only make sense in retrospect, often a long time after a particular kind of music has expanded to include sounds and styles its label fails to include. This is the case, of course, with 'gothic' music. During the form-ative heyday of gothic music in Europe and the United States, it was

Photo courtesy of Dan Schneider

aLiCe

"I like 'Coma White,' because it's an accurate description of the reasoning behind much drug use in younger years. He seems fairly intelligent. But his capitalizing on something that was meant to remain underground and sometimes scorns its own capitalization was rather a slap in the face to a lot of goths. When I first heard him, I thought he was a poseur, and a terrible musician. I still feel that way."

Angel "I respect him as a businessman. He is very intelligent and articulate. Some of his music is good. His live shows are amazing to watch, very theatrical."

biogoth "I rather liked the first couple of MM albums, but after that it got silly and self-indulgent. Honestly, I think they're kind of irrelevant these days."

✛

Johnny Formaldehyde "I can't stand his followers. He knows how to make money. But he's not goth, and bastardizes the goth look for shock value. It hurts the goth scene, because now we have all these kids in MM T-shirts and white face paint claiming to be goth and

called—rather unimaginatively—'Postpunk.' To many, Postpunk referred to the abandon of political posturing in addition to the more melodic turn in sound. Postpunk music replaced a rage directed against the outside world with a lyrical introspection that bears some similarity to the psychological focus of Gothic literature. The ephemeral nature of music rags and fanzines is the reason why no one really knows how this music, originally typified by eerie guitar effects, strong bass lines, and morbid lyrics, came to be called 'gothic.' (Some fans maintain the label was first deployed in print by NME [New Music Express], who borrowed the term from one Siouxsie Sioux while she was describing her band's sound.) Yet the music's lyrical preoccupation with love and death and the deliberate 'spooky' theatrics of many Postpunk bands are the most likely reasons for why the label 'gothic' stuck.

"Although the history of gothic music is usually told with numerous references to the UK scene in the early 1980s (Bauhaus, the Batcave, and so on), musical artists in the United States unquestionably contributed to gothic music and gothic aesthetics long before the release of 'Bela Lugosi's Dead' in 1979. Arguably, the first 'goth' was Screaming Jay Hawkins, an R&B artist from Ohio most known for his 1956 ditty 'I Put a Spell on You,' in which he obsesses about a lover in drunken howls and moans. The huge underground success of Hawkins's single in the US led him to adopt the onstage voodoo chic for which he is most known. Hawkins's spooky theatrics did not emerge again until the mid- to late sixties with bands like the hearse-riding Tombstones from Canada, mostly as a part of the mainstream whitewashing of R&B music. Indeed, one element that is frequently absent from discussions of gothic music is its reliance on musical elements that originated with people of African descent (e.g., the reggae bass lines of *Bauhaus*'s albums).

"As with rock music in general, many sounds often identified as part of the gothic music repertoire have their origins in the United States. The 'acid rock' and 'art rock' genres of the late sixties and early seventies, in particular, introduced a number of somber songs that we might label 'pregoth.' Jefferson Airplane, for example, experimented with gloomy melodies and chilling lyrics in a number of their songs, such as 1967's 'White Rabbit,' a popular cover among gothic bands. The Velvet Underground, however, are likely the most significant precursor to the emergence of gothic music in the West, despite the fact that the band was short-lived and only released a meager four albums before their breakup (a career path that would be repeated by Bauhaus a decade later). The band's first album, *The Velvet Underground and Nico* (1967; it's the one that features Warhol's cheeky, obviously phallic, banana on the cover), contains a remarkable number of influential songs that proved to be many years before their time: with John Cale's eerie viola, Lou Reed's monotonous drones, and Nico's mysterious moans, songs like 'All Tomorrow's Parties,' 'Venus in Furs,' and 'The Black Angel's Death Song' showed a much darker brand of songcraft that would inspire the Postpunk and so-called New Wave movements in the late 1970s.

"Despite these important American influences, gothic music is unquestionably a British import, however much we might claim it is repackaged. One part Hawkins and Lou Reed, one part New Wave (as Punk was originally dubbed in the US), one part British Punk, and one part Glam Rock (especially David Bowie), American goth began to take hold in two different sorts of venues: punk clubs and disco clubs. The music did develop in the US in ways that are stylistically distinct from what we might call 'Eurogoth.' On the East Coast, the darker Punk of bands like the Ramones would become associated with gothic subculture and inspire even darker punk bands in Europe such as the Damned. It was the tongue-in-cheek 'ghoul rock' or 'Deathrock' movement in San Francisco and Los Angeles, however, that marks a uniquely American version of goth. In the early eighties, bands like T.S.O.L., 45 Grave, and the more musically limited Misfits (actually from Lodi, New Jersey, but frequently lumped into the Deathrock subgenre), mixed gloomy chords, gothic topics, horror-show theatrics, and, for some, rockabilly riffs, carving out a sound and aesthetic that gave goth a comic-book spin. Combined with the more serious-minded California Deathrock acts like Kommunity FK, the California scene created the kind of supportive culture that sustained and nurtured the most influential American goth band to date: Christian Death.

"Formed by the late Rozz Williams in Los Angeles in the early 1980s, Christian Death started as a morbid punk band and evolved into a distinctly unique enterprise (currently managed by the very hairy and sex-obsessed guitarist Valor, to the chagrin of many early waifified and twinkified Christian Death fans). Lyrically, a preoccupation with religious themes gave the band a thematic focus beyond the mere 'doom and gloom' of other Deathrock and goth acts in the 1980s. Williams and a re-

making the majority of people think what they're about is goth."

cypher

"Manson is a genius at manipulating the media. Writes some good songs, does a fine stage show. Had he not attained the success he enjoys, he would be much more popular in the goth scene."

Johnny Formaldehyde "I can't stand his followers. He knows how to make money. But he's not goth, and bastardizes the goth look for shock value. It hurts the goth scene, because now we have all these kids in MM T-shirts and white face paint claiming to be goth and making the majority of people think what they're about is goth."

Katwoman "His public image is very silly, but I like it, and I do like his songs and videos. Interviews reveal him to be an intelligent, well-spoken showman, making a clear distinction between his public image and real life. However, if I knew a thirteen-year-old was listening to his music, I'd explain that Manson's fantasy is not how you should actually live your life; life really isn't about shocking people all the time."

Lisiblac "No one who entered the goth scene before 1990 will identify this band as goth, guaranteed."

Nadia "I can see why he appeals to younger people, but I don't listen to his music myself. I find it rather sad that the prevailing social conditions and moral climate in the US has forced Manson to adopt a 'pantomime bad guy' persona that I feel is beneath his obvious intelligence. All the same, I admire him for taking on the Moral Majority."

Ravenheart "I remember when he was just geeky Brian and hanging around Orlando clubs. I think he is a walking gimmick. Nothing against him or his fans, I just don't care for his stuff."

Reynaldo "Who says Manson is a goth band? I thought he simply made cool alternative music."

Taoist "I like his music a lot, and what he says in his lyrics, but I think he's exploiting the goth aesthetic to make money, which is kinda ironic considering the aesthetic is art–not money–driven."

Thyssen "He is a hypocrite, a guy who uses ideas and the creations of musicians from more than twenty years ago, repackages them and sells them as something new. Manson is crap."

Zerstoerte "I like his music, and I think he's a brilliant media whore, but overall he really is a twit. He's done more to bring negative attention to the gothic community than made it more acceptable. The inflated ego isn't very attractive either."

volving number of contributors developed unique musical arrangements and experimented with spoken word, giving their music a kind of artsy (if not playfully pretentious) feel lacking among their Deathrock cohorts. Blasphemy and obscenity soon became the choice aesthetic of the band, which helped to increase their popularity among the gothic faithful in the United States and Europe. After the demise of their popularity, similar sounds and arrangements would be explored and furthered on small record labels, principal among them Cleopatra, which has helped to keep a number of Deathrock bands on vinyl and which continues to promote newer, electronic innovations in goth (e.g., Switchblade Symphony, Rosetta Stone), and the now defunct Tess Records, a label that promoted more European-sounding gothic bands. Tess bands like Faith and the Muse, This Ascension, and Autumn dropped the obscenity and blasphemy in favor of the more 'ethereal,' Romantic stylings becoming popular in Europe. (The back catalog has since been picked up by the Metropolis label, which is most known for its EBM [electronic body music] and Industrial acts).

"From the 1990s to the present, US gothic music has continued to evolve newer sounds. Although Deathrock remains an important subgenre, the second most influential musical development stateside is Darkwave, an expansion of the rather limited gothic repertoire into electronica and, in a way, the US answer to the 'ethereal' subgenre that developed in Europe (e.g., Dead Can Dance). Anchored by Sam Rosenthal's now New York–based record label, Projekt, Darkwave music is less rock and more roll, supporting bands who tend to emphasize folk songcraft, hushed vocals, ambient experimentation, and synthesized sounds more akin to the brief 'shoegaze' moment in alternative rock than the punk styles of early gothic music. Significantly, whereas Deathrock is largely centered on male vocals (45 Grave being an important exception), women have a much larger role in Darkwave and ethereal goth music. Projekt bands like Love Spirals Downward and Lycia are among the most popular of this subgenre.

"Of course, this brief chronicle would not be complete without mentioning those acts that some consider goth 'crossovers,' particularly Nine Inch Nails and Marilyn Manson. Most goths would consider Nine Inch Nails 'Industrial rock,' and Marilyn Manson 'heavy metal.' In part, denying Marilyn Manson and Trent Reznor the goth label has to do with the absence of key 'gothic' sounds (eerie guitar effects, bass high in the mix, and so on). But denying these acts the label is also an attempt to resist the mainstreaming of 'goth' by goth fans. Although recent NIN material is thematically and musically Darkwave (e.g., 1999's The Fragile), Reznor's past musical history continues to place him in the Industrial rock or Industrial dance category. And despite his use of gothic aesthetics and lyrical themes—especially the blasphemy shtick more intelligently explored by Christian Death—Manson is doggedly denied gothic status by goths because of what is perceived as a kind of stylistic and aesthetic theft. For many goths, Manson's failure to produce anything other than heavy metal, Industrial rock, or glam rock means he has stolen a gothic look and aesthetic without promoting the gothic musical tradition, an unforgivable sin for the gothic faithful."

When it comes to Marilyn Manson, *The † Section*—and likely most goths—are completely split down the middle. No other musician seems to evoke such extreme emotion. Feelings about Manson are intense, and many of *The † Section* hold both positive and negative feelings.

What does Manson think of goth? He tells us in his autobiography, *The Long Hard Road Out of Hell*.

origins of the species

Six goth bands discuss what it's like to be a goth band. These are the boiz and gurrls in the trenches, recording the CDs and the music videos, performing the shows, creating the music goths love to listen and dance to.

Bella Morte: "Gopal and I [Andy Deane] started the band because we were pretty much the only goth kids in town. We needed a creative outlet and happened to have a few broken amps and a drum machine lying around. We've been around for over five years now, though we didn't get very serious until a couple of years ago. When we started I was playing guitar and singing, but we decided that having a guitarist would free me up on vocals. We brought in a Punk named Frizzle who stuck around for better than a year before leaving to form his own Oi! band. Then we brought in bn to cover guitar and he stuck around for a couple of years before leaving to start a family. Our latest guitarist is Tony Lechmanski, and it looks like he's going to be here for a long time. Now we need to find a drummer."

Photo by Jan Powell

BELLA MORTE: www.bellamorte.com
Charlottesville, VA
Band Members: Andy Deane, Gopal Metro, Tony Lechmanski
Releases: Remains; Where Shadows Lie
Style: old school goth, deathrock, darkwave, synthpop
Selected discs and videography:
• Remains
• Where Shadows lie
• The Quiet

Photo by Marc Metz

FEAR CULT: www.fearcult.com
Hollywood, CA
Members: Matt Riser, Van Shock, Secret Sin, Nikki Star
Releases: A Bouquet of Songs; Your Darkest Romance; Drop Dead (EP); various compilations
Style: gothic-visual-cyber-death-rock
Selected discs and videography:
• A Bouquet of Songs
• Your Darkest Romance
• Drop Dead
• She Loves Me Not
• Visionary Complex

Photo by Albert Strano

MASOCHISTIC RELIGION:
www.masochisticreligion.co.uk
Montreal, Quebec, CANADA
Members: Mitchell D. Krol, Mopa Dean,
D'errol Flynn, Julie Seddon Faris, Martine
Matthews, Harry Simpson
Releases: Sonic Revolution–Evolve;..
.and from this broken cross. . . our
misery. . . ; The Litanies of Satan;
limited editions: Burn in Hell; Prelude
to the Apocalypse; In Noctun Concilliam
(with Annahav); The Raven & others;
In a Nightmare without Cease; The Piano
Style: Deep goth, scary goth, cerebral goth
Selected discs and videography:
• THE VAMPIRE
• The Litanies of Satan
• The Piano
• The Raven and others...
• And from this broken cross our misery
• Sonic Revolution–Evolve
• Burn in Hell

Fear Cult: "The band was started by me [Matt Riser] some ten years ago in Arizona. I've always been involved in some form of artistic expression, and this was just another way to present my art. I've never thought of myself as a musician; it has always been purely art to me. Why I feel the need to create things such as Fear Cult is a mystery to me, and I've stopped even trying to figure it out, I just do what I'm compelled to do, and I'll let the rest of the world try to decipher the reasoning for it. There have been numerous incarnations and changes throughout the history of Fear Cult. First of all, it started out as a solo project, and over the years has slowly grown into a full-blown performing band. Various members have come and gone, and the sound has changed and evolved quite a bit. But for the most part the same ideas and philosophies of the original concept are all still alive. And samples and synthesized sounds have always been present."

Masochistic Religion: "I [Mitchell D. Krol] was playing in a punk band in the late eighties, and found the Punk thing to be a bit confining and wanted to do something else. I was doing a lot of drugs, getting heavily into the S&M scene, and spending a lot of time with my friend Malissa X. One dark and stormy night I played her some of my music, and it really turned her on. Next thing I knew, we were having heavy sex, and doing music! I mean, it really worked! So we came up with this concept of a Masochistic Religion, a sort of dark S&M theater thing done to music. All the lyrics were about sex, death, religion, pleasure, and pain, and the show was heavy, real, and probably illegal, but we didn't care; we were young, stoned, and horny, and there was nothing like it out there. It went on like that for a while, until I lost Malissa, and changed the concept a bit. Our first release was in 1988, a tape called *Cosmic Dancer;* that was after Malissa split, and Andy Yue joined the band, but we were around before that. I've been in the band since the beginning, but with every incarnation it evolved, and continues to evolve. After Malissa, I straightened up for a while, and the music became a bit more rock 'n' roll. I've heard it called our Velvet Underground period, but I thought we were just noisy. We recorded a pile of music then, and were playing all the time, famous for smashing our instruments and destroying clubs."

Sera de Morte: "I am an artist who performs and makes CDs to share my music. This is a profession. . . . It's what I do. I started on mp3.com with

Stifffff Kitties. Very popular with the goth mp3 crowd. As I was the sole writer and producer of Stifffff Kitties, I'm taking it solo now."

SEVEN 13: "It was in the summer of 1997 that I [Amanda Adams] began seeking out individuals to help bring my compositions to the life that they so desperately cried out for at the time. I began working with a gentleman by the name of Teisan Russell. He collaborated on several of the pieces. The first name of the band was actually Coven 13. It was in 2000 that we decided to change the name to SEVEN 13. We believe the name represents the balance and unity present within our music."

Umbra et Imago: "Umbra et Imago were founded in 1991 by me [Mozart] and from the very beginning had a concept of mystic, erotic S&M-oriented music with strong visual elements. There were several changes in the lineup. The first two albums were of a much more electronic nature. After the second album came a dramatic change when all the other original members—Michael Gillian, Nailz, Torsten B.—left. I relaunched the band in 1995 and Lutz Demmler joined me as songwriter. Nowadays he is also producing the band. The current lineup has been stable for about four years now."

playing polyphony

Bella Morte: "My first record was a live KISS album! And you know, I still love that stuff . . . just never could get it out of my system. My introduction to underground music came by way of metal and Punk, with goth following a few years behind. As for training, I studied opera for about five years."

Fear Cult: "When I was three, my older brother and I were given lessons on the violin. I have only vague memories of this, mostly consisting of someone placing my fingers in the appropriate spots on the instrument. I can also recall myself standing in my living room screeching out something that resembled 'Twinkle, Twinkle, Little Star.' Years after that my mom forced me to take piano lessons, which I absolutely hated, and pretty much blew off."

Sera de Morte: www.stiffffkitties.com/
Yourtown, USA
Members: Sera de Morte
Releases: Choose
Style: gothic attitude with
Industrial/dance beat
Selected discs and videography:
• Witches Dance
• Mya's Book of the Dead

SEVEN 13: www.seven13band.com
Boston, MA
Members: Amanda Adams,
Lauren Doucette, Kenneth Michaels,
Brian Verrochi
Releases: Book of Shadows; Unleashed
Style: Melodic, progressive,
darkwave rock
Selected discs and videography:
• Unleashed
• DRINK
• Book of Shadows

Umbra et Imago:
www.umbraetimago.de
Karlsruhe, GERMANY
Members: Mozart, Lutz Demmler, Freddy
Stürze, Migge Schwarz, Lisa and Nadia
Releases: Träume, Sex und'Tod; Infantile
Spiele; Gedanken eines Vampirs; Mystica
Sexualis; Hard Years; Machina Mundi;
Mea Culpa; Dunkle Energie; Die Welt
Brunnt; Die Hand Gottes; Speichel und
Blut; Ein dunkler Traum
Style: Gothic-metal
Selected discs and videography:
• Dunkle Energie
• Mea Culpa
• Träume, Sex und Tod
• Infantile Spiele
• Gedanken eines Vampirs

Masochistic Religion: "I started with violin and contrabass in school, and at the age of thirteen discovered the guitar while on acid at a party somewhere. Since then, I am self-taught on cello, piano, bass, and various stringed and percussion instruments, and of course now the computer. When I first picked up the guitar, theory didn't interest me. I listened to rock and roll, and wanted to play rock 'n' roll—why bother with books or lessons? I picked up the theory thing later. My father was a bit of a beatnik, and my mother into jazz and blues. There was always music playing in the house, often scary music, and when I went out, I had a radio glued to my ear."

Sera de Morte: "Piano since three years of age and a B.A. in music performance."

SEVEN 13: "My musical background started very early in life at the age of four. My mother decided to teach me the keyboard scales on her accordion. Yes, accordion. She laid it sideways on her lap and began teaching me. I graduated to a piano and started lessons immediately."

Umbra et Imago: "I am an autodidactic learner. In '93 I ran a small place called Spirit Café near Karlsrühe and a small label, Spirit Records. My band before Umbra was Electric Avantgarde, and we wore Rococo clothing. Now I am also involved in the management of *the* goth club in Karlsrühe, Kulturruine, where Twilight Studio, the studio I have with Lutz, is also based. It's a perfect home base for a band. I never studied music, and I have no classical background. Lutz and I have our own kind of language when we are in the studio. In the last years I have also produced a lot of newcomer bands, most of which are Goth Rock or Medieval Rock."

sound philosophy

Bella Morte: "I wouldn't say that we have one defining philosophy. We have quite a few different themes running through what we create. We tell lots of stories about ghosts and zombies, for example. We try not to mention anything that would pinpoint a specific time in history as well, which gives the songs a kind of timeless feel. And while there are a lot of mellow goth acts and a lot of Deathrock acts, few tend to cover as much territory in the scene as we do. We love our diversity of sound."

Fear Cult: "The main philosophy of Fear Cult is the age-old idea of doing what you want when you want without letting other people stop you."

Masochistic Religion: "Our philosophy? Sex & drugs & rock 'n' roll. Reality sucks, make your own reality. The band members have always just followed their hearts. It just worked for us. I guess you could say we follow the nineteenth century ideal, the Baudelaire concept of beauty in decay, poetry in sadness. Or Poe, he had it down. They both died poor. Music is like any other art form, any composition, it has a beginning, a middle, and an end. It just depends what colors you use to paint it. What words you use to say it. And always remember: it can have quite an impact, good or bad. We write the songs that make the whole world sing . . ."

Sera de Morte: "The need to be heard and recognized is universal. Maybe by my efforts with a major label release, I can open the door for goth to be heard by a more diverse audience. People want this, and no one has given the goth community, my family, any real major push in society . . . but we're here."

SEVEN 13: "We believe that music can, does, and will effect change. We do our best at every show. We never feel that one show is more important than any other. Music is our art, our fortitude, and being given the opportunity to share it with our fans is the best reward."

Umbra et Imago: "One thing Freud discovered that really struck us: Everything in our lives is about sexuality. S&M culture is the most intellectual way to cultivate sexuality by adult role-playing games. Nietzsche said that there are just some people beyond color bars, operating at a different speed. They don't have that sense of being cattle, and they drop out of their role and become outcasts. As such they will be crushed to death by the masses, or they can become outstanding personalities, especially in the arts. Religion in itself, in our eyes, contains a strong intolerance, even fascist elements, which keep leading to bloody orgies in which human beings are ideologically oppressed. God doesn't need any hypocritical religion. All those elements are things that every thinking person should be able to make up their mind about; if you want to call that philosophy, please do so. We call it healthy common sense! There is a certain quality to gothic people, their way of questioning in depth, not believing everything they're being told, defining themselves by certain characteristics and appearance, in a way casting themselves out. They also develop some kind of more intellectual sexuality that is feared and loathed by society just as much as the goth scene itself. Umbra et Imago has been a driving force in that development, at least in that this form of sexuality is taken for granted within the scene."

the good, the bad, the unbearable

Bella Morte: "The best parts? The shows of course, and meeting the fans afterwards. As for negative, I'd have to say that getting to California and finding that we only had thirty dollars between us was a little scary, but really, not too much bad stuff has come our way."

Fear Cult: "The creation process is the most rewarding and positive. It's that moment when you hear the finished recording of a song that you can't even believe you yourself wrote. I don't think there is anything more rewarding than creating something beautiful. I think the most negative experiences come with all the "business" and "politics" that are involved with a band. Sometimes it becomes really hard to keep everyone happy and excited during the down times. There is pressure from within the band, as well as from the Label and even the fans. Also there is just a lot of work that needs to be done like photo shoots, press releases, Web site updates and things like that which are really not related to the art of creating songs and are often rather boring and tedious. It often feels like you spend 95 percent of your time doing these kind of things and only 5 percent actually having fun as a band. Ultimately you are doing something that most people in the world only dream about. You are on stage performing, and traveling, meeting and becoming associated with some of the most interesting people on the planet. And on the flip side it's a ton of work. You tend to miss out on a lot of things due to a recording schedule or rehearsal schedule. While everyone else is out in the club having fun, you are backstage getting ready for a show. But I think it all evens out in the end."

Masochistic Religion: "Being on tour playing shows and seeing the world rocks. The worst part? Being in a tour bus. Or dealing with record companies. I've had my fair share of insane fans, some harmless, some not, but that's too creepy to get into. As for being in a band, anybody from any band will tell you that *This Is Spinal Tap* is closer to reality then we would like to admit! The first time we used pyro onstage, D'errol was controlling the blasts, but he missed his cue, and lucky me was standing in the middle of a twelve-foot column of flame. Apparently it looked incredible to the audience, and just as I was catching my breath, he did it again! Foooofffff! Look, it's a flamin' goth! I don't know how, but I didn't catch on fire, even though I had very flammable hair that day. Needless to say, I built a foot controller for our pyro after that, and control it myself now. It's weird, when you create a piece of music, and release it upon the world, you no longer own it. It has a life of its own, making its own relationships, hurting, or enlightening others, changing lives, whatever. Then, when you see it again, it's as if it grew up on its own, and has its own stories to tell. . . . I grew up in Masochistic Religion, and I'm almost an adult now."

Sera de Morte: "Well, the positive is I met my current producer, Kim Morrissey. I've learned so much about music and the record business from Kim. Negative? I did a show in a bar in Florida. The crowd was *great*, but the sound, promo, even getting paid, from a packed house, was a nightmare."

SEVEN 13: "Every show that SEVEN 13 puts on is described as a 'journey through life.' We take the audience through many emotions such as love, hate, lust, jealousy, joy, and wonderment. Because of our unique presentation, we have received wonderful drawings that one fan made for each song after seeing our show. That was truly a gift."

Umbra et Imago: "Being able to express and share my feelings this way is the best part. Having to make compromises when you're really into something sucks. I think some really scary experiences can occur with some fans who have totally lost themselves and look up to you as some kind of god. They see everything in you that they are craving but can never reach because they've already lost themselves. There is no way to communicate with them, and I can tell you it's not so easy to deal with. But there are also a lot of positive experiences that come with working with the band. . . . Extreme experiences that lead to new lyrics are a special privilege if you're an artist in the public eye, but psychic and physical stress are the price of being a 'star.'"

URLs

Ed Kline's music lists
www.kzsu.stanford.edu/eklein/

Richard Wagner
www.users.utu.fi/hansalmi/wagner.spml

Enigma
www.enigma.de/

Loreena McKennitt
www.quinlanroad.com/

Deacon Syth's Cerebral Confines (poetry)
www.syth6.tripod.com

Angels of Addiction
www.aoa15.tripod.com

Thomas Thyssen
www.nightmarezone.de

This Vale of Tears
www.tvot.be

Pee Wee Vignold c/o Sonic Seducer magazine
www.sonic-seducer.de/

Joshua Gunn's music page
www.lsu.edu/faculty/jgunn/music.html

Marilyn Manson
www.marilynmanson.com/

Dark Side of the Net internet gothic radio list
www.darklinks.com/dnetradio.html

Bella Morte
www.bellamorte.com

Fear Cult
www.fearcult.com

Masochistic Religion
www.masochisticreligion.co.uk

Sera de Morte
www.stiffffkitties.com/

SEVEN13
www.seven13band.com

Umbra et Imago
www.umbraetimago.de

6

SON OF MUSIC
OF THE MACABRE

We can dance if we want to . . .

music mags and their raison d'être

Goth music magazines are the lifeblood of bands. They advertise and review CDs and videos where, otherwise, goths might not be able to find out about them unless their local DJs receive a copy. Another source is radio, and there are few local goth radio shows, although more and more alternative radio programs are happening, especially Internet radio. *Dark Side of the Net* has a great list of internet gothic/dark/Industrial radio programs.

Five goth magazines that focus on bringing music to their readers discuss what they do and why they do it.

Ascension Magazine (formerly *Ascension*) (Publisher: Alex Daniele, Crescentino, Italy): "The publication started in the summer of 1998. During the nineties I wrote reviews and articles for various Italian alternative gothic magazines. I always loved gothic magazines from the UK, USA and Germany—more open-minded than in Italy. My former working partner said, 'Hey, you just bought a PC. Why don't we start a new goth magazine?' *Ascension* was born! I took it over in 2002 and renamed the publication *Ascension Magazine*.

"Initially I just wanted to try to put out something new and, hopefully,

Copyright by Ascension Magazine

complete, in Italy. Now, the main focus of my work is to become less underground and easier to find by everybody in Italy. Using just one word, I wish and work for a larger *distribution*. All over my country. I'll never become rich with *Ascension Magazine*. It would be great if one day it becomes my work. Now it's just my hobby and my passion, but . . . argh! . . . it takes eighty percent of my free time!"

Comatose Rose magazine (Publisher: Azriel J. Knight, Calgary, Alberta, Canada): "I started this magazine on my own, first as a rant zine online in 1999, then it switched mainly to music in 2000. The name changed to Sidestream, then Pandemonium. The print version came out 2002. I've always been a big fan of music of one kind or another, and figured doing reviews would be a good way to express how I feel about the artists, and to give them exposure.

"You give a thousand people a Web site, maybe forty will really go through a lot of it. But give a thousand people a paper magazine, and the rate of people reading it is much higher. We still have a few things online, a rant here and there, coverage of events. Currently, we are the only Canadian gothic Industrial print magazine in existence, and we are trying to live up to that title."

Elegy (Editor: Alyz Tale, Boulogne, France): "Several musical magazines are edited by the musical Press Group CPES Editions. Nathalie Noguera-Vera, editor of the group, decided they should create a gothic mag in France at the national level. *Elegy* was created in 1998 simply because there was no national magazine for the 'dark' scene in France. The magazine is sold with a free CD sampler. It was black and white at the beginning but soon became color.

"We fill the need of a dark mag in France. Our purpose is to inform people about bands, classic and famous ones, but also new bands, and artists, both known and less known, all in the dark scene. It's difficult to maintain a magazine like this, because the market is small. Everybody knows that we are living in a difficult period—terrorism, wars, etc.—a time when spare-time activities are far from being part of people's priorities. On the other hand, people need to survive, and to dream, and music and art can be a good refuge. I see more and more 'dark' people in the streets and at gothic clubs."

GOTHIC magazine (Publisher: Martin Sprissler, Sigmaringen, Germany): "I started the magazine in 1993. I got to know Jörg, who had been publishing, or rather photocopying, a fanzine under that name. He had nineteen issues out and was about to end his achievements. I was there, already DJing for five years, with a hobby interest in taking over *GOTHIC-Magazine* (yes, the title is in English). I'd convinced A.M. Music (who released my first CD) to publish the magazine, which they did. I added the concept of releasing a CD compilation along with each issue in order to present the bands interviewed with their music. It's pretty common nowadays but was new back then. At first we were available exclusively in train stations and airports in Germany, Switzerland, and Austria. Since issue 24 we include 8 postcards inside the mag as a bonus.

"It's fun to do and readers get their kicks too—they wouldn't buy *GOTHIC* if they didn't, would they? We exist to inform, to entertain. It hasn't been awfully hard for the magazine to survive, but you cannot ride a dead horse. If you start a goth publication with the priority of spreading your personal opinion and that has no basis within your readers, then it surely won't exist for too long."

Photo by www.newgrave.com

Newgrave (Publisher: Matt Riser, Hollywood, California, USA): "I started this magazine in 2000 because all other magazines sucked hard. There was absolutely no support or coverage for the underground and obscure bands. All the gothic magazines at the time (and still some currently being produced) were just embarrassing to be associated with. They were reporting on a scene that was so different from mine, so different from what got me into the gothic scene in the first place. They made the gothic movement seem like a total dorkfest full of wannabe vampires and Renaissance Faire rejects. If these publications had been my first exposure to this subculture, I would never have given it a second thought. I couldn't stand it any longer, so I created my own magazine that would feature articles on things that were of interest to me. Apparently other people also wanted the same thing, because the magazine has been successful.

"There are a lot of hard-working bands getting absolutely no respect or media coverage by other magazines. Also, I wanted to make the gothic scene appealing to a new generation. When I was a teen, my first exposure to the gothic scene was through *Propaganda* magazine. It totally blew my mind. I guess I wanted my magazine to have the same effect on some unsuspecting youth. A print magazine is expensive to produce, so there needs to be some kind of funding—advertising—outside the magazine's sales. Unfortunately, you only get advertising from companies if you promise to interview or feature their band or product. With only a few exceptions, I refuse to work this way. I think the magazine loses all credibility and becomes run and controlled by advertising money. Next time you look at a gothic magazine and wonder why they decided to interview the lame-ass bands they do, just keep flipping the pages and you'll see the nice full-page ad that ultimately paid for that interview. Also, it's hard as fuck to get the distribution deals."

why go on . . . ?

Ascension Magazine: "We fill the simple need for 'information' that the Italian goth community needs. We don't care if something is popular or not, if something sells or not. I'm very open-minded. Even the smallest grain of sand is part of a desert. And we are just a little little bit of sand!"

Comatose Rose magazine: "We're a missing piece of the puzzle, really. The average large city has at least one goth night, a few bands, some Web sites, but no magazine. Not in Canada, anyway. I like a challenge. I took a road trip to Vancouver to see a Frontline Assembly concert. I brought seventy-five copies of the mag and handed them all out within an hour. Everywhere I looked there was someone sifting through a copy, two or three people huddled together in a corner with a lighter . . . It was overwhelming to see so many people holding something you worked so hard on. Intimate."

Elegy: "The need we fill is the same for all underground communities—to inform about music and artistic events. I mean, you cannot find information about the dark scene on TV, in the newspapers, or in the mainstream mags, and the goth community wants to know about the last record of this or that band, wants to read interviews with their favorite writers, wants to know about the next goth festival or concert in their town. I think the needs of the gothic community are simply the needs of passionate people. We provide people, gothic or not, information in the newspaper kiosks, even in the small towns, about the dark scene. We help to develop this culture. The goth culture often has a bad image in the mainstream; there are a lot of clichés, and many stupid things are said. I hope that people who are not part of the community but who read *Elegy* change their mind and see it for what it is. That is to say a real, beautiful and interesting musical and artistic movement."

GOTHIC magazine: "We make people aware that there's life inside the scene. If you had just the possibility to go to your same old club on weekends to dance a little and gossip about the same issues over and over, the day would come a lot sooner when you're just fed up with it all, and you'd turn your back on the sad old goth scene. My mag keeps readers updated, and provides opportunity for them to make up their own minds about what's going on in the scene itself, especially on a larger scale than that of the home club."

Newgrave: "I think the goth community has lost sight of what makes it great. You go to a club and you hear synth pop music. Most of the clothes have become so uniform and off-the-rack boring. The scene as a whole seems to be just a watered-down, middle-ground version of what it could be. I think with *Newgrave* I give the scene that burst of fresh air that it truly needs. I never take the safe or predictable route. I support the underdog, and the obscure. With *Newgrave,* you never know what you'll get. I go to great lengths to obtain articles and interviews, and take many of the photos myself to maintain a level of quality and ensure my content is exclusive. For instance, *Newgrave* is the first US publication to report on the Japanese visual kei movement in a positive light."

goths converging

For goths, forming the tiny percentage of the population that they do, plus being spread out all over the world, the need to meet and greet those such as oneself under a full moon can become painfully paramount. Goth Meetup Days have become popular events around the world, set up on the Internet by locals so that those in the same city can put a face to the Internet handle. It's a start.

Corporations, and like-minded groups convene; why not dark brothers and sisters? The Internet has become the lifeblood for many goths, especially for those who are isolated by geography, or in contact virtually but in reality live worlds apart. The Net provides lists for information ex-

Copyright by Darkmedia GmbH, photo by Peter Schilling

50 Ft Queenie
Photo by Nicole Aucoin

C1 - Chicago 1995 While many people talked about organizing an international gathering of net.goths, it took Chicago goths Gothpat (now a London, UK goth) and Heather Spear to finally do it. Held in the back of a sports bar, where Convergencites had to make their way past rowdy sports fans, C1 featured: Arcanta, The Machine in the Garden, Seraphim Gothique, Sunshine Blind, The Wake, Garden of Dreams, Trance to the Sun, Lestat, Mephisto Walz, and Lycia. This was the first opportunity for many net.goths to meet one another in real life, and the general consensus was, let's do it again!

C2 - Boston 1996 Cusraque took the ball and kept it rolling. This swashbuckling club promoter organized three nights of dancing and bands at Boston's Man Ray club, featuring acts Johnny Indovina of Human Drama, Switchblade Symphony, Sunshine Blind, Valor's Christian Death (who turned out to be more trouble than they were worth), You Shriek, and One of Us. A buffet dinner at the Middle East, a fashion show featuring designs by alt.gothic's Lady Bathory, and a tour of Boston's lovely cemeteries rounded out the activities.

C3 - San Francisco 1997 Midwest to New England, it seemed only appropriate that C3 be held on the West Coast, and what better place than beautiful San Francisco. For two nights, the sounds of Battery, This Ascension, Sub Version, Kill Sister Kill, Darkling

change, and announcements, making it an invaluable tool for goth promotions. It also provides forums for interaction, from serious discussions to silly chatter to bitch sessions, aka flame wars. Goths around the world can communicate with one another.

Darkness, face to face

Goth convention organizer Macross Ascendent discusses two annual North American Goth gatherings, Convergence and Gothcon.

"Convergence is an annual reunion of extended family. Friends from all over the world make the pilgrimage to whatever place in North America the event is taking place in and spend the weekend—and in many cases longer—partying, drinking, talking, attending tours and seminars, shopping, drinking some more, and having the time of their lives indulging in sweet debauchery.

"At its best, Convergences are truly magical events. The addition of bands, DJs, and other scene celebrity entertainment is icing on the cake, but in no way the central focus of the event [Goths meeting Goths]. The themed Masquerade Ball on Sunday night began with C5 and is a popular regular event. Attendance on average is around the 800-person mark. Convergence was created for and by the users of the alt.gothic newsgroups—it's basically alt.gothic's party, but everyone is welcome.

"Gothcon is a band- and music-focused event, run entirely by a single promoter and her volunteers. The first Gothcon was held in Atlanta, Georgia, in 2000. The next two were held in New Orleans, with about 600 attendees each year. Events included numerous live performances and DJ nights, a vendors' room, and discussion panels. Gothcon was advertised as a nonprofit event dedicated to raising money for charities. Within the last year several volunteer and company sponsors requested proof for tax purposes and clarification and verification that donations had been made to the charities they claimed they were sponsoring. To date, an investigation into the event and its promoter, Snow Elizabeth, continues amid rumors that a fourth Gothcon is being planned."

Probably the largest regular gothy event in the United States is Dracula's Ball, run by Patrick Rodgers of Dancing Ferret Concerts. The group—around for eight years—produces Nocturne, which might be the biggest weekly gothic/Industrial night in the United States, held in Philadelphia. They also run a retail store, and the record label Dancing

Ferret Discs, home to goth bands the Cruxshadows, Nosferatu, Neuroticfish, The Dreamside, Paralysed Age, and others.

Patrick says, "Dracula's Ball is sometimes billed as 'the largest regular gothic/Industrial event in the country,' although the promoter's earlier tagline, 'largest event of its kind in America,' is perhaps more appropriate. Music is provided by two guest DJs, and two guest bands, which have included such (inter)national acts like the Cruxshadows, Neuroticfish, the Dreamside, Seraphim Shock, Rasputina, and Godhead. Vendors hawk gothy wares such as veils, leather goods, chainmail, and original dark art.

"The crowd, typically up to two thousand strong, is a refreshingly diverse mix of hardcore goth club veterans, vampire subculture enthusiasts, fetishists, horror fans, strippers, SCA members, and some folks who are just genuinely curious, many of whom wind up becoming regulars at their local goth clubs. Besides coming from varying backgrounds, the crowd is racially diverse to a degree not often seen in goth clubs, and as the Ball is an all-ages event, there is variety from Kindergoth to Elder goth as well. New faces are always in abundant supply, in large part due to the fact that most patrons aren't actually from Philadelphia (around half the crowd drives two-plus hours to reach the Ball). While some goth elitists turn their noses up at the amount of 'new blood,' most people find Dracula's Ball to be a major social event, and the bar is always packed with the East Coast's A-list of promoters, DJs, and band members.

"Dracula's Ball takes place four times a year in Philadelphia. Our twentieth anniversary celebration was held on Halloween 2002, and one lucky attendee won the big prize: a trip for two to Transylvania!"

In Europe, goths meet at music festivals. Sizewise, there is nothing in North America comparable to the mega Euro goth festivals. Music writer Pee Wee Vignold provides a behind-the-scenes peek at one of Germany's biggest annual goth events, the M'Era Luna Festival:

"Once a year the airfield of Hildesheim-Drispenstedt in the very heart of Germany becomes the center of attention for gothic and goth-affiliated people from all over the world. That's when Sonic Seducer's M'Era Luna Festival calls the black-hearted to celebrate themselves for two days and two nights.

"Friday afternoon at four P.M. the first festival visitors enter the camping site to set up their home for the weekend, a weekend of forty bands on two stages, two endless party nights at the aircraft hangar getting hundreds and

Thrush, Seraphim Gothique, the Razor Skyline, and Wench filled the gorgeous Maritime Hall. Other events included dancing at the Trocadero, a Mad Hatter's tea party, comic book signings by the beloved Jhonen Vasquez, creator of <u>Johnny the Homicidal Maniac</u>, and a cemetery tour that led to hell.

C4 - Toronto 1998 The C4 ball was first started rolling by Matt Ardill and Siani Evans, then picked up by the C4 committee, consisting of Sheryl Kirby, Greg Clow, Siobhan NiLoughlin, and Charlotte Ashley. Performances from Masochistic Religion, Faith and the Muse, Rhea's Obsession, the Changelings, My Scarlet Life, and An April March as well as dance music spun by DJs Greg Clow, Michael Salo, Todd Marylace, Lady Bathory, Lord Pale, Antithesis, and Tapestry. Highlights included a reading at Savage Garden by vampire writers Nancy Baker and Nancy Kilpatrick, a tour of Castle Loma, dinner at the Movenpick Marche and shopping tours through Toronto's immense downtown retail districts.

C5 - New Orleans 1999 Heather Spear teamed up with G.E. Addams of Mere Mortal Productions, Misha Sand, Harry Konidisiotis, and Connor Preciado to bring us C5 to the beautiful city of New Orleans. By all accounts the most widely attended Convergence to date, it featured the bands New Dawn Fades, Falling Janus, Cut.Rate.Box, Ex Voto, The Cruxshadows, Mentallo and the Fixer, and Clan of Xymox, as well as a bazaar and art show, an elder-goth cocktail hour and the Rougaroux's Costume Ball.

C6 - Seattle 2000 The C6 team of Jilli, Professor Pan Satyricon, Vomvamuse, Luna, violet weary, Fluke, Midnyte, Cerberus, the Mysterious Voice, and wendolen created an itinerary that included a meet'n'greet, a visit to the Kiva Han coffeehouse, a tour of underground Seattle, a cruise, fashion and art shows, and of course, the bands. Music was provided by Attrition, Trance to the Sun, Unto Ashes, Faith & Disease, Voltaire, and surprise guest Peter Fucking Murphy! and by the DJs Slowdive, Hana Solo, Mistress Catherinna, Scary Lady Sarah, Fross, Batty, Arcanus, and Macross.

C7 - New York City 2001 New York City received the winning vote, and organizers Angel Butts, Batty, Bloodlotus, Bob Westphal, Carrie Carolin, Carrie Laben, Carrin Welch, Claire Archer, Clifford Low, Daednu, David Hogan, Dragon Edward Garou, Joseph Max, Lainie Peterson, Miguel Fernandez, Todd Zino, and Trystan L Bass presented The Unseelie Court on the weekend of August 17–19. Music was provided by Coil, Clair Voyant, Snog, Deep Red, and Neurepublik. Additional events included an absinthe party, meet 'n' greet, discussion panels, cloisters picnic, merchant bazaar, swap meet, fashion show, and museum tour.

C8 - Montreal, Quebec 2002 Siobhan NiLoughlin took the helm once again with coconspirator Casper Von Bittergoff and a small army of dedicated volunteers. Features included a haunted dinner theater, fashion workshop, writers panel with Nancy Kilpatrick, Sephera Giron, Edo VanBelkom, Michael Rowe,

hundreds of goths into the groove, shopping sprees of the third kind, and meeting with the 'stars' that have grown out of the underground scene.

"While some might still think the twelve-year-old Wave Gotik Treffen, which paints Leipzig black for five days every May, is the event that best reflects the current state of the European goth movement in all its variations, within only four years more and more people feel that M'Era Luna has become the place to be.

"Unlike Leipzig, where the attractions are splattered all over the city and a huge amount of organization, logistics, infrastructure, and endurance is needed to get to the right place at the right time in order to join all the events you don't want to miss, M'era Luna concentrates on one spot—a spot big enough to hold the more than 20,000 visitors who come every year to see the hottest bands in the gothic world. The forty bands that come here from all over the world each year define the present range, and the three generations of goth.

"First there are the Elders, to which belong well-known UK legends remaining from the eighties, such as the Mission, Fields of the Nephilim, Gary Numan, and even though obviously trying to rid themselves of the everlasting goth label sticking to them, the Sisters of Mercy. They share two venues—the huge, outdoor main stage, and the smaller indoor stage, set up in the adjacent aircraft hangar—with acts of the 'second generation' that emerged during the nineties, such as Project Pitchfork (Germany), Covenant (Denmark), VNV Nation (UK), Suicide Commando (Belgium), or Das Ich (Germany), HIM (Finland), the 69 Eyes (Finland), Oomph! (Germany), and Marilyn Manson (USA), acts that all began in the underground and have become mainstream chart players without losing their credibility by selling out—they're just becoming more and more popular. Of course most of the music of the second generation still happens outside the mainstream attention. Berlin-based Blutengel and the Mexican maniacs Hocico are just too weird ever to become part of 'the outside world,' no matter how hard the fashion scouts of H&M are trying to milk the scene, and that's exactly what they are most appreciated for. And even if the bigger-selling acts like Belgian Johan van Roy's Suicide Commando ever sell enough units to become 'pop' one day, they will be viewed in a similar fashion to how the Sex Pistols are seen now.

"The last third belongs to the newbies, who often have to face big expectations from the audience and always do their best to prove worthy of their slot on the festival bill—for example, Norwegian Industrial rock love machine Zeromancer, who opened the hangar stage of the first ever M'Era Luna Festival in 2000 and returned one year later to do an afternoon show on the main stage because they gained a reputation as a dynamic and sexy live act that knows how to thrill their audience, male as well as female. In 2002 the newcomer most talked about was Sulpher (UK), the four-piece band gathering around Rob Holliday and Monti, who gained their first credit for co-producing the defining Gary Numan Y2K comeback, *Pure,* and shook the sleepy UK scene with the release of their stunning debut, *Spray,* a lean, mean Industrial metal machine that creeps along then hits you 'harder than a prison fuck' (as the band's shirt-backs state). And then there's Pzycho Bitch, whose hard-edged and noisy electro-Industrial brings fresh aspects to 'Future Pop' (as Ronan Harris of VNV Nation likes to call it). They dominate the electro scene, not only by the appearance of their enticingly beautiful but rather evil-looking red-headed female singer S.I.N.A., who gives that musically rather violent genre a little bit more sex appeal.

"One of the traditions as well as the main attractions of the still-young festival is the signing sessions at the *Sonic Seducer* music magazine booth, where the festival audience has a chance for personal contact with their favorite bands, such as VNV Nation, Paradise Lost (UK), Wolfsheim (Germany), or even platinum sellers HIM and their charismatic androgynous singer, Ville Valo, whose appearance at the booth gives a strong impression of what it was like back when the Beatles ruled the world. They too appeared here on an afternoon slot two years ago, right after their breakthrough number one single "Join Me," which as a part of the *The 13th Floor* soundtrack made them famous overnight in Germany. In 2002 they returned as celebrated headliners with not so many hearts left to conquer anymore.

"In the end each and every one of the bands has a history worth telling, and they all connect here at the M'Era Luna Festival, where it's not only about playing, but also meeting and greeting the fans as well as their 'colleagues.' This is typical: watching backstage L'Ame Immortelle singer Thomas Rainer hurrying from his dressing room followed by Flux and Dero from heavy rocking Oomph! to watch the show of their old heroes Soft Cell, who a minute later receive a standing ovation as they are guided onto the stage.

Stephanie Bedwell-Grime, and screening of Daniel Richler's Reach for the Crypt. Also, tours of Montreal including the cemeteries, and the second biggest in-joke in convergence history, Captain Matt's Armada featuring Axel. Live performances by Mara's Torment, CMAFA, Bella Morte, This Ascension, Cinema Strange, the Chaos Engine, Bordello, and Swarf. DJs Fross, Macross, Doc Pain, Mr. Black, Todd Clayton, Sexbat, and Scary Lady Sarah kept the throngs dancing throughout the weekend.

C9 - Las Vegas 2003 800 goths descended on Sin City and the Flamingo Hotel for a weekend of debauchery and reunions. Mandalay Bay's rumjungle and Red Square were taken over. Daytime: exploring Vegas's Strip, getting married (there were five known C9 weddings!), a goth-clothing swap, visiting the Jackpot Bazaar, which features 50+ merchants. Plus an open mic with spoken word poet Clint Catalyst. Evening: Entertainment at the historic Huntridge Theater; a fashion show; music by Reverb TV, Babylonian Tiles, and bootle. Well-known DJs from the US and UK spun everything from Apoptygma Berzerk to Lionel Richie at Saturday's Area 51 dance party. Sunday night: Performances by Frankenstein, Android Lust, and the Last Dance, and the now infamous after-hours party—attendees took over the hotel's two large hot tubs for insane fun.

C10 - Chicago 2004

"*Sonic Seducer* music magazine publishes regular editorial announcements beforehand, and also brings out the official festival schedule—100,000 copies are given away free each year. But the highlight is always the filmed documentary of the festival for a covermount video CD that *Sonic Seducer* sticks to the inside of the magazine's Christmas issue each year. It features live footage from the shows as well as behind-the-scenes shots and vivid interviews, which often show a whole different side of the artists.

"Many visitors use the festival itself as a shopping occasion. A market fair carries nearly every goth need, from stickers to jewelry, books to boots, records and CDs to bondage equipment, from mead to absinthe. Whatever the black heart desires, one of the traders who come from all over Germany is sure to have it. As long as the music plays, you'll find the market crowded with creatures of the night.

"The nights belong to the hangar parties, where several DJs keep people dancing until dawn. The festival opens with the first party, which takes place on Friday night. You'll spot the faces you've seen in the crowd as well as those of the artists, journalists and managers who worked behind the scenes or onstage during the day. Bands like the 69 Eyes, Clan of Xymox (Netherlands), or Project Pitchfork are always seen partying until the morning hours, but even after the bands return to their hotel rooms, the party continues at the camping site.

"And the bottom line is, that's what M'Era Luna Festival is all about: partying. Enjoying yourself. And music, of course. goth music, that is. And all that that involves."

dancing the ghost

It's undoubtedly the nature of goth music that encourages goth dance styles, styles recognizable everywhere you go. Anything this familiar is up for satire, which Kai MacTane and Ann Killpack manage very well on the hilarious Web page *How to Dance Gothic*, which includes illustrations and a rating system.

clubbing the night away

Goths dance in clubs, and London's Slimelight is one of the oldest goth clubs in the world, extant since the 1980s. The closest tube stop is the appropriately named Angel station.

Photographer Stephané Lord gives a camera-eye view of Slimelight.

"It's down an alleyway, no, not even an alley, in a very industrial-looking building with no sign at all. Well, the sign says ELECTROWERKZ; it's a paintball club during the week. If you don't already know where it is, you probably won't find it unless you see goths gathered outside. Most of the time there's a small waiting line.

"You can't get in unless you're a member, and Slimelight boasts about 10,000 members worldwide. If you're not a member, you have to ask a member to sign you in—each member can sign in two people. If you want to become a member you need to fill in a form, pay your money, and have two members endorse the form.

"The building is an old warehouse with cement walls. There are three floors, and you enter at street level. The second floor plays Industrial and Techno, and the crowd there is more Cyber. Goth music is played on the top floor, but they also now do synthpop. A large part of the clientele travels from floor to floor. Sometimes there are shows on the Industrial floor. There is not much in the way of decoration, but they do use a bit of lighting for effect.

"What makes Slimelight special is the people, and they come from different parts of Europe; it's easy for people from France and Germany to get there for the weekend. You see plenty of Cyber goths, but also old-fashioned Victorian goths, and a few of the old Batcave goths are still visible. There is more variation than at most goth clubs.

"What is especially British about the club is that people seem to talk to each other. They are friendly, not so timid with strangers, and I find that quite interesting. One of the oddest people I have seen at the club was a lady in her forties, directly from the New Wave era, but whose look incorporated funky science fiction elements. Peculiar, and I liked it.

"Slimelight is always trying new things. Because they are open till around seven A.M., a few years ago you could order breakfast at the end of the night at the club."

Not all goths are happy with shifts in music. Gossips club in Soho now features Malice Underground nights. Stephané says, "Two guys started it because they were pissed that Slimelight moved a bit away from pure goth music. The bar has a gothic event once a month and draws older goths, not much of the Cyber crowd. It's very Old School goth. One of their special events was named 'London After the Slimelight.' Then, recently, Slimelight decided to rededicate the 3rd floor to gothic music. It's been well received."

Types of Movements for Goth Dancing from the How to Dance Gothic Web page
With thanks to Kai Mac Tane and Anne Killpack

Hand and Arm Movements
Washing the Windows
Changing the Light Bulb
Sweeping the Floor
Stuck in my Coffin

Washing the Windows

Changing the Light Bulb

Sweeping the Floor

Stuck in My Coffin

Foot Maneuvers
With Catlike Tread
My Artificial Hip Joint
Testing the Scratching Post
Which Way is the Exit?
"Ow! I Cut my Wrists!"

the goth father speaks

One of the great contributions to goth music, to goth in general, has come not from a band, but from the incredible Mick Mercer. His groundbreaking books, which include *Hex Files* and the more recent *21st Century Goth*, have expanded goth awareness. Goth is now an international and intergenerational phenomonon.

Mick, from the UK, is a terrific music fan, and it is his knowledge and love of dark music that has inspired much of his writing. But oddly enough, Mick does not see himself as goth. "Nope, never in the accepted sense. I have never had *any* interest in fashionable things, so never got into the fashion, and having been a 'Punk' before 'goth' started, there is a gap there . . . but when people attack goth or laugh at it, something inside of me instinctively rears up angrily, because this is something I love that is being derided. I don't care about the scene element of goth or the bitchiness, I care about the music and the ideas."

Mick explains what enticed him into the goth music world in the first place. "It's what *all* my other interests have always been about, since I was a child, so when it came along it made sense, basically, and that's a positive effect for something to have. Growing up near a weird church with a cute graveyard, preferring horror mags and ghost stories to traditional books when I was small, and then being hugely disinterested in everything other than horror and comics while at school, where the only literary works that interested me were *King Lear* and Joseph Conrad's *The Secret Agent*, it was that world, and the themes of death and the outsider, which were the only things to directly appeal. A teacher who understood why I was so bored at school then plonked a copy of 'The Rime of the Ancient Mariner' in front of me, not for the words, but for the illustrations, which were by Mervyn Peake, and that led to *Titus Groan*, whereupon I was immediately inspired to become serious about being a writer, when before I had only dabbled!

"Musically, the vast majority of stuff around was dross, then Punk happened. This was incredibly direct and exciting but after a few months lacked substance, for me, and I was looking for something else, which manifested itself in bands like Gloria Mundi, early Ultravox (when John Foxx was on vocals), and Adam and the Ants, then began expanding from there. This music was both cerebral and violent, which I liked.

"A load of bands naturally started creating a more developed, emotional form of Punk, with their own preferred ideals and inspirations, and those naturally started to be noticed for their darker style. This was perfect, just what I was waiting for."

Hex Files was Mick's third book, following close on the heels of *Gothic Rock*. "I'd started a Punk fanzine in 1976 called *Panache*. By 1978 I was freelancing for a music paper, and in 1980 for a magazine called *Zigzag*, which was run by a total idiot. That folded, but I'd been able to cover lots of the early goth bands in that. By now I'd given up temporary work doing crap jobs, and was making my living, such as it was, by being a writer, and mainly concentrating on Punk, New Wave, and any element of goth that was emerging. I went on to *Melody Maker*, but a new publisher asked to start *ZigZag* up again as a national monthly magazine, and I was editor, ensuring that all goth material was covered. When the real goth era mushroomed, with the rockier bands to the fore, it was very big in this country [the UK], and that's how, and why, I did the *Gothic Rock Black Book* in the eighties, which was a fairly straightforward music-publisher book. They saw that goth was big, wanted a book on it, and so asked the only journalist who was writing in Britain about the subject as though it mattered. That did well, and was noticed by a guy called Sheldon Bayley at Pegasus, a publisher in Birmingham. He lured me up there to edit a monthly mag called *Siren* and wanted to do a book, *Gothic Rock*, which also ended up having an American print, via Cleopatra. That's the one that spawned several CD compilations of the same name on Jungle/Cleopatra, which people always assume I get royalties for! (Maybe I've been a bit dim with business, but I got paid for doing sleeve notes, and nothing else.)

"Anyway, Pegasus went bust, so no royalties there, but it had been fun doing a book about goth that was riddled with humor, even though that pissed lots of goths off who had become seriously po-faced by that time ('91–'92), and the bands appearing included chronic Sisters and Nephilim copycats, so I was pretty bored by that. The experience of then working for a couple of other publishers of music titles left me so disenchanted with all things musical that I even stopped my fanzine in 1992. I still wrote, but mainly for goth fanzines, while doing work for a record company, which was unspeakably dull.

"Then I asked a publisher if I could do a bigger, better goth book, which would become *Hex Files*. This was Batsford, a traditional publisher, who normally did books on history, social matters, embroidery, chess . . . any number of rather serious subjects. They did a great job with *Hex Files*, but also went bust. I was in talks with them about other books but nothing came of it."

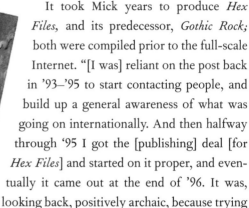

Courtesy of Mick Mercer; Hex Files photo by Andy Cameron; 21st Century Goth photo by Stéphane Lord

It took Mick years to produce *Hex Files*, and its predecessor, *Gothic Rock;* both were compiled prior to the full-scale Internet. "[I was] reliant on the post back in '93–'95 to start contacting people, and build up a general awareness of what was going on internationally. And then halfway through '95 I got the [publishing] deal [for *Hex Files*] and started on it proper, and eventually it came out at the end of '96. It was, looking back, positively archaic, because trying to keep up to date with addresses and details of bands was pretty difficult, especially as you couldn't keep writing to people to check up on them. The costs were prohibitive! If I hadn't been prepared to spend *everything* I had doing it, I couldn't have finished the thing at all. There was no real data-bank of info anywhere to refer to, and having agreed to also include sections on vampires, fetish, and pagan elements—because so many people were expressing an interest in those—meant I was then having to find as many publications that were leaders in their fields that also included details of other fanzines for that genre."

Mick's books have been labors of love. "It's only the people. I have made friends from that time who I am still in contact with. Now and again you also meet people who say that that book [*Hex Files*], or *Gothic Rock*, helped introduce them into the music because they lived somewhere that had no scene whatsoever. That is always one of the overriding factors that keeps me going, apart from my own interest in the subject. When people are so honest and quite emotional about it at times it just makes you feel humble to the point of queasiness!"

His early books are now out of print, but he plans on printing revised and redesigned versions on CD-ROM. Fortunately, Mick's newest book is still available, with a wonderful cover photo by Québec photographer Stephané Lord. "*21st Century Goth* is a review of over 6,000 Web sites of bands, clothes businesses, goth people, goth sites, zines, resources, regional guides, visual rock, webrings, sites of interest etc. It looks for quality and for new things, and works as a far more instructive aid to people than any of the biggest Web site resources because they put nothing in context, only lists. There may be a compilation CD to accompany it, as there always has been before—that isn't settled yet. Goth books will, providing *21st Century Goth* succeeds, be every two years from now, plus I have a series of books, including goth material from the eighties that most goths will never have seen, which I will release on CD, and will only be available via my Web site. I also have a few books on CD on other subjects coming."

Because Mick has had such a long-standing love of and in-depth knowledge on the subject of goth music, he also has a strong opinion about its future. "If it doesn't change in certain ways it could die, especially in Britain. To change, it *needs* to change, fundamentally, in how it reaches people.

"The scene in the eighties twice reached such heights (first indie, then mainstream) that it was easily twenty times the size it currently is in the UK, probably more. The idea of a large band selling 50,000 albums is a pipe dream these days. Goth bands were the staple diet of any indie label, they were the most popular form of live bands during the early to mid-eighties, but all that has gone.

"Most forums rarely discuss music to any great degree, so I don't really visit them on anything approaching a regular basis. You can flip back though a month's postings and find hardly anything beyond social discourse, which is how the Net obviously benefited goth in the first place, and remains its saving grace. The communication aspect helped goth stabilize when it could have gone under, due to the general media ignorance and avoidance of anything goth, but I think it must be time for it to move on.

"Ironically, it is envy which eats into the goth scene more than anything, with elitists holding court, and people being branded not fit to be in one clique or another. Considering how small the scene is, outside of Germany, or how scattered, even in the biggest potential territory, America, it's a wonder anything ever gets done at all. Quite why this parsimonious approach should exist and still flourish seems positively weird to me, but once a source of tension arises within any part of a scene in a noticeable way, it balloons up, flourishes, and is never forgotten. I have never got involved with any of that and try and look for the best in people and developments, and that distance, I believe, makes my detached observations more worthwhile and pertinent, and sensibly so, and with my wide range of experience in the media and with labels, indie promot- ers . . . I see where the possibilities lie and in how easily things can be ef- fectively manipulated in ways that those who have always concentrated on how the business machinations of goth grind very carefully along can- not sometimes even believe. To many it seems there is an insurmountable hurdle to overcome for goth to become popular on a large scale again, which is rubbish.

"We have big problems in the UK because the ignorance and self- obsession of music journalists meant they turned readers off, leaving ti- tles to fold, which wasn't a result of the Net flourishing, where no natural focus on music exists, just a myriad of smaller opinions. Music journalists on paper could have saved themselves by writing about goth and the more credible forms of rock, such as all the post-death-speed-thrash-nu metal. If, to give a perfect example, *Melody Maker* had covered that dur- ing the nineties and had simply put on an extra five to ten thousand read- ers a week (quite simple when *Kerrang* was fortnightly), that would have represented a huge increase of approximately 25 percent and the publish- ers would never have folded the title. As it is we have only one paper, which *still* doesn't have the sense to go down this line and covers brain- dead pop manufactured by major labels with an audience under fourteen in mind, who aren't going to buy music papers anyway! Those who don't learn the history of the past (the demise of *Record Mirror, Sounds,* and then their stable-mate *Melody Maker*) are doomed for unemployment within two years.

"It leaves our music scene with no way back once it goes. The radio and TV don't bother, and people will withdraw into regional interests, which is bizarre, but stupidity is at the root of it all, because the magazines which succeed are the metal, music, plus the dreary monthlies like *Q* and *Mojo,* which concentrate on big established names, but get a readership because fans are interested in music, not in music journalists.

"It also astonishes me how apologetic the UK goth scene is—whereas during the nineties, goth bands played goth gigs, and that was pretty much that. They never slugged it out on the indie circuit the way indie bands do. To get a deal, an indie band will routinely be doing gig after gig every month in the hope of attracting passing A&R attention from individuals too dopey to listen to demo tapes. It means goth bands get a tiny audience when the majority of indie music is duller than it has been since the mid-eighties, and yet goth isn't there to present a viable alternative, while forms of rock are.

"Curiously most bands seem happy with sporadic gigging, suspicious of advice, as though this hobby-horse of theirs *is* only a hobby. Hopefully people will set their sights higher now, and I want to give as many hints as I can through my Web site on ways in which the music business can be manipulated, but that's all in the future. For the time being I'll just cover what I find exciting and hopefully convey just why I believe other people will also."

One particular bone for Mick is just how much both goths and goth music are *not* appreciated by the world at large. "It still *amazes* me that people don't get it: that goth is *unique*. It remains the only musical form that articulates many different areas of your life, of things that interest you, affect you, and shape you. And as your interests change there are then new areas of goth which can also become naturally relevant to that. It is for life, because it always adapts. If you look for new things, new forms, you will succeed.

"Other genres of music tend to be about something, with the link generally being something you feel, but that's all—yet if you are interested in literature, film, art, visual stimuli of various forms, goth has a relevance that wouldn't appear within other forms, exhibiting such broad, welcoming facets. They really are all inextricably linked, and it's all down to which particular elements you mix and match.

"Also, assuming they aren't put off by the petty-minded superiority of the minority, then newcomers should find it all-encompassing to the point where they need to make certain decisions. You naturally enjoy it the more you get older, as you learn from mistakes, or you're merely one of the fashionable types, which has the highest dropout factor, where once the clubbing ends so does any serious contemplation.

"To me the music comes first. These are bands who don't expect to make it, in the expected sense, and create their music purely for the love of it, and that still hasn't even penetrated the ludicrous skulls of UK music journalists, or in most other countries I imagine. This music is far more exciting than anything indie currently offers, or has for years, and yet goth bands haven't even begun flaunting themselves.

"It still isn't taken seriously, which will change. Bands *will* be able to prove they deserve to be taken serious, and I will still be writing stuff people are confused by, taken with, or angry about ten years from now, by which time everything will have improved massively, or have died. Personally, I'm banking on the former."

URLs

Ascension Magazine
e-mail: ascension@libero.it

Comatose Rose Magazine
www.comatoserose.com

Elegy
www.elegymag.com

GOTHIC-magazine
www.gothic-magazine.de

Newgrave
www.newgrave.com

Photos of Gothcon 2001
www.darkart.net/gothcon/gothcon.htm

Photos of Convergence 8, 2002, Montreal
www.noctivagant.net/c8pics.htm

Dracula's Ball
www.draculasball.com

Vampire Condoms
www.vampirecondoms.com

Sonic Seducer—M'Era Luna Festival
www.sonic-seducer.de/

Wave gothic—Germany
www.wave-gotic-treffen.de/start.html

Goth Am—Netherlands
www.gotham.nl/

Projectfest 02—Philadelphia
www.projektfest.com/

Whitby Gothic Weekend—UK
www.wgw.topmum.co.uk/

Industrial Festival—France
www.membres.lycos.fr/industrialfest/

How to Dance Gothic
www.gothpunk.com

International goth club listings
www.vamp.org/Gothic/clublist.html

Stephané Lord
www.necrobabes.org/darkfairies/

Slimelight
www.slimelightlondon.com/

Gossips Club
www.gossips.co.uk/history.html

Mick Mercer
www.mickmercer.com

iΠtoxicaΠts aΠd otHER stimulaΠts

Absinthe by the six-pack!

existential questions for goth bar and club owners

A common wail from club owners is: "Goths don't drink!" This is a subculture not afraid to order a Shirley Temple, or cranberry juice and Perrier. Those who do drink have, for the most part, preferences.

What's the most popular goth drink and how often do goths drink it? Basic beer and/or wine. Occasionally to frequently.

The world floats in beer, but some brewers like to focus on a dark element. The Raven Beer—advertised as "The Taste is Poetic"—was apparently first produced in the Black Forest region of Germany. Now, it's made in Baltimore, Maryland, in honor of Edgar Allan Poe (who lived and died in Baltimore—see Chapter 11), and his evocative poem "The Raven." Other beers brewed around the world with idiosyncratic names include: Dead Guy Ale and Rasputin from Rogue Breweries of Newport, Oregon; Arrogant Bastard (demonic label) and Gargoyle from Stone Brewing Co., San Diego, California; HopDevil Ale from Victory Brewing, Downington, Pennsylvania; Fin du Monde (End of the World), Maudit (Dammit!) and Ephémère (Ephemeral), from Unibroue, Chambly, Québec; Gargouille (Gargoyle) from Quatre Temps in Québec; Rigor Mortis and l'Alchimist, from the brew pub Dieu du Ciel! in Montréal, Quebéc; Bishop's Finger ale from the UK's oldest brewer, Shepherd

Neame, Faversham, Kent; La Mort Subite (Sudden Death), Br De Keer Smaeker, Belgium; Duvel (Devil), Moortgat Brewery, Breendonk, Belgium; Louwaege Hapkin, named after an axe-wielding count, from Belgium; Judas, Brauerei Alken-Maes, from Belgium; Belzebuth, advertised as the strongest lager beer in the world, from Brasserie Jeanne d'Arc S.A., Ronchin-Lille, France; La Bière du Démon (The Devil's Beer), "12% of diabolic pleasure," from Les Brasseurs de Gayant, France; Trompe la Mort (Cheat Death), from Brauerei Schwabisch Gmund, Germany, with the reaper in the fog on the label.

Wine, especially red, is a perennial goth favorite. After all, red wine claims elegance, sophistication, and has the added benefit of resembling blood.

wine of the undead

Vampire wine image courtesy of Michael Marchant

One wine that stands out for many of *The † Section* is Vampire Wine. Michael Marchat owns the company that imports Vampire Wine, and also sells the energy drink VAMP (sold at Hot Topic). Like the vampire itself, Vampire Wine has a long and complex history, full of twists and turns, laced with supernatural elements, a tale worthy of a novel. "In the summer of 1985 while driving cross-country from LA to New York late at night, through Death Valley, I encountered a Mysterious Being at a gas station. He somehow knew that I had just finished reading *Dracula* for the very first time, and he urged me to go ahead and establish a Vampire Vineyards. We had a long conversation, and afterwards I wasn't sure if I was hallucinating or if it was real. The idea stayed with me.

"In the summer of 1985, I went to England with the intention of returning in two weeks. Instead I met my wife to be, Lisa Dominique, fell in love, and I stayed seven years. During the summer of 1986, I was pitching a film to Paul Ranieri, a friend of mine, while we were drinking some good Italian red wine. He wasn't biting, and then, the idea of Vampire Wine came back to me. I told him about it, and he agreed to put up some seed money. At that time, I knew practically nothing about the wine business. I was a lawyer in the music business. I made some inquiries to buy wine from Romania, a Communist society at that time. There was a government organization in charge of exporting all wine from Romania, and I explained that I wanted to export some wine to America. They told me that they already had an importer in America (Pepsico), and they didn't want to export to anyone else. I then asked if I could buy some of their wine for England. They told me they also had an importer for the UK, and that they weren't interested. Undaunted, I then got samples from Hungary, but I didn't like the wine. I was looking for a real full-bodied dry red wine, but I didn't really know which way to turn.

"Then suddenly one hot balmy summer evening in London, I saw the same Mysterious Being I saw at the gas station in Nevada. I was at one of my wife's rock concerts, when out of nowhere, this being comes up to me and hands me a bottle. 'I have what you are looking for,' he said. He gave me the bottle along with a business card, and vanished. The next day, I drank the wine. It was a good, extremely full-bodied red wine, 13 percent in alcohol, produced in Algeria. I called the number on the card. An Englishman answered the phone. He didn't sound like the being I had met twice, but he knew about the wine. He worked for one of the largest French wineries and he offered to arrange to bottle it for me. We subsequently met and made a deal. It took a while to put together the design elements, but finally in the winter of 1988 I arranged for some Vampire Wine to be shipped to London. The first 50 cases were sold to Alice Cooper and his English record company. He had a new album coming out, and they wanted to offer a gift to various radio DJ's and promoters.

"Since I had no experience in the wine trade, business was slow. Still, a loyal following began to emerge. The wine sold steadily at one of England's most upscale stores, Selfridges. Nevertheless, sales were small. Most people were not really interested in an unknown Algerian wine.

"In 1989, while having lunch at an Italian restaurant with the manufacturer of the cardboard coffins (when Vampire Wine was first released, we sold each bottle in a black cardboard coffin), I was drinking a good Sangiovese di Romagna. I thought it was delicious. While Nigel went to the bathroom, the Mysterious Being materialized, handed me a card and said, 'It is delicious. Go there.' He handed me another business card and simply vanished. The card contained the address of a large Italian winery not far from Verona, Italy, home of Romeo and Juliet. I made contact with the winery, and they put me onto their London agent. I ended up selling the remaining Algerian Vampire Wine, and buying the Sangiovese Vampire

Wine. I changed the packaging; the gold in the label and on the coffin box became red. The Italian Vampire sold better than the Algerian Vampire.

"The wine attracted more and more business. One day I received a call from Kathleen Ramsland, who was an assistant working for Anne Rice. Somehow she had gotten ahold of some of the Vampire Wine, and they wanted some for one of Anne's parties.

"At another summer rave in 1991, I had another conversation with the Mysterious Being, who appeared behind the bar in an empty tent. 'You look like you could use some of this,' he said, opening and handing me a bottle of Lucozade, an energy drink. Before I could take a sip, he then proceeded to tell me the time was ripe, and to go to Romania and seek out the vampire wine from there. Not knowing if I was talking to an illusion or myself, I protested, 'They don't want to sell me wine!' The Mysterious Being reassured me, 'They will!' And then he vanished. "In November of 1991, I traveled to Transylvania with a friend. He and I rented a car and drove to Brasov, a small town at the foothills of the Transylvania Alps. The road wound up and down a mountain and was extremely dark; they had no street lights. Fortunately the bottoms of the trees were painted white to help us see the way. We heard wolves as we drove through the countryside.

"We headed to a bar to try some local wines, and made a friend who thought he was being gracious by pouring some of his Pepsi-Cola into our red wine. 'It makes it better,' he said. The Berlin Wall had fallen but many Romanians were still afraid to talk to Americans. Still, we learned that under Communist rule, the Russians put them on a quota system, and the Romanians produced wine to meet the quota. Quality didn't matter. The best quality Romanian wine went to Pepsi. The wine left for the domestic market remained undrinkable by western standards.

"We met with the people from Vinexport, the Romanian official agency in charge of exporting wine from Romania—the same people who did not want to consider dealing with me before. When I told them I wanted to buy Romanian wine and call it Vampire Wine, they thought I was crazy. 'Who would buy such a silly thing?' they asked. There was a younger guy at the company, Basil, who thought it just might work. He had gotten married a mile from Dracula's castle and was well-read in English. Basil made arrangements for Bob and me to visit numerous wineries. The management at each winery thought I was crazy. We tasted some pretty good wines, the ones held back for export. We went to one winery where we found a reserve cabernet sauvignon that I fell in love with. I was all set to go with that one, and then I explained what we were going to call the wine. The winemaker became furious. He was too proud of his wine to let me call it Vampire Wine. I tried to explain through our interpreter that by calling it Vampire, people would be attracted to it. He didn't understand, and we had to choose another wine.

"By the beginning of 1992, I had a US importer lined up to purchase the first batch of Vampire Wine from Transylvania. My wife and I moved back home that year. In 1995, we finally began to import Vampire Wine into the US from Transylvania."

Michael has had a ton of goth-positive response to his wine, like the club promoter in New York's Alphabet City "who told me, 'How cool, a wine for goths!' I think there is a need for beverages with a wicked edge, something different from the everyday assortment of beverages. I like to think we offer the beverages of choice for the goth community. The packaging of our products seems to uniquely fit the goth style."

Importing Vampire Wine has been rewarding for Michael other than financially. "I've always enjoyed wine, but like so many other young people, I found the people who sold wine to be dull and boring. These same people, who dominate the wine industry, proclaimed that there would not be a market for Vampire Wine. It's fun proving them wrong."

"Writhe and Shine" comic
Copyright by Robert Tritthardt

the green fairy is goth

It's always been legal in Spain and the Czech Republic. The British just realized in 1998 that it never was banned in their country. Absinthe was born in Switzerland and lived to its fullest in France before it was murdered.

Extract of Artemesia absinthium. It's just a shrub, called wormwood in English. They used it in the Middle Ages to treat intestinal worms. Absinthe was allegedly invented by Dr. Pierre Ordiniare in 1792 as an all-purpose medicinal. In the late 1700s, Major Henri Dubied bought the recipe from the Sisters Henriod and began brewing the green beverage that combined wormwood with exotic-sounding herbs like juniper, melissa, angelica, nutmeg, anise, fennel, and hyssop, which created a bitter

Photo courtesy of Hugues Leblanc

ABSINTHE PARAPHERNALIA

The Absinthe Museum in Auvers-sur-Oise, France displays Toulouse-Lautrec's absinthe spoon. This museum was founded by Mme. Marie-Claude Delahaye, a lecturer in cellular biology, who in 1983 wrote the Bible: *Absinthe: History of Absinthe*

ABSINTHE-FLAVORED WINE RECIPE

courtesy of the Gothic Martha Stewart

2 tsp. dried wormwood
2 pints port
2 tsp. hyssop
2 tsp. lavender
2 tsp. marjoram
2 tsp. peppermint
2 tsp. sage
2 tsp. thyme

All herbs are dried. Steep herbs for one week in the port, then filter and bottle. Serve mixed with sugar cubes and water.

drink that he gave to soldiers. The effect was mental clarity and increased libido, a fine combination. Dubied sold the recipe to his son-in-law, Henri-Louis Pernod, in 1797, who set up the Pernod-Fils absinthe factory in Pontarlier, France in 1805.

Absinthe enjoyed about thirty-five years of a heyday before it met an untimely end. Yet right from the start this magical drink appealed to artists. During *l'heure verte* (the green hour), Gauguin, Toulouse-Lautrec, and van Gogh took to the drink, as well as Baudelaire, Apollinaire, Rimbaud, and Satie, who also claimed it enhanced their creativity.

Absinthe requires ritual. A small amount of absinthe is placed in a large and lovely bulbous or egg-shaped glass. Special spoons are used—in the past they were sometimes silver, often pressed tin, the bowl of the spoon perforated in a decorative fashion to form *des flèches* (arrows), *des fleurs* (flowers), or *la croix* (cross); a modern spoon owned and prized by absinthe connoisseur Wolfgang is shaped like the Eiffel Tower.

Because absinthe is bitter, and tastes a little like licorice—it resembles the Pernod you can buy everywhere today—it requires modification. To properly drink absinthe, a sugar cube is placed on the perforated spoon and water drizzled over the sugar. As the sugar melts into the liquid, the absinthe turns from sea green to a milky green—the first of its magical transformations. Absinthe in the past was a minimum of 75 percent alcohol (150 proof), and water was added three or four to one to dilute it, filling the glass three-quarters of the way up. A variation on the ritual is to place the sugar cube onto the spoon, dip it quickly into the absinthe, then set the sugar on fire. The alcohol burns away via the lovely flame that melts the sugar through the holes in the spoon and into the drink. Sometimes, the entire contents of the glass is lighted, which, of course, burns away much of the coveted alcohol.

The French have always been a café society. Lingering on the *terrasse* of a Montmartre café while sipping a glass of absinthe for an hour or more is the stuff of which high romance is formed. Absinthe can produce wondrous effects, a kind of dream-state filled with melting images. It became the drink of the Belle Epoque (1871–1914), reeking of naughtiness and charisma. Wildly popular—millions of gallons a year were sold—and less expensive than wine, it soon replaced wine as France's national drink.

But as with any intoxicant, overindulgence is easy and can lead to problems for some, and it did. Hallucinations were known to turn ugly. Convulsions and fits occurred. In a large enough quantity, and because of the high alcohol content, kidney failure was reported—even recent cases have occurred with the resurgence of this delirious drink's popularity. And back in the late eighteenth and early nineteenth centuries, disreputable manufacturers were known to color the cheap stuff with copper compounds and fortify it with methanol, both toxic.

The prohibitionists of the day blamed absinthe for every conceivable problem: high unemployment, marriage difficulties, breakdowns of religions, government, and every other institution, all leading to delirium, madness, and even death. Van Gogh cut off his ear under the influence, and look what happened to Oscar Wilde!

All of this kerfuffle culminated in a pivotal moment. In 1905, Jean Lanfray, a Swiss farmer, murdered his family. Just as today, the media reported the most sensational facts—Lanfray was on an absinthe binge. What was not reported was the fact that he had also consumed several bottles of wine, and many shots of brandy as well. The abolitionists used the event, and by 1914 absinthe became illegal almost everywhere.

Many believe the ban was fueled and paid for by the grape growers, who had suffered severely under crop failures for years due to an infestation of the phylloxera insect. They needed a defeatable enemy, and absinthe sales outgrossed wine.

In reality, thujone, the basic compound in wormwood, is poisonous—in massive doses. Wolfgang believes: "The whole thujone story is a hoax created by the prohibitionists of the time. There's a load of thujone in sage, but did you ever hear about psychoactive and poisonous turkey stuffing?"

Because of its infamous history, absinthe carries a mystique like no other alcoholic beverage. Every darker subculture since the ban has discovered it. Goths seem obsessed with it, and it's almost a badge of honor in the goth universe to have drunk absinthe. Most of *The † Section* have tried it.

Nadia brings up a valid point about this most romantic of beverages: "Have you seen how much it costs?" A good bottle of absinthe from Spain, with wormwood, plus shipping costs can run to $100 US. And, of course, it is illegal in most countries, which prohibits importation.

And one favorite haunt of any goth visiting that charmingly decaying city of New Orleans is Jean Lafitte's Old Absinthe House in the French Quarter, dating back to 1807.

THE † SECTION AND ABSINTHE

jetgirl

"I had absinthe for the first time when my friend who visits from England smuggled me a bottle. I took it with me when another friend and I went to New Orleans for vacation and we shared it there."

Deacon Syth "I was at a small artsy cafe called Milk. I was in a strange depressive mood and decided to see why Shelley, Byron, and Wilde love it so much. It was intoxicating (in more than just the obvious sense) and I found I felt strangely euphoric."

Hardrock Llewynyth "I've drunk quite a bit. Spanish absinthe is too sweet, and too heavily anise-flavored. Czech absinthe is almost exclusively Windex, with the exception of Sebor, which is my favorite absinthe. Sebor has a wonderful bitterness with a nice balanced herbal nose with anise almost unnoticeable. French La Bleue absinthe is a pleasant balance of sweetness and bitterness, not overwhelmingly anise."

DJ Ladybee "I have drunk absinthe on a few occasions, mostly at parties, some of which were specifically absinthe-tasting parties. The only time I felt anything more than 'Ew, this tastes shitty!' was the first time, in which I experienced the sort of dissociative amusement at everyday objects/occurrences, described by writers like Wilde. I remember laughing for maybe ten minutes at the sight of a moped, thinking it the most absurd thing ever."

Prosthetic God: "No damn green fairy has visited me yet!"

Cemetery Crow

"It's a stiff drink that makes my liver go nuts if undiluted. Moderation is the essence of drinking absinthe."

Sire Cédric: "I drink absinthe on a regular basis. It is still illegal in France but easy to find in Andorra. I love the herbal taste of it, it is a strong alcohol but it does not have any particular effect on me, like no hallucinations, except sometimes heavy headaches."

The Crow: "Are you kidding? I grew up in the absinthe-producing valley, in the French part of Switzerland where the real undercover absinthe is made. I always have a bottle at home for friends. I love it, but don't drink too much of it–you don't want to go bananas."

The ritual of drinking absinthe, with its special glasses and spoons, the antique bar-top dispenser with brass taps from which the absinthe dripped, the fountains that added water, the ornate matchstick holders that were a crucial part of the café world, has made acquiring the accoutrements into almost a fetish. London's charming Bar Absinthe serves a variety of absinthes, and also pastis (absinthe without the wormwood), which is much easier to find, and far less expensive. On display are original absinthe items and the tools of the trade.

Original absinthe paraphernalia have become rare, high-priced collectibles—a pressed tin spoon from the late 1800s can easily sell for $50. But this is a realm that suits goth sensibilities: a drink that can enhance creativity, or cause liver failure. A world of dreams and magic, or nightmares and sorcery. Romance combined with danger equals appeal. More than one goth has dug up an old recipe for absinthe and brewed a batch or two, or drunk a friend's home brew. Or, more frequently, tasted a pastis.

Wolfgang is a goth with a passion for absinthe. He has tried about twenty of the modern commercial absinthes, and has tasted one authentic absinthe made by Jules Pernod. He says that none of the modern absinthes can compare to the original, although some rare homemade and artisanal brews are pretty good. "Modern absinthes are made from mixing essential oils with alcohol, and they taste more like pastis than anything else. The best antique absinthes were made by steeping herbs in alcohol and then distilling it. The distillation was later colored and other herbs added. To my knowledge, only one Spanish brand, Sagarra, really distills it. Unfortunately their coloring step isn't right, which leads to a pleasant but unauthentic brandy taste."

There are many reviews of commercial absinthe brands at the *La fée verte* (the Green Fairy) Web site, as well as recipes and sources for wormwood and other supplies.

Wolfgang confides: "Drinking absinthe gives me an anachronistic and almost historical pleasure. Doing the ritual and drinking is akin to a meditation. It forces you to take your time, like those who were sitting in the French cafés. It gives you a pleasant and clear-headed kind of drunkenness."

weed vs. spice

Far outweighing ordinary tobacco in the mystique department are clove cigarettes, fragrant Indonesian imports, aka kretek.

Kretek cigarettes are a blend of 60 percent tobacco and 40 percent clove spices, plus a "sauce" of spices. Sometimes the tip of the rolling paper is dipped in saccharine to enhance the sweet taste. They look like regular cigarettes, although some use dark brown paper or a corn husk. Legend has it that the name "kretek" comes from the sound the cloves make as they pop through incineration.

Clove cigarettes were invented in the 1880s by Haji Jamahri, a resident of Kudus. An asthma sufferer, Jamahri rubbed clove oil on his chest to ease the discomfort of his breathing difficulties. Clove oil was also known as an analgesic in the west, often rubbed on the gums to alleviate toothache or the pain involved with teething in infants. Apparently it was a short leap for Mr. Jamahri from clove oil on the chest to rolling crushed cloves into cigarettes and smoking the spice. Jamahri experienced remarkable results and sold his discovery locally to friends and neighbors through pharmacies, since these cigarettes were considered medicine. Naturally he did not live long enough to open a clove cigarette factory and massively profit from his discovery.

Somehow his recipe found its way into the hands of those entrepreneurs who mass-produce blends of tobacco and cloves. Then, around 1912, a young fellow named Seeng Tee began adding flavorings such as chocolate, vanilla, nutmeg as well as cloves. He'd worked for a kretek manufacturer but soon set up his own business and grew rich producing prerolled clove cigarettes.

Not all goths smoke only cloves, but many like one now and again. *50 Ft Queenie*, for example, is "a nonsmoker, but I do love cloves. They're my special indulgence once in a blue moon."

No major studies have been conducted on how clove cigarettes affect overall health, but according to the US Centers for Disease Control and Prevention, clove cigarettes, which contain 60–70 percent tobacco, produce twice as much tar, nicotine, and carbon monoxide as regular American cigarettes. The active ingredient of cloves, eugenol, is a topical anesthetic used in dentistry. Eugenol numbs the throat and impairs the gag reflex, which means smokers may not feel the harshness and consequently inhale more deeply and hold in the smoke longer, leading to respiratory problems; but this has not been substantiated by studies.

Regardless of whether or not a goth smokes, and how harmful clove cigarettes might be to their health, the consensus is almost 100 percent that

Mistress Hades

"First you take a drink, then Linda Blair takes a drink, then you are out shouting at trees in the high street! I loved it!"

Miss Lynx "It didn't do a damn thing for me—I actually wonder if it had any wormwood in it at all. It tasted kind of like NyQuil."

Azazelle

"I made some myself, and have had experience with other people's offerings, both homemade and commercial. It never tastes good."

Xefiel "Never! That drink is used to kill faeries, you know!"

there is nothing quite as romantic and evocative as the scent of cloves wafting through the air as one enters the dark domain of a goth club.

natural vs. pharmaceutical

As with any individual maturing, many goths no longer use illegal drugs, although they employed them in the past as a means of exploration, which is, after all, a staple of being goth. It's a common refrain as stated by *Slave 1*: "I've done almost all of them. I'm older now and have too many responsibilities to do them anymore."

And with maturity comes self-awareness. *C.B.* admits, "I used to take drugs, but I've got a compulsive nature. That's why I don't go to casinos either!"

The power of a negative experience—if it doesn't kill you, it can cure you—is that it might lead to change. *Daevina* confesses, "I took drugs to escape from my sadness and try to dull the pain of adolescence. It didn't work; it just made me more screwed up, and I was hospitalized."

Goth has never been a heavy-use drug culture, regardless of media presentations. And for most of *The † Section* who indulge, marijuana is or was their drug of choice, used infrequently. *Ravenheart* speaks for many when she says, "I don't do any [other] drugs anymore, just pot, and rarely. I have seen so many lives ruined or lost to drugs. People say they do drugs to escape reality. I say, make your reality so fucking cool you *never* want to escape it."

URLs
Vampire Wine
www.vampirewine.com

Raven Beer
www.ravenbeer.com

Rogue Breweries
www.rogue.com

Stone Brewing Company
www.stonebrew.com

Victory Brewing
www.victorybeer.com

Unibroue
www.unibroue.com

Shepherd Neame
www.shepherd-neame.co.uk

Moortgat Brewery
www.duvel.be

Louwaege Hapkin
www.hapkin.be

Brauerei Alken-Maes
www.alkenmaes.be

Brasserie Jeanne d'Arc
www.orpal.tm.fr/Ebelz.html

Mme Marie-Claude Delahaye
www.eabsinthe.com/lafee/mmedelahaye.htm

Old Absinthe House
www.oldabsinthehouse.com

La fée verts
www.feeverte.net

Wolfgang recommends
www.isuisse.ifrance.com/absintheauthentique/index.htm

Bar Absinthe–London
www.netlinewebservices.co.uk/absinthe/contact.asp

Indonesian Clove Cigarettes
www.indonesianclovecigarettes.com/index.htm

LOVE IN THE POST-LOVE AGE: DOMESTICATING THE GOTH WITHIN

Men! (Women!) You can't live with them, and you can't bury them in a shallow grave without breaking your fingernails!

courtly (not Courtney) love

The Indian poet Vallana (ca. A.D. 900–1100) wrote "Who could save me from plunging into a sea of shame but the love god, who teaches us how to faint." But long before that, the Latin poet Ovid (43 B.C.–18 A.D.) wrote: "So, I can't live without you or with you." Both expressed goth sensibilities. Love tainted with heartbreak is a cornerstone of the goth lifestyle.

Like everyone else on the planet, goths long for love. What makes them different is that they expect disappointment. Partly it's squarely facing the age we live in, and partly the nature of the beast—independence is often the antithesis of commitment, it seems. On the other hand, if wielded properly, it can contribute to lasting love. Rabid individualists are skilled at finding alternatives for themselves, even in *amour*.

Marriage in the past (and still in much of the world) was the traditional match made for advantage that families engaged in. Love grew, or not; it didn't matter, since union was for procreative purposes. Either way, love was certainly not a reason to join together! History and literature are both

Courtesy of X-tra-X

saturated with the teary stories of unrequited love, doomed love, forbidden love. But something happened in the fourteenth century that sowed the seeds for intimate love as we understand it today.

Romance (from the French word *romanz*, meaning: derived from the language spoken by the Romans) referred to a specific type of literature. It involved tales of chivalry, usually set in the court of King Arthur, and the escapades of knights and their ladies. Queens, duchesses, countesses, and ladies of the court loved such poetic stories, which featured women in prominent and romantic roles—compared with *Beowulf*, which focused on male warriors. Eleanor of Aquitaine, queen first of France, then of England, and her daughter Marie, Countess of Champagne, two strong proponents of the arts, supported these romantic troubadoural poems, commonly termed "courtly love."

Courtly love was modeled on the feudal relationship between a knight and his lord, and dictated that the knight owed his lady the same obedience and loyalty, although in reality she might not know he existed. Consequently, the lady controlled the relationship. Such love ennobled the knight, inspiring him to great deeds in order to be worthy of and win her (platonic) love.

Back then, everyone understood that courtly love was idealized love, not something one attempted to apply to real relationships. This was a behavioral model for the lords' unmarried younger brothers, who owned no property and hence could not marry, but might still find their sisters-in-law hot. Some scholars speculate it helped keep them from wandering the countryside and raping women.

"Lovesick" knights (Ovid described love as a sickness) often sighed, turned pale or flushed, suffered fever, or were unable to eat, sleep, or drink.

Romance for the modern terminally romantic cynic elicits all of these reactions and more.

Courtly love has come to infect relationships, so that today we hold this as the epitome of real love (with the addition of sex). But, of course, normal relationships cannot sustain such lofty ideals for long. Naturally, when love crashes and burns, all the dried roses in the world cannot mend a broken heart quickly. Goths are used to broken hearts, and they sleep with despair. They have learned to take the time to heal before moving on to become once again a romance victim.

sex and the single goth

Goth is a sexy business, a flirty subculture. Almost all goth boiz and gurrls exude a kind of sultry eroticism tinged with danger. More than half of *The † Section* identified themselves as heterosexual. Another 29 said they are bisexual, although the bulk of those are in heterosexual relationships—for now. Five of *The † Section* are gay or lesbian. Two declare themselves as polysexually oriented, meaning they are open to all combinations and genders. One of *The † Section* is transgendered.

Sex is the biggest thrill in the lives of most people. It's when we get to put all the bullshit aside and expose our physical and spiritual nakedness to another humanoid. Having sex with someone means we temporarily deeply touch another, and are touched by them on a variety of levels, all of which emanates from skin contact. Consequently we are for moments no longer alone in the universe.

Because of that, sex, as we all know, is fraught with peril. Repressed feelings may surface and can lead to emotional or physical violence. Childhood traumas get reenacted, sometimes retraumatizing. Power struggles ensue. Sexual jealousy frequently leads to possessiveness, and rejected love has too often led to murder. Sex is a nasty business, not simply as the Puritans assured, because of the exchange of bodily fluids which made it a "dirty" act for them outside of marriage, but because, let's face it, sex makes people insane.

Despite knowing the risks in our heads, we all pursue the act anyway, happy as the Fool in the Tarot deck to blissfully stroll toward the edge of the cliff, sometimes walking directly into a trauma just waiting to happen. Anything for that amalgamation with "other."

Much of our lives is spent finding our other half or soul mate so we are no longer utterly alone. But the minute we find them, our energy funnels into keeping them with us, or escaping as fast as we can! As difficult as sex is for most of us, those double outcasts of the collective—gay, lesbian, and gender benders who are goth too—suffer twice as many problems.

love among the runes

It is not easy to meet a desirable other, especially once you've left school, where everyone is your age, and most are single, too. When people hit the adult world, things change, and the older you get, the fewer options you have, although technically you should possess more self-confidence.

REMEMBERED GOTH COMMENTS DURING INTIMATE MOMENTS

- I can't see a damned thing. I'm gonna have to take off the sunglasses.

- I was going to blindfold you but I didn't want to smudge your eye makeup.

- Is that your skirt or mine?

- You want to put your pet snake where?

- What a romantic Nietzschean move on your part, my little Über-kink.

- That better be white candle wax you're dripping on me; the black candles leave stains.

- What the hell!? Did you put Floodland on REPEAT?

- Are your pubic hairs normally that color, or do you dye them?

- Do we have to take our Docs off?

- My ampallang's caught in your labia ring!

- This thing is so small. . . why don't you get a bigger coffin?

- I love seeing your black fingernails against my pallid skin.

- Shhhh! I think I saw headlights past that grave.

- Damn, there's nowhere to attach the handcuffs to in this coffin.

- Can you please play dead?

Sky Claudette

Photo by Swan Justis

THE † SECTION ON FETISH PLAY or SM

Azazelle "I've been to fetish clubs and had fun. And the fashions are great!"

biogoth "I've tried sex with costumes on; mostly they get in the way. A little bit of pain during sex (giving and receiving) is sexy to me. A lot of pain is just, well, painful."

C.B. "I've tried it a bit, but more with women than men. Mainstream men say they're attracted to it, but in real life it scares them. I like men in women's clothing, and extremely uncomfortable furniture."

Cemetery Crow "Goth is a fetish. I've done SM as an art form. I hate the fact that it's fashionable nowadays, and exhibitionists have made it a laughable practice for the egotistically extroverted."

The † Section said two-to-one that it is hard finding a long-term partner, although many felt it's fairly easy to unearth a warm body. There are any number of reasons, but one is simply the logistics of environment.

Clubs are certainly one way for goths to meet ones such as themselves for possible romantic interludes, if not lifetime love affairs. Of course, clubs serve alcohol, and other intoxicants are sometimes available. When the music dies and the lights come up, goths find it appallingly easy to find themselves wandering into the dawn with someone whose eyeliner has smeared in an unesthetic manner, and whose name may be a mystery not worth solving.

No matter how much *The † Section* revile the one-night stand, it is a staple for the young and horny, and most concede it is a necessary evil. As *Nadia* says, "A one-night stand is an interesting human mirror and an excellent fillip to the vanity. Occasionally the sex is good, too."

The modern way to expand horizons is the Internet, which overflows with matchmaking possibilities. But can a soul mate be found in virtual space? Of the fifty or so of *The † Section* who have dated through the Internet, nine had bad to terrible experiences, like *C.B.* "Great! Now I can meet even more losers from the comfort of my own home! The guy lied when he said he liked cats, lived alone in a house . . . Turned out the thirty-six-year-old was afraid of cats and lived alone—*in his parents' basement!* He didn't even have his own phone line! Also found out he was writing to a friend of mine the whole time!"

Despite Internet mating's reputation, twenty-eight of *The † Section* have dated someone they met online and have had satisfying experiences. About one quarter of them are currently living with a mate they met through the Net.

Internet relationships can go either way. Two long-term net.goths (see Chapter 9), with years of experience under their virtual belts, talk about their experiences.

Macross: "I've slept with a few people I've had conversations with on IRC [Internet Relay Chat], but not specifically because of IRC; simply

'Oh, you're so and so,' and then we moved on to being real world acquaintances and sharing physical attraction."

Cavalorn: "Sure, I met a lover online through a goth channel. She was in America, I was (as ever) in the UK. We eventually met up, clandestinely, since though I'm polyamorous, she wasn't, and was in a relationship at the time. We had three sexually intense days, following which everything went directly to hell. We're friends now, though we don't talk much. It's the one and only time I've ever been involved with someone already involved and her partner didn't know and approve. I'd never do that again."

crossing the leather line

Goth lends itself nicely to the tough-love look of fetish. The crossover is easy and (almost) painless. Goths wear dog collars and fetishwear, and sometimes carry S&M gear. Black leather and latex are already in the closet, the props often hanging on the wall.

Fred H. Berger of *Propaganda* magazine (See Chapter 2) says about the goth/fetish connection, "People unfamiliar with the gothic/fetish movement have looked at *Propaganda* and were amazed that such a widespread and vigorous subculture could possibly exist in their midst."

At one time a fetish had to do with voodoo, with magic, and meant an object that carried a spirit, as in supernatural. It wasn't a big leap to making shoes a fetish, since the stilettos that pinups like Betty Paige wore in the 1950s certainly carried the spirit of the wearer. But many centuries before Miss Paige was a gleam in the camera lens of fetish filmmaker Irving Klaw, the Chinese created the mother of all foot fetishes. The feet of girls of nobility were bound when they were children, ensuring that they would not grow larger. As well, some of these girls were forced to walk over pottery shards to break foot bones. This practice of keeping the feet as small as possible ensured a lifetime of pain for these women, who could walk only with difficulty throughout their lives, but were wealthy enough to be carried.

Any object or article of clothing can be a fetish—it's all in the eye of the beholder. And fetishes are usually erotic.

Fetish has evolved into a catch-all word. Fetishwear is as much a trip for the wearer as for the observer, and it is almost always expensive. Fetish today also encompasses sadomasochistic play. *Sado-* comes from the Marquis de

DJ Caluna "My boyfriend is a nylon fetishist. My ex was a latex fetishist. I love SM. Can be very exciting!"

Lisiblac "Most of my experience is with the gay leather crowd. Goth fetish parties are fashion shows."

Malinda "I go to fetish parties because I enjoy the style of dress, and find sexual fascination with garter belts and corsets. I often go in a 'Satan's cheerleader' outfit, or a vinyl nurse dress. I see people who need their fetish to enjoy sex and I don't think that's healthy."

Marcelous "I'm trying to get my girlfriend to order me around and hit me and stuff, but no luck so far."

Paola "Hot candle wax is my main form of perversion."

Rois "I find corsets, heels, and the occasional chain or clampy thing to be incredibly sexy and will incorporate these into as many outfits as I can. Bondage is fun. Sensations are better. Pain doesn't do it for me."

Taoist "I came from the fetish scene before getting into goth. I mostly like the physical torture side rather than the 'headfuck' domination thing. It's liberating. There's a fair crossover (fetish/goth), particularly Carnival of Souls—goth bands and DJs with a fetish atmosphere and dungeon equipment."

Courtesy of X-tra-X

Sade's potent writings about cruelty inflicted on others for the pleasure and gratification of the inflictor. *Masochism* was coined from the surname of Leopold von Sacher-Masoch, author of the novel *Venus in Furs*, the story of a man giving himself over mentally, physically, and spiritually to the woman he is devoted to, for her to do with as she will, which ultimately includes the final masochistic indulgence when she abandons him completely. S&M in reality is quite different from those classic works of fiction, or even popular modern erotica like *The Story of O* by Pauline Réage, Anne Rice's *Sleeping Beauty* trilogy, and the series *The Darker Passions* by Amarantha Knight. In the real world, S&M play is usually only undertaken with mutual consent. Safe words are used to stop the play when the "bottom" has had enough, and the "top," the one in charge, is responsible for making sure nobody gets seriously hurt. Trust is crucial.

Public play happens at fetish clubs, not at goth clubs, although there are goth fetish nights—Toronto goths have been holding a monthly goth/fetish night at Reverb for five years. Whips and chains come out. Bottoms are spanked and paddled, and boots (and other things) licked. Costuming is a big part of a fetish night out.

Goths for some reason seem to have more fun with these activities than traditional fetishists. It's not unusual to find goths at fetish clubs laughing, and taking turns as to who is on the receiving end of the riding crop. Pure fetishists are appalled by such behavior, but it goes with what goth is about; they take the "play" in fetish play seriously.

Fred Berger, who has chronicled goth/fetish, says, "The only constant is change. *Propaganda* has progressed from punk/hardcore to goth/glam to goth/Industrial to goth/fetish to transgender/transgression and has always done so with passion and vision. Each of these phases has represented a new frontier of rebellion, a new mode of self-destruction. If it's pierced and tattooed, fanged and fishnetted, bound and gagged, fagged and in drag, it's that much more cannon fodder for *Propaganda*'s ongoing war against the status quo." This is a good description of the goth experimental nature in general.

One other aspect of fetish play for goths is this: goths like their fetish play mixed with sex. This is a fetish purist's nightmare—fetish is erotic, but not necessarily sexual. A pro dominatrix will be the first to tell you her clients are there for the pain, the humiliation, the power exchange; it's not prostitution and she doesn't have sex with clients. But for goths, who by their nature blur lines, fetish without sex is like a night without moonlight. You can still enjoy the darkness, but it's only half as good.

marriage or mirage?

Legal marriage for many goths is not a prerequisite for happiness, and couple love does not necessarily lead down the aisle. Over 99 percent of *The † Section* sanctioned cohabiting with a lover prior to or in lieu of marriage. Being goth is no more a prescription for a doomed relationship than being a CEO of a blue chip company. And it just might be that, while goths too will often undergo a starter marriage, by the second time around they usually know themselves fairly well, which increases the chance of a union's survival.

Goths value individualism, and when it comes to joining with another for the longer term, they often seek out alternatives to mainstream weddings, everything unusual, from clothing, to music, to the written nuptials themselves. The Neo-Pagan ceremony of handfasting is one popular alternative. Almost one third of *The † Section* identified their religion as Pagan or Wiccan (See Chapter 13).

Handfasting is a ritual joining, derived from Medieval ceremonies around the world, particularly those of Ireland, Wales, and Scotland. Historically, handfasting is not a wedding, but a ceremony celebrating and affirming the intention to marry.

The eighteenth-century writer and poet Sir Walter Scott wrote this about handfasting: "When we are handfasted, as we term it, we are man and wife for a year and a day; that space gone by, each may choose another mate, or, at their pleasure, may call the priest to marry them for life; and this we call handfasting."

In Neo-Paganism and Wicca, handfasting can be a substitute for marriage, an alternative that is especially attractive to same-sex couples and those in multipartnered relationships, where legal marriage is prohibited. The ceremony can embrace a theme, for example, Celtic, Teutonic, Druidic, goddess, Norse, winter solstice. One ceremony, called the blood-binding wedding ceremony, involves the bride and groom each holding a sword. They fill a goblet with wine, then each pricks a finger and lets a drop of blood fall into the goblet. When the wine is drunk, the blood-bond is secured.

Handfasting involves rituals that allow the old gods to bless the union

Slavel

FROM A BLOOD-BINDING HANDFASTING CEREMONY

Like a stone should your love be firm. Be close, yet not too close. Possess one another, yet be understanding. Have patience with each other for storms will come, but they will go quickly. Be free in giving of affection and warmth. Have no fear, and let not the ways or words of strangers give you unease, for the Gods are with you, now and always.

of two or more people. It also employs traditional practices, recipes for foods, and party favors designed to be in tune with nature, and to bring good fortune to the couple.

The Gothic Martha Stewart (see Chapter 8) says, "When my husband and I were planning our wedding, we wanted a rather gothic-Victorian style for the event. You can't buy gothic-Victorian wedding decorations and clothes off the rack, so we created our own. And then I wrote everything up and put it on my *Gothic Martha Stewart* site." She suggests gothing up a reception with candlelight, dried roses, and red frosting on the wedding cake with spiderwebs and bats piped around the edge. "A hearse as a getaway vehicle might freak out guests, but the alternative of a horse-drawn carriage could be a good thing!"

Traditional weddings with a goth flair are offered here and there, especially in the United States, for instance, the Viva Las Vegas Wedding Chapel, and by Chaplain Bob of South Florida, for those who want a heavy Christian spin on the ceremony. A few countries offer non-

---

DRYING ROSES COURTESY OF THE GOTHIC MARTHA STEWART

MATERIALS:
- fresh roses
- pushpins
- rubber bands or string
- hair spray
- silica gel (optional)
- plastic container (optional)

Try to get the roses just before the heads start to droop and before they've lost any petals. Remove leaves around the bottom of the stem. Take two or three roses and gently twist a rubber band or string around them near the stem, making a very loose bunch. Push a pushpin into the wall that's out of the way of people and pets, preferably near a heating vent but not facing a window. Hook the rose bunch onto the pushpin with the rubberband. Wait about two weeks until the roses are completely dry. Lightly spray each flower with hair spray so it doesn't fall apart.

This simple drying method will cause the roses to shrivel somewhat and the color will darken. Bright red roses usually become the color of dried blood, while white roses become a yellowy parchment color. If you wish to preserve the color, size, and shape of the fresh rose, you will need to completely immerse the rose in a plastic container of silica gel, which is available from craft stores. Follow the manufacturer's instructions carefully and keep the gel in a safe place away from food and pets.

Dried roses can be used singly or in bunches in vases, jars, or bottles. Or gather bunches together with wide ribbon and hang on the wall or work them into bed hangings. You can also snip off the heads and hot glue them onto things like jewelry boxes, picture frames, wreathes, straw hats, etc. Or just the rose petals and make your own potpourri for sachets or around the house.

heterosexuals the opportunity to marry, for instance, Denmark, Iceland, and Canada. But it is only in New Orleans that a coffin-making shop on Burgundy Street morphed into a wedding chapel offering goth weddings and handfasting ceremonies for opposite and same-sex couples. Goths can marry in the chapel, or at the St. Louis I Cemetery—but not at night; gates are locked at 3 P.M.

Former San Francisco chef and Las Vegas card dealer Reverend Tony Talavera, owner of French Quarter Wedding Chapel, says "Normally, in Louisiana, there is a seventy-two-hour waiting period for a license, but couples can walk to City Hall in the French Quarter and apply for a waiver—it takes one hour." The Reverend Talavera believes goth romanticism blends nicely with "the existing romance and mystique already in New Orleans."

Whether getting traditionally married or having a handfasting ceremony, the union of goth to goth inspires a huge fantasy. The image of Morticia and Gomez swathed in cryptlike elegance, floating along a graveyard path strewn with dead rose petals, enjoying a gargoyle-topped wedding cake, and retiring for the day to a satin-lined coffin built for two is a dark dream to be cherished for eternity.

It was Queen Victoria herself who started the trend of wearing an all-white wedding gown, when she married Prince Albert, the love of her life. Prior to that, a woman wore a dress with some color, usually just her best dress. Goths, it seems, manage to spin her tradition in their own manner, and black is a favorite color for wedding gowns.

The Dark Angel has been dressing brides and grooms in England for seven years. Carri Keill's romantic-clothing design company "evolved from an amalgamation of other businesses with a new designer." She says she was more goth in the 1980s. "It was a huge part of my life back then, and in those days I did live the lifestyle to the extreme."

The elegance of the clothing on display at the Dark Angel shop reflects Carri's goth history, with high, midnight blue ceilings, Victorian-style pale gold papered walls, floor-to-ceiling windows draped in gold organza and velvet, black iron railings with fleur-de-lis finials, elaborate chandeliers, and gilded mirrors over the fireplace.

Another wedding specialist in the Goth world is Enigma Fashions, opened five years ago by Jay and Diana Drake of California. Diana was "hardcore goth in my younger years, absolutely." Now, "my passions and lifestyles are goth or preppy goth."

Enigma Fashions' collections for both men and women came out of Diana's love of dressing up. "I have always liked to dress up but found it very hard to find gothic clothing that would be elegant enough but still maintain my true identity. And while there were great gothic clothing designers out there, no one filled that niche. After designing a few dresses for myself and getting great responses from even regular folk, I decided it [opening the business] was worth the risk taking.

"Gothic bridal clothing is scarce," Diana admits. Seventy percent of her customers are goths. "Every item we design is made by a high seamstress or a master tailor, which means we can alter an existing design, customize the colors and fabrics, and even create a one-of-a-kind design for a customer." Enigma Fashions' best-selling items are from their Apparitions Collection, specifically the gowns called Josette and Bryana. Most of their gowns and men's fashions are named.

Twenty-five-year-old fashion design student Christina Dettmers of Germany is a passionate seamstress who always wanted to own a costume business. Nehelenia Designs—named after a Pagan goddess—burst out of her imagination four years ago. Christina is fascinated with period movies, particularly fashions from the 1800s and clothing with a "darkly romantic period appeal."

She says she "had my black-only phase, but I realized I am too multicolored to restrict myself to just one color. My opinions might gel with 'goth' but I hate to be characterized by a single word."

Christina's favorite periods are "English Regency, eighteenth century, and the bustle era. I also love to do movie repros." To make a garment, she does a lot of research: "Internet, movies, visits to museums, libraries, etc. I stick closely to the original garments and patterns to get the most historical authenticity."

Nehelenia Designs is popular among European goths "Because I recreate garments from the Gothic era, and from period movies that goth customers have been searching for, like gowns from *Interview With the Vampire*. And I offer plus sizes!"

Currently she is working on the most unusual garment she has ever created, "an Empress Sisi of Austria crinoline gown with movie stills from the German *Sissi* trilogy printed all over the front, and the back is covered in blood and newspaper articles announcing that the empress was murdered!"

gothlings

One reason goths in love enter into long-term relationships and marriage is to procreate. When the mainstream thinks of goths at all, they do not envision them with children. Even most goths know few, if any, goth parents. This is a realm that goths frequently grow into as they age.

If goths fantasize about having children, it's often along the lines of somberly humorous hollow-cheeked waifs like Wednesday Addams. In a world where black equals morbid, dressing children in outfits the color of raven feathers becomes a controversial issue. Six goth parents from the Web site Gothic Parents talk about their children, and what it means to be a goth parent.

SkunkGoth (Newcastle-Upon-Tyne, England): "Lilith (four) looks lovely in her purple satin frock with the lace trim; just don't let her near your neck, any axes, sharp implements, small boys . . ."

EireGirl (Minneapolis, Minnesota): "February (seven) dresses herself goth. I bought her a pair of knee-high boots and she loves to wear them with black tights, black skirt, and black shirt. London's (six) favorite clothes are his black jeans and his blue shirt that says GERMANY on the front. He loves his jammies that have spiders on them. Parker (four) likes to wear his Halloween shirt with bats on it, and his favorite jammies are ones with witches, ghosts, and spiders. We don't force it upon them. They choose for themselves to dress the way they do. There's not a whole lot out there in the way of goth clothing for children, especially boys."

Rain (Columbus, Ohio): "Isabella's (one and a half) first professional pictures were taken in a velvet leopard-print dress we found. She has a black baby sling, a PUNK PRINCESS T-shirt, and a Hot Topic shirt that reads: WHAT ARE LITTLE GIRLS MADE OF? FISHNET, BATS AND ALLEY CATS. We found a medieval dress on eBay."

Mellybee (Sleepy Hollow, New York): "I don't make a special effort to dress Connor (two) goth. That stuff can be hard to find and more expensive. However, he has many black outfits, and a number are specifically goth, such as black overalls with a skull on them, black onsies with various sayings. His stroller, diaper bag and anything I can get are black. You can't get disposable diapers in black, or I would buy them."

Saintnic (Sydney, Australia): "They do wear dark clothes or black combined with bold colors. Tain (3½) had a bat mobile, and a few vampire toys and lots of books that are gothy. Brittany Raven (11) dresses herself."

GOTH BABY NAMES

The most popular goth baby name according to the Name That Goth site run by Penny Dreadful:

Winter

Wintre

Wynter

Wintre

Wyntre

Blodeuwedd (Bay Area, California): "I feel that forcing your children to dress in any particular fashion is oppressive. I allow Taylor (ten) to pick out her clothes, even when she chooses something I deplore. Taylor has many dark 'gothic' outfits that she wears on occasion. She adores Wednesday Addams and loves to have her hair in braids. A couple of years ago she asked me to dye her naturally light hair pink. I did not do it because I didn't want to face flak from her school. Later I gave her a flaming red streak for Valentine's Day. Surprisingly, the school said nothing!"

Goths who dress goth often draw stares, and sometimes negative criticism, but when children are involved, the responses can verge on abuse. Many goth parents have experienced rejection from other parents or society at large simply because they and/or their children dress goth.

Blodeuwedd: "Once, while working at a makeup counter, I mentioned to a woman customer who had her young child with her, 'I have a beautiful six-year-old daughter.'

" '*You* have a child!' the woman uttered with disgust on her face. 'Oh my God! Imagine what she'll look like when she's older!'

"I told her, 'Probably whatever she wants to look like, because unlike some people, I've taught my child that it's what's inside a person that's important.' "

EireGirl: "We live in a very snotty suburban area where the other parents kind of give us that 'they let you be a parent?' look. I get people asking me if they can pray for me."

SkunkGoth: "I look like a thug; people seem to prefer to keep their casual opinions to themselves. Where discussion takes place, I can hold my own intellectually. People seem more interested and positive about my parenting commitment."

The other goth parents—*Saintnic, Mellybee,* and *Rain*—generally feel accepted by the collective regarding how they dress. Sometimes it's the level of self-confidence a goth parent puts out, but the open-mindedness of the community in which they live plays a part.

The arenas where goths are most vulnerable because of how they look involve bureaucratic institutions, like the courts. *EireGirl* has had a serious negative encounter that has affected her life. "When I went to court during my divorce and custody battle, my ex-husband kept bringing up the fact that I was goth, and went out to goth clubs, etc.—never mind that the majority of the time that I went out the kids were with him. I believe the court discriminated against me because of it. I worked Monday to Friday, an eight-to-five job where I was home with my children every night, whereas my ex worked a job as a DJ in a college bar. Somehow he was more acceptable to the judge than me. I didn't have much of a chance, since the court was in a small town in a very small county. We have joint legal and physical custody, but they gave him primary custody. I have to pay him child support even though he lied about how much he makes. I went into court and told the truth. I dressed nicely, black pants and a pink shirt, but I could tell the judge was biased."

Family relationships for goths can go either way. Relatives are the people who should be most supportive in a cold, cruel world, but sometimes home is the last place where they let you in. None of the six goth parents have had serious rejection from their parents or in-laws, although they haven't received 100 percent acceptance either. *Blodeuwedd*'s mother thought she'd " 'grow out of' being goth. Once I moved to California, they changed, and now claim to be completely proud of me." As did *Saintnic*'s parents, who "thought it was a phase. Ten years later they are still hoping I will change; otherwise, they are used to it. I have a sister who is goth." *Rain* says, "My family tells me that I need to dress more like a parent and less like I'm going to a party." *EireGirl* is the exception in terms of family. "I love my family. They are very supportive, and we are very close."

The gothic lifestyle undergoes major alterations when children come into the picture. Children change the dynamics of a relationship, or in the case of a single parent, of a life and lifestyle. All of the goth parents feel this is so.

SkunkGoth: "Bars? Clubs? Oh yes, I remember those. These days I'm glad to be in bed by ten P.M."

EireGirl: "[It's tough to] find a babysitter who will come watch the kids. Most people don't understand that clubs and concerts start around ten or eleven P.M."

Mellybee: "We used to sleep until noon on weekends; now we get up at 6:30 or 7 A.M. every day. And sometimes being outwardly goth is just too much effort for me—let's face it, it's not always the most low-maintenance look."

Rain: "I stopped wearing excessive jewelry because I was afraid she would get scratched on my spiked collar. I also had to take out my belly button piercing when I was pregnant."

- Always take advantage of stereotypes that work in your favor and play along.

- Know, and never cross, the boundaries of tolerance in appearance for your specific profession.

- Check out how others dress in the company before interviewing.

- Wean them in—establish mutual respect and then slowly show your true colors (or in this case, lack of colors!).

- Maintain a professional stance. Dress and act appropriately for meetings. Sometimes you need to make sacrifices to stay ahead.

- To help make sure you are taken seriously, try to make your first contact via e-mail or phone.

- Dress in a manner that is comfortable for your coworkers (within reason). Compromise enough to establish a good working relationship with your coworkers.

- Speak to your HR representative and learn your rights! Technically I can dress in drag (as long as it is something a woman could wear to work), and legally they can't say anything to me. Of course that does not mean they won't figure out another reason to fire me! So know your rights and also know the limitations of those rights.

Goth, being a lifestyle given to appreciating life and respecting all aspects of it, lends itself well to good parenting. Being goth is liberating to an individual, and reinforcing as a parent.

Saintnic: "We dealt with judgment from our parents about being different. I think we are more relaxed."

Rain: "I love being a Momigoth. I tend to focus on individual strengths instead of a false ideal that many people have for their children."

Mellybee: "I'm a happier person since I discovered the goth community. It gives me an outlet and expression for negative energy, and makes me feel at home and understood in a way I never did before. That makes me a better, more understanding parent. Never give up what you are to be a parent. If anything, be more what you are, so you can be happier, healthier and an example of strength for your child."

EireGirl: "I am more understanding, more patient, and probably a little more fun. I think most goths have better morals than most other people out there."

Blodeuwedd: "If anything, being goth allows me to recognize the freedom that comes from being able to truly express oneself. I try to remind myself constantly that each of us deserves to be ourselves without retribution, or flak."

working goths

Whether goths couple or not, somehow, the rent has to be paid, and that usually involves work. The shortage of professional mourner positions is appalling. And contrary to what the mainstream likely imagines, goths are usually employed, and not necessarily in low-paying jobs. Brocaded jackets, velvet capes, and full-body cyberwear do not come cheap, and unless one is being supported by well-heeled, indulgent parents, money must be earned to maintain this lavish lifestyle.

John J. Coughlin (known by his Internet handle Dark Wyccan) runs *corporategoth.com* under his umbrella site, *waningmoon.com*. He started the site because "I knew I could not be the only 'freak' out there who has to deal with balancing work life with a gothic lifestyle. I created the site initially as a place to share ideas and to let others know they were not alone. I am humbled to see on the mailing list alone—our 'virtual water cooler'—we have over 600 members, with 1,000 registered altogether.

"Goths in their thirties and late twenties today have a decent job. A large percentage work in the technology field, or are in art/fashion. These folks have passed the 'trend' stage we all go through and found a true reflection of their lifestyle and personality. There are also a few lawyers, and a medical doctor as well, although it is harder to maintain a gothic identity in such jobs. From what I have seen, the typical goth is quite intelligent, well read, and able to appreciate art in many forms. There is so much talent in the gothic community, and it is a shame it often goes unrecognized."

Being goth and working for a corporation engenders specific problems. John has had trouble being taken seriously. Fortunately, his reputation precedes him. "By the time people see me, they already know I know my stuff, but when dealing with new consultants, there is always a point where they can't see me as a manager, so they have a hard time accepting that I am. Usually once they start working with me, they see past our differences, but when they can't they only hurt themselves, since their job often relies on my cooperation."

Other problems border on the edge of harassment. "Some used to assume I must be into wild parties, so when I would sleep in my office because I did an all-nighter to fix a problem, I would hear comments like, 'Oh, you were probably out partying and couldn't get home.' And since I'm male yet have long pointed fingernails, which I color from time to time, people might assume I am gay or into kinky sex. I know many female goths have to contend with more sexual harassment because of this. Their look might be perceived as a welcome mat for such advances."

Does a goth working for a corporation constitute an oxymoron? "Back in the eighties," John says, "we had a romantic notion of living this underground lifestyle but as we got older, reality set in, and we began to search for ways to be ourselves and enjoy what the 'mundane world' has to offer. If I hear the 'sell-out' accusation, which is rare, I just shrug it off. I know I am being me, and that while I may compromise to some extent to keep a steady job, I never once sacrificed my self-identity."

Which leads to a good point John makes in terms of his definition of goth: "Those of us who need to dress more corporate know that ultimately what makes one 'goth' is not the clothing or the paraphernalia, but rather a certain disposition. We may like to express ourselves through our clothing, but when you take it away, we are no less goth, and when that is the case, we were not gothic to begin with!"

What not to Wear to a Corporate Job

courtesy of Amy of the corporategoth.net site:

- So many people wear crosses to work, but I still tuck my pentacle in.

- Leather should be confined to shoes or jacket.

- Black lace blouses are fine but wear something more modest than a bra or corsette underneath.

- Excessive facial piercings frighten people. Leave the jewelry at home.

- Learn to conceal your tongue ring when you talk.

- The torn fishnet stockings should probably get left at home.

- No visible garter belts.

- Avoid wearing skull jewelry (besides, it's rarely done well enough to keep you from looking like a lame teenager!).

- Leave the animal bones at home.

- Stiletto heels should stay in the closet. Your Docs are more comfy anyway!

a home could be a castle

Goths need to nest, but there's definitely a dearth of affordable Victorian mansions. Finding a Victorian, or even a funky home to rent or buy—à la the *Amityville Horror* house—is not so easy, and they are rarely reasonably priced. True Victorians or Arts and Crafts–style homes have been gobbled up by yuppies either enamored of the past or of inflating property values. Some at least restore these amazing relics to their original glory, while others gut and waste.

Goths live in a variety of locations: at home with the parents, in a room in a house shared with others, in a studio or warehouse loft space, in an apartment, in a rented or owned house. They generally like to goth-up their abodes.

Trystan L. Bass, of Silicon Valley, is the Gothic Martha Stewart. She has run her Web site full of crafts and decor tips since 1997, before the "real" Martha Stewart had her site up. "Over the years, I've gotten quite a few misdirected e-mails. People have asked me about Martha's sheets and towels. They've said things like 'I saw this project on your show last week—can you help me find this material?' These e-mails boggle my mind. How can you possibly confuse my site—all black and red, with the word *gothic* in big, bold letters, not to mention the disclaimer and a whole FAQ page saying that I'm not connected to Martha—with her official site? I just send them a terse reply, and ship them off to Martha's site."

Trystan says it was conversations with friends on the Usenet group alt.gothic.fashion that inspired her to begin. "We had been trading home decoration and craft tips for a while. I was already a fan of Martha Stewart's TV show and magazine, especially her Good Things. These are usually small craft projects that reuse things around the house or stuff from thrift stores (or, as she calls them 'tag sales'—I rather doubt she's set foot in Goodwill!).

"My ideas are all born of what I do to make my own home look and feel better. Until recently, I'd been a renter and couldn't paint or make any large-scale changes. Plus, I've always been on a tight budget. So I do everything I can with fabric and thrift-store finds. I also read a lot of home decorating books and magazines, and I'm thoroughly addicted to *Home & Garden TV*, along with shows like *The Christopher Lowell Show* and *Trading Spaces*. These all give me new ideas. As my life changes, opportunities for new projects arise."

Trystan uses her home as an example of how to goth-up decor, with photographs on her site. And much like her idol, the Gothic Martha Stewart suggests: "Don't bother with what's trendy, and don't care what other people think. Life's too short for that nonsense. Stick to what you love and you'll never go wrong—that's my advice to anyone, goth or not."

Edemonium, in Paris, is run by Barbara Perrier. The shop, nestled in the home of gargoyles and Euro dragons, is located in a sixteenth-century building composed of stone walls with iron bars at the windows, a cast-iron porch, and columns and moldings throughout the interior. "It is an intemporal and peaceful atmosphere," Barbara says of the three-year-old shop.

An artist herself, Barbara likes to feature macabre work by artists and designers. The majority of her customers are goths. "This is a place where people come who want to decorate their interior, even to have specific pieces made for that purpose." The worst part of owning the shop is the ordinary people who stumble in "and think I'm a witch!"

The four-year-old online shop Dark Reflections Designs specializes in black mirrors, scrying mirrors, coffin frames, coffin boxes, and cast items. Owner Micah Medway had worked as a custom picture framer for seven years. "One time I had a coffin-shaped Bauhaus poster, from the New Orleans reunion show. I built a coffin-shaped frame for it, and some friends wanted me to build them one . . . The business blossomed from there."

Everything sold at Dark Reflections Designs is handmade by Micah, whose clientele is split between goths and Pagans. Her most unusual item is the coffin clock, which she makes in Hollywood, where she creates all her designs, "in the guesthouse I built with my landlord in the backyard!"

wicked meals

Eating, even among the cadaverously lean, is fun. Dinner parties are de rigueur in the goth world. Setting a mood with a bloodred brocaded tablecloth, silver candelabra with twenty-four-inch black tapers, frankincense wafting through the air, Dead Can Dance oozing from the CD player, and coffin-handle napkin holders contribute to the ambience that turns a goth meal into a soirée.

The † Section offers a few unusual gothish food suggestions, from the plebeian to the exotic:

Azazelle: "Shaved black truffle with white asparagus, fugu, ancient red wine with dust and cobwebs from the cellar still on the bottle!"

BLACK (AND BLACKISH) FOODS

- black beans
- black pasta (colored with squid ink)
- black radish
- blackberries
- black rice (Forbidden Rice from Thailand)
- black silky chicken

biogoth

Photo by Andrea Dvorkin

UNIQUE COLLECTIONS OF THE † SECTION

aLiCe "I collect bottle caps from every type of beer I've had, and T-shirts from most of my favorite bands.

Ariana

"Little coffins."

Cemetery Crow "I collect metal grave markers, tombstones shaped like crosses, and any plastic thing made in the shape of bones, skulls or mummies."

Jetgirl "Dead roses (oh boy, do I have dead roses!), art, photos, and weird lamps."

Johnny Formaldehyde "Tacky religious things (like black velvet paintings with glitter blood of Jesus)."

Madame X "Whips, pewter figurines."

Malinda "Stonework, romantic paintings, porcelain masques."

Cemetery Crow: "Everything I serve is dead anyway. How about a black caviar, gray aspic in my brain mold, Forbidden Rice from Thailand [which is black], blackberries, and bloodred Vampire Wine."

Madame X: "Call of Cthulhu calamari, Heart's Desire stew prepared with the heart of the beast of the chef's choice, Blackened Fungus Olé, Blood Clot strawberry Jell-O with strawberry schnapps, cranberry and grape juice, and Transylvanian Vampire Wine."

Mylucretia: "Bleeding heart cake."

Vena Cava: "Sugar skulls, red wine or cranberry juice."

Paola: "Black pasta [blackened with squid ink], black bean salad, black soy youba, a dark red Italian wine—some wines are so dark they are almost black."

a hearse, or a PT cruiser?

Most of The † Section want to own a hearse. Or a PT Cruiser, the most accessible car that resembles a hearse. Richard Goulet and Claudine Verstraelen, co-owners of the goth shop Cruella in Montréal, own both. The PT Cruiser is more practical, but the 1979 Cadillac Miller Meteor hearse is more fun although, as Richard says, "Every time I turn the key, it costs me $10 in gas!"

Taoist owns "a black PT Cruiser 2-liter limited edition with blacked-out windows and steel kickplates, and a solid pewter skull gearknob."

Jetgirl and Medea have goth friends who own a hearse, as does TankBoy, who says, "It requires constant maintenance." Gypsy is "saving up for a hearse right now!" And while Amanda doesn't own a hearse, she has driven one: "I actually picked up a 'special delivery' for a funeral home at the airport in a hearse for the funeral home I was living in at the time."

Nevermore is the only one of The † Section who actually possesses a hearse: "A black 1971 Cadillac Fleetwood M&M hearse. Doesn't run too good. Burns lots of oil, and the transmission is flaky."

familiars

Goths are overwhelmingly pet lovers. Pets can take the place of a partner or children, and they can add animation to the décor. Goths have been known to cohabit with all manner of creatures, the most common, not surprisingly, cats (although there may be more fish). The most common cat color is . . . black! The favored cat breed is the exotic Sphinx—named because of its resemblance to ancient Egyptian cat sculptures. The first of these hairless mutants was born in 1966 in a Canadian litter of Rex kittens. The Sphinx, often described as the most loving of cats, has enormous ears that give it the cross-species look of a gargoyle. They are a popular breed, but being pure-breds, out of the price range of most goths.

Other animals that goths smile favorably upon are panthers, skunks, rats, and wolves, treating them with respect, viewing them as kindred spirits. Many goths find spiders and lizards fascinating, although insects per se are not high on the list of adorable creatures to share your home with.

Many Goths hold a special spot in their heart for ravens, crows, and bats.

Ravens and crows—those shiny black birds that in so many lands symbolize death—are interchangeable to most people. Both belong to the Corvidae (crow family), which includes about 100 types of birds, of which only forty or so are crows. Ravens, with an average length of twenty-four inches, are larger than crows, and have a wedge-shaped tail. The crow's tail is fan-shaped. Ravens tend to be more solitary than crows; the latter like to fly in packs called "murders." Ravens are purported by ornithologists to be the most intelligent birds on the planet, with a large, complex, and varied vocabulary of sounds they use among themselves. They can imitate almost any sound, including the human voice. Edgar Allan Poe said about ravens, "Though the birds have a wide variety of sounds and calls, they may not be willing to divulge their secrets to us."

Unfortunately ravens and crows are also harbingers of the mosquito-borne West Nile virus, since they are one of the species whose death from the virus is noticed first.

About 1,075 species of bats have been identified—the only flying mammals, and the only vertebrate animals that fly at night. Bats come in second to rats and rodents as the most diverse mammals on the earth. The two cutest bats might be the epauletted fruit bat (Epomophorus wahlbergi) of Africa, commonly called the "flying fox," weighing about three ounces, and the dog-faced Egyptian fruit bat (Rousettus aegyptiacus), which weighs in at a slightly larger three and a half ounces. Most bats eat fruit or insects—roughly one half their body weight in insects each night; without bats we would be overrun by insects. Vampire bats (Desmondus rotundas) are small—their bodies about the size of an adult thumb (two and three quarters inches long, with an eight-inch wingspan). Indiginous to the tropical and subtropical areas of the Americas, they live in colonies and

museumbitch

"Little lamps that hold tea lights. I also have a small collection of oil lamps, including one of a woman where the flame comes out of her outstretched hand."

Nevermore "Movie maniacs and hearse toys. Also, funeral items, desk fountains, chalices, and horror movies."

Nimue "I collect art from a woman who makes gothic things like black roses with thorns, mirrors with skulls, skull candleholders. The woman does not want to give her name."

Ravenheart "Things with ravens, dragonfly stuff (since childhood I thought they were spirits) phantom crystals, corsets, tarot cards, which I have been reading since age fourteen."

Sire Cédric

Photo by Andy Julia

"I collect religious icons. I want to collect coffins, but will need a lot of room for that."

Suzanne

Photo by Linda McRae

"Antique dresses and shoes."

The Crow "Fangoria and Orkus magazines, candleholders."

THE † SECTION ON MARRIAGE

Calista Waterwoods "I'm engaged and [intend to have] a medieval wedding."

DJ Ladybee "Unmarried, antimarriage. I live with my lover and am bisexual."

Hardrock Llewynyth "I currently have a fiancée who is the most incredible woman in the world, and two wonderful girlfriends. I'm a transgendered bisexual. I want to get married as soon as I can afford to, yes. Though my commitment to my fiancée is such that we are married in all but name now."

are strongly bonded socially; bats that go hungry on the nightly outings are fed by their mates through a regurgitation process. They live about nine years in the wild, and up to twenty in captivity. Bats mate year round, and usually produce one offspring annually. Vampire bats can maneuver on the ground as well as in the air, and can crawl or fly side to side and backwards. They feed on the blood of animals and require about two tablespoons each day, which they get by making a small incision in their prey and then lapping rather than sucking the blood—anticoagulants in their saliva prevent clotting. Vampire bats need the red blood cells only, and begin excreting the plasma, which their bodies cannot utilize, before they finish dining. Like all bats, they locate their prey by smell, sound, and echolocation (analyzing echoes from sound pulses), and possibly by heat. Currently vampire bats are on the endangered species list.

keeping up with the Addamses

Goth-interest objets d'art abound, especially on eBay, that virtual memento mori ("Remember you must die!") heaven. Goths around the world can bid on human skulls, Victorian hair jewelry, antique crucifixes, rosary beads, and funeral flags from the early 1900s.

Necromance is a goth legend. Home is the store on Melrose Avenue in Hollywood, which resembles a Victorian curio shop. Necromance has been in operation for a dozen years, and goths make pilgrimages to it when in Los Angeles. Nancy Smith, the owner, also sells on eBay. "I have loved skulls and skeletons, monsters and ghosts all my life. I thought it would be nice and dreary to be around this stuff all day, so I opened the store," which she describes as "the Disney Haunted Mansion meets the Natural History Museum." Besides jewelry made of animal bones and teeth, Necromance is the place to find a spider paperweight, glass eyes, or a fruit bat preserved in formaldehyde for the kitchen counter. Nancy also sells cool T-shirts, like L.A. CORONER; MOTEL 666; and the famous two-headed skeleton Necro. "There are stores that sell human bones and stores that sell Victorian mourning jewelry, and stores that sell coffins. What makes us different is we sell it all!"

Miriam Melanson of Vancouver's Flaming Angels Designs, creates much of what she stocks in her three-year-old shop. One unusual items is the "bloody cross pillow." Miriam says, "We are unique because we are product developers, not crafters or sewers. I spend countless hours devel-

Courtesy of Damien Glonek and Ed Long

oping product ideas as well as designs for these items. We don't just produce the latest version of the hottest, latest thing; we go beyond that."

Julie Pedersen, owner of *Shaddow Domain Gothic Treasures* in Idaho, sells items she scours the planet to find. "I do make some of my own products, and have begun production of mugs and other printables." Her most popular item is "the Devil Duckies."

Rare, expensive, one-of-a-kind antiques, for instance, mourning pins for the morbid sewer, and old morticians' embalming equipment, can be had from the online shop Gothic Rose Antiques, which operates out of Petaluma, California.

Goths have a great sense of humor, and love toys. Inkubus Art and Objects sells everything, from clothing to decor, and they have plenty of goth oddities, like Raven the Goth Girl Nodder, and the Brain Mold, for making an unusual aspic, and sugar skull molds, which can also juice up a goth high tea. Owner Malaise Lindenfeld—who recently moved her six-year-old operation from Florida to New Hampshire—also sells the artwork of Czech artist Adolf Benca. One of her most precious memories is of a young boy who used to come in to the shop and would "buy something, then stay a while and we would talk; he complained about his parents, and his life in general. I tried advising him, being a parent of a boy his age myself, so I understood what his parents felt and could explain it to him. A few months later his parents came by to thank me for being a positive influence."

Miss Lynx "Since my partner is female, it's not likely to be an option for us. We may have a Wiccan handfasting though."

Nevermore "Engaged. We're getting married on Halloween, and honeymooning in Salem."

Slavel "Engaged to my wonderful man. Wedding will be more cyber/vintage."

Sky Claudette "Vlad and I live together. Being bound by a piece of paper is a form of slavery. A growing percentage of people who marry divorce. Relationship should be a form of truth of love, not a piece of paper that can perish in a fire. The only way we could see ourselves being officially joined is through an old-fashioned Pagan wedding, which has the significance of being bound by blood. We are extremely spiritual."

Lestat de Lioncourt "Never believed in marriage...well, at least not in the Christian way. But making a pact with someone to stay forever by her side sounds really really romantic."

Mistress Hades "Yes, I'd like to get married. I'm very old-fashioned. A reception in London Dungeon."

Raven "I have a boyfriend. I'd have like about five nine-year-olds in faerie wings for my flower girls, and I will have black rose petals."

cypher "We actually had a Victorian theme wedding. Top hats, ascots, canes–at least eighty percent of our guests made some attempt to dress for the theme and they're still complimenting themselves."

DUSK "My dress was purple. Our rings are Celtic rings, in silver. We had a nice goth party. We had a honeymoon in California where we saw the whales."

Emily Bronte "We had a Pagan handfasting in the woods and a legal ceremony in the Chinese tomb at the museum."

Jetgirl "Divorced now, but we had our ceremony in a cemetery. Complete with us coming out of the coffin that my friend drove there in his hearse. An Enokian priest married us and we had all the goth accoutrements. It was filmed and shown on <u>Wild Chicago</u> when we were interviewed for the show. Also used some of the footage in one of our music videos. It was pretty outrageous and cool."

Ravenheart "I had my wedding in a tiny little white storybook church with stained glass windows in Gothic arch shapes, with lots of tattooed, makeup-wearing, pierced-in-places-I-can't-imagine band members I work with in attendance. Honeymooned in St. Augustine, where there were some cool old cemeteries."

The † *Section* are overwhelmingly collectors, and it's not unusual that many collect the same things. Collectibles from Tim Burton's movie *The Nightmare Before Christmas* are hot. And the grimly adorable Living Dead Dolls are very popular with goths in general.

Ed Long and Damien Glonek of New Jersey began creating Living Dead Dolls five years ago. Damien says, "We never really set out to cater to goths, as our roots were planted in horror films. We just did what we wanted, and it just happens to work well in the goth community." Ed adds, "Our dolls are a lot less romantic about death. That's why I am so surprised that they are so well received in the goth community. I think it is refreshing to see that they [goths] actually have a sense of humor."

Damien and Ed licensed sales and distribution to Mezco Toyz, but continue to design all the dolls themselves and oversee production samples of the dolls and the other items they've branched into, including mini dolls, stationery, journals, barware, and the adorable Living Dead Doll pencil sharpener where, to sharpen the pencil, the doll head is stabbed in the eye.

"One of the reasons we think Living Dead Dolls have been so successful," Damien says, "is because there has never been anything like them on such a level before. And we do what we want to see and don't try to guess what the next 'it' will be." Ed says, "I think people have been waiting to see something like this for a long time, and finally someone had the guts to do it, and do it right." Damien adds, "It's great to be able to infect the world with our bit of sickness!"

URLs

French Quarter Wedding Chapel, New Orleans
www.frenchquarterwedding.com

The Dark Angel
www.thedarkangel.co.uk

Enigma Fashions
www.enigmafashions.com

Nehelenia Designs
www.nehelenia.de

Gothic Martha Stewart
www.toreadors.com/martha/

Gothic Parents Web site
www.gothicparents.com/

Necromance
www.necromance.com

Gothic Rose Antiques
www.gothicroseantiques.com/

Flaming Angels Designs
www.flamingangels.net

Shaddow Domain Gothic Treasurer
www.shaddowdomain.com

Inkubus Art & Objects
www.inkubus.com

Edemonium
www.edemonium.com

Dark Reflections Designs
www.darkreflectionsdesigns.com/

Cruella
www.cruella.ca

Corporate goth site
www.waningmoon.com/corpgoth/

Living Dead Dolls
www.livingdeaddolls.com/

rinaedin "Gay and living with my life partner. We're handfasted—same thing."

Zerstoerte "I'm happily married to my best friend—we never dated, he just asked me to marry him five minutes before I got on a plane to the Netherlands when I was moving there. I wore a medieval bell-sleeved gown I purchased in the Netherlands, loads of black eyeliner, and a satin floral headpiece. We had a formal reception for the family, and a separate reception for friends at Sanctuary: The Vampire Sex Bar, later that night."

Xefiel "Broken mirrors, magic items.

Artwork by Hunter Gough

WHEN GOTHS RELAX

Hauling out the crushed velvet lawn chairs!

surfing the dark side of the Internet

Woe to the goth who does not partake of the Internet! For he/she shall be relegated to the humdrum of real time with all its imperfections!

The Internet is probably the largest source of entertainment for goths of the industrialized world, and the percentage of goths on the Net is high, with newsgroups, chat channels, and thousands of goth Web sites available for the consuming. This virtual goth haven offers contact, from local to international, with the like-minded, all beyond the speed of light.

One of the best goth sites has been the online goth magazine *gothic.net*.

Darren Mckeeman is the delightfully cynical mastermind behind the highly successful six-year-old Web publication. "Gothic," says Darren, "stood for clanky chains and ghosts in castles long before Joy Division started whining.

"*Gothic.net* was started by a bunch of Internet professionals as a response to the crush of their day jobs. We all love horror fiction, so we decided to publish short stories online. I got the domain name and suggested it to my friends after spending a bizarre weekend in Niagara Falls in the entourage of Poppy Z. Brite and Caitlín Kiernan—sometimes I say it came out of a drinking contest with Ramsey Campbell that we both lost horribly. Horror writers are cool!"

Darren admits that it's not easy running an all-goth Web publication. "It's hard finding good help. Most of the people who work for us are goth-as-fuck. Because of this, they are also notorious flakes. It's great for trade shows where we are the center of attention, but often it shows in the fact that we skip editorials, cut corners on coding. Our machines are all recycled from trash heaps. It hasn't been that hard to keep going, though. I put this down to the fact that we're just better than the average goth at this. [We're] publishing something to print out and read on the toilet."

Running *gothic.net* has a lot of advantages, including nominations for awards, and parties! "We have outrageous parties—the last one in Hollywood we had this guy who played Leatherface in *Texas Chainsaw Massacre 3* as a bouncer!" But what really makes it worthwhile for Darren are the accolades from publishing peers, and the e-mails he receives from grateful goths. One in particular touched him. "Five years ago, an e-mail from a thirteen-year-old girl in Kentucky came in that's still stuck to my fridge. It says, 'I love your webzine, it gives me a reason to live. I'm your fan for life.'"

Another popular net magazine is *Dark Culture* (formerly *The Gothic Preservation Society*), run by Mistress Cinka, also on the net for six years. "Initially I had this mad plan of ridding the world of Marilyn Manson and his preteen minions. [joke!] I fantasized about creating my very own magazine. I wanted to create a place where people of a gothic/dark nature could come together, share their thoughts, their artwork, meet people. I wanted to create sort of a literary community. I'm also attempting to not only focus on the past (music and artists), but current events, up-and-coming. I try to maintain a balance between old school and the new school."

Mistress Cinka says, "I've been in the [goth] scene for twelve years. *Dark Culture* is my heart and soul. I couldn't love it any more than I do. Sometimes I feel we're 'the little site that could,' and this gives me hope." She prides herself on integrity. "We don't kowtow to record labels, we try to tell it like it is, and everyone's invited. As the goth culture waxes and wanes, I want *Dark Culture* to be part of what keeps the scene breathing. Our best review is from Mick Mercer in *21st Century Goth*: 'You will actually need a brain inside your head for this one. It isn't soporific in any way."

Grave Concerns e-zine focuses on music. Julie Johnson from Albany, New York, started it four years ago in her spare time. She's a grade seven and eight Spanish teacher. "I wanted people to get to know bands, both the smaller and the better-known bands. If someone reads an interview or a review and finds out about a new band they might like, that's great. I really want to help the bands."

Seven years ago, Julie says she did not know she could write. Now, besides *Grave Concerns* e-zine, she has also contributed to *Black Monday* magazine in London, *Sideline* magazine and *Gothic Beauty*. "Gothic bands and fans are really driven," she has observed, "and have a great dedication to the scene. There is something about the gothic scene; we are very hard workers, and I feel we don't have big egos like other subcultures. The Internet is a great tool for goths to come together. One of my most enjoyable experiences is forming with Joshua Heinrich our band Orangabelle 5, after we met doing only my second interview when I had my original personal page, *Gothgirls Web of Gothic Darkness*. We have since released four CDs together."

The Internet is alive with good goth sites. Some of the best general sites are *Dark Side of the Net; Gothic Resources; Scatheweb; A Study of Gothic Subculture: An Inside Look for Outsiders.* There are also some wacky and/or macabre Internet sites that goths love, like *rotten.com*. One Web site that appeals to the dismally inclined who like their morbidity with a dash of humor has a free e-mail newsletter, *Morbid Fact du Jour*, sent by the mysterious Comtesse DeSpair, who "sits in sullen silence at *The Asylum Eclectica*, located at The Castle DeSpaire in the Valley Dementia, Catatonia."

Courtesy of The Comtesse Despair

The Asylum Eclectica is a Web site begun six years ago when the Comtesse was "at home nursing a broken arm sustained when foolishly I attempted to Rollerblade. I started the Web site as a narcissistic outlet to indulge my obsessions. It also helps fill my artistic urges, although, in truth, over the years I've become much more of an archivist." The site features macabre sections filled with grim facts often presented with Morticia Addams–style ghastly humor, for instance: Morbid Fact du Jour (which can be sent to your e-mail box for free); Malady of the Month; My Brush with Morbidity; All Things Dark & Gruesome; Garretdom; and the Morbid Sightseer.

Her mailing list is enormous, and the Comtesse updates it regularly. She feels aligned with all morbidly inclined souls across the planet, including goths. "Those of us who find the dark side of life fascinating have to deal with a certain stigma thrust upon us by society. You're not supposed to take enjoyment in reading about horrifying things, crack morbid jokes about tragic occurrences, willingly seek out images of death. It's very gratifying when you stumble upon people who share a dark worldview, with whom you can be honest about your interests without having to worry about the white coats coming with a straitjacket. It's a great feeling to find kinship with others when you've been told you're an aberration." The Comtesse does not consider herself goth, although she "dresses in black" and her house is "filled with skulls, crows, *Nightmare Before Christmas* memorabilia, dark art. . . ." She laments, "I greatly admire goths, and sometimes wish I could join in the fun . . . but I think I'm destined to forever be an outcast among outcasts."

She sees her work as a service to the macabre-minded. "My site allows a forum for the preservation of the darkly arcane. For example, there aren't many sites out there where morbid nineteenth-century newspaper articles are actively collected. My site also helps keep psychopaths from getting bored, which can only be of great benefit to *all* segments of society! I probably should receive a Medal of Honor!"

net.goth

When it comes to goth on the net—Internet chat lines and channels, Web rings and newsgroups—two self-confessed net.goths discuss what it's like. Cavalorn, thirty-four from the UK, has been a net.goth for seven years. He runs New Aeon Books, an online metaphysical bookshop. Macross Ascendant, twenty-eight, from the US, has been a net.goth for twelve years. He hosts an Internet radio show for *impradio*, and also oversees the Alt.Gothic newsgroup's annual party, Convergence.

Courtesy of X-tra-X

defining net.goth

Cavalorn: "A member of the gothic subculture with net access, who participates in Internet-based gothic communities."

Macross: "The origin of the term *net.goth* is a sarcastic joke attributed to SexBat and other 'founding' members of the alt.gothic newsgroup. Over the years it's become a generic term describing anyone gothic who also uses the Internet to communicate. I'm an old-school hardass, and I firmly stand behind the Usenet alt.gothic newsgroup usage being the only thing that makes one a net.goth. Everything else is just goths on the Internet [wink]."

online chatter

Cavalorn: "I don't use Web-based chatrooms at all. I use IRC (Internet Relay Chat), on undernet, #gothik, #gothick, efnet and in the UK on #uk_goffs, which is usually abroil with relatively inane conversation. But topics come and go. They are rarely about anything exclusive to gothic culture, more about sex, humor, or both."

Macross: "I used to spend too much time on undernet and efnet, #gothic, and related channels. I've happily recovered from that period of my life. Chat rooms are the never-ending international tournament of bullshit. It's anonymous, ambiguous, and cheap, like a Teflon coating for personality disorders."

up- and downside of internet gothing

Cavalorn: "Participants generally are highly intelligent and have an excellent sense of humor. My friend Boo asked me to tell you the best thing is the cyber.pOOn [cyber sex]. Another friend, Ratty, says the best is you 'don't have to see the bad clothes and eye makeup.' The worst part is definitely the politicking. Alliances form, relationships evolve and fragment, emotions are frayed, and the camaraderie suffers for it."

Macross: "The best is leaving the house and finding something to do with real people in a real destination. Using all the senses and muscles instead of only the eyes and fingers. The worst? Doing nothing, producing nothing but methane and waste water, losing touch with reality, friends, and the short time we all have as mortals."

Cavalorn: "Three words. 'Sexy death chicks'—or 'sexxy deth chix,' as we like to spell it . . ."

Macross: "Low self-esteem, laziness, escape."

scam or spam

Cavalorn: "I realized that the woman I had thought I was talking to and flirting with was in fact a man who had stolen her identity. I did the decent thing and e-mailed her to let her know what happened."

Macross: "Realized I had wasted nearly a year of my life sitting at home or at work alone in front of a computer typing to people I didn't really know or like instead of spending time with my friends and family in the real world. I neglected myself, my friends, my family, my job. My attitude and my life were a sad state of affairs. Wallowing in self-pity and pretending to live and rule in an imaginary world of text is as addictive and destructive as any chemical narcotic, maybe even more so."

love and hate relationship with the machine

Cavalorn: "I don't hate my computer at all. It's a tool, not a narcotic."

Macross: "Back in the 1920s, the leaders of science and industry thought that harnessing the power of coal to generate heat and create steam to power engines was mankind's greatest achievement, and that no other achievement could ever surpass what had been accomplished, thanks to coal. About coal they wrote, 'Anything is possible.' I regularly consider replacing my desktop computer with a lump of coal, as I suspect I would at once be far more productive."

virtual gaming

Although *Medea* says, "I would rather socialize on the computer than play games," many goths play computer games. Among *The † Section*, the overwhelming favorite is *The Sims,* short for *simulations,* a computer world that can be interactive via the Internet with other players, and allows players to construct and guide the lives of virtual people. It's the modern world's Victorian dollhouse. Most of *The † Section* have good things to say about *The Sims. Marcelous* says, "It's a great game, if you fix it up first, download some gothic people and accessories." *Angel in PVC* admits, "I like to control their lives." For *Rois, The Sims* is a tension release: "When I'm really cranky, I kill them eight at a time and work out my frustrations that way. Most other games give me vertigo."

Mistress Cinka, editor of the net.goth magazine *Dark Culture*, shares an article she wrote on *The Sims.* "About two years ago, my younger brother had me check out a computer game entitled *The Sims.* I thought it was cool enough, but what got me hooked was seeing the cute little goth Sim my brother had created . . . scary enough, it looked like me. I was gone. I began playing like mad. I had no concept of time. Day turned into night. If I saw the quiet blue light of morning, I knew I'd been playing too long. After a few months of insanity, I went cold turkey . . . that is, until the latest expansion pack came out.

"*Sims,* short for *simulations,* is a game that allows the player to create an entire world from scratch. The graphics are fairly advanced, and character actions are often frighteningly lifelike. You must care for your Sims; feed, clothe, educate, and make sure they get to the bathroom. Sims even have a varied amount of careers to choose from, complete with paycheck at the end of the day.

"In many ways, playing *Sims* is like playing God. There are few limitations and many variables. You control a Sim's personality (astrological sign), their environment, their interactions, and how well they do in 'life.' Sims can be gay, straight, or bisexual. They can get sick, fall in love, suffer from depression, have babies, leave home, get into fights, and yes, die. I've even heard of spontaneous Sim combustion. From hair color to wallpaper, you design nearly everything. Very little is left up to chance. It's sort of like the board game *Life,* but far more complex.

"Several expansion packs have granted *Sims* access into new worlds, like a downtown area, and Vacation Island. Players across the globe have spent their free time creating a countless number of skins (clothes, hair, face, body type) along with thousands of objects (anything you can find in your house and more). The quantity is staggering, and there is no real way to describe it in its magnitude. Simply, it's a very fun, but very time-consuming game.

"Goth Sims are not hard to come by, and are scattered all over the net.

Davis

"The story we have now is so complex,
and it's great."

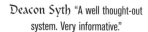

Deacon Syth "A well thought-out
system. Very informative."

Gypsy

"I love V:TM. I'm oh-so Toreador!
I love the gothic, romantic style.
And the options."

⊹

Hardrock Llewynyth
"Mostly for the politics."

⊹

WantonBlood: "[White Wolf
role-playing games] put you in a world
of darkness where supernatural is a
matter of everyday. Also, everyone
dresses funny so it is amusing."

One of the best is *Ophelia's Little Page About the Sims*. Her site is beautiful to look at and her skins are truly unique.

"For more dark skins, see *Evil Sims*. Here you'll find Father Karras (*The Exorcist*), Evil nuns, Anton LaVey, Alex from *A Clockwork Orange*, Elvira, and a bunch of other horror/sci-fi personalities. Woo fun!

"*The Sims Resource* has a vast array of gothic skins as well. You'll find *Buffy* (entire cast), general goths, several punks, and hundreds of other dark personalities. *Darkside of the Sims* has a small but nice-looking collection of vampire Sims, along with an Evil Alice.

"In essence, since you have utter control over your Sims, you can make them into anything you want. Many goth players design vampire crypts, haunted mansions, Medieval castles, or simply modern homes with every gothic convenience. Some players act out story lines, and others play for the sake of playing.

"Sometimes God is a vengeful God. As ruler over your Sims' lives, you have the power to kill them. Check out *The Guide To Kill Sims*. There are several ways in which to murder your Sims. One of the more popular methods is fire. When a Sim dies, the Grim Reaper floats in on a cloud of skulls, waves his hands, and carts the body away. A small urn or tombstone is left in your Sim's place. Your house is now haunted! *Sims Slaughter* has even more ideas for Simicide."

Goths have other favorite, traditional computer games they like, for example, the graphically stunning *Alice*, created by American McGee. *Quake* and *Doom* are two of the more popular games.

But computer games are not universally loved. *Lestat de Lioncourt*, one of *The † Section* goths, sometimes reacts physically to some computer games. "I like *War Craft 3*—check out the undead and the night elf clans, pretty gothic and druidic."

And there's always the traditional: *Goth: A Horror Trivia Board Game* is a Trivial Pursuit for the darkly inclined.

∂ark RPGs

An excellent movie from Chile that depicts the connection between goth, vampires, and role-playing is young gothish director Jorge Olguín's *Sangre Eterna* (released by Fangoria Films in North America as *Eternal Blood*). Not only that, but the movie gives other goths a good look at how Chilean goths go clubbing.

By far, the most popular real-time role-playing game for goths is *Vampire: The Masquerade*, from White Wolf gaming. The company's World of Darkness series includes *Werewolf*, *Wraithe*, and *Mage*, but *Vampire* has extra appeal for goths. The vampire game is really a complex masquerade party. People get together and assume a character, then dress up and act out that character, sticking to the rules of the world. In *Vampire: The Masquerade*, the premise is that all vampires are descendants of Cain [who, in the Bible, slew his brother Abel, Adam and Eve's other son]. Those whom Cain begot are first generation, and their children second gen, and so on. All vampires belong to a clan, of which there are several, such as Brujah (tough witches), Nosferatu (the original resuscitated corpses), Toreador (the beautiful and artistic ones), and so on. Players pick a clan and a generation. They must also decide if they want to play with the Camrilla (generally the good guys), or the warlike Sabbat (generally the bad guys). Both sects live hierarchically in a city ruled by a prince who is constantly being overthrown, usually through political intrigue. It is an intricate world, based on aspects of mysticism, philosophy, and spiritual disciplines gathered from cultures from around the globe, and White Wolf has published tons of books of rules and information on all of the above. Each game played has at least one storyteller, who is the arbitrator of the world's rules.

Role-playing games give participants, especially the young, a chance to learn the possibilities of interaction in the real world by role-playing in a safe and contained environment they can go home from afterwards. Role-playing can assume the position that fairy tales fulfilled in the past—a story that shows something of human actions and interactions, with wins, losses, obligations, and rights, as well as consequences of actions. And in the same way that fairy tales altered a bit from place to place and the ending could go any which way depending on who told the story and what moral he or she focused on, role-playing ends differently each night.

Some goths are against role-playing games, such as *Lord Madd*, *Madame X*, and *Malinda*, who says "I see the whole idea as an opportunity to lose who we really are and pretend to be something we never can be. Honestly, if I get hit on by one more teenage boy who thinks he's a vampire (eternal acne, how sad would that be?), I'll scream." *TankBoy* "used to play as a kid, but they're boring now. People are much more fun to play with. Tactile dark room full of fuzzy comfy things anyone?" *museumbitch* says "They put me

Individuation "I mostly went to hang out with my friends, and because I had a crush on a Chicago boy who used to come down to play. He's a friend of mine now."

Miss Lynx "I've played many World of Darkness games like Vampire, Werewolf, Mage, Changeling. Also Shadowrun, and Runequest. I enjoy gaming because it's a nice escape into a fantasy world, which helps alleviate work stress, and also it's a way to exercise my creativity. It combines the best of fiction writing and improv theater."

Slavel "Vampire was okay. Cheesy, though."

the evil one "I had a short stint with Vampire. I don't have the patience it takes."

to sleep!" And for *Paola*, "The very idea bores me. I'd rather read a good novel than hear friends conjure up a bad spoken-word plot!"

relaxing with comix

Charles Addams drew the Addams Family cartoons for *The New Yorker*, where they appeared from 1935 to 1988. The morbidly funny characters we now know as Morticia or 'Tish; Gomez; and the grimly adorable Wednesday, among others, went on to their own popular TV series in the sixties, made several movies, and were reincarnated for another TV series in the 1990s. They are cherished images for goths.

But the most beloved comics in gothland are those created by Neil Gaiman. Goths adore his mega-award-winning *Sandman* world. *Miss Lynx* admires him "for turning comic books into a real work of art." *Kate* feels that "his beautiful fantasy world intersects with the world I live in." *Slavel* credits Gaiman with making "the most effort to create a modern mythos or fantasy, due to the impact that *Sandman* made in art and literature."

Neil Gaiman doesn't really know why he is so popular with goths, but speculates, "I suspect it's because I don't try to write for them [goths], but I do write characters and places and things that they can identify with. Most of the fiction people have given me to read 'aimed at goths' is terribly earnest and depressing. Most of the goths I know like funny—even if their tastes in humour tend toward the dark—and they like real."

Neil admits he was never really goth. "If I was ever part of a movement, I was a punk. (We didn't have goths back then.) If I was five years younger I might well have been a first-wave goth, and if I was fifteen years younger I might be a goth now. Instead I'm just an author with a rather monochromatic wardrobe, and a mind that wanders towards graveyards."

He sees goth as a natural phenomenon. "Truth to tell, I suspect that goths are born, not made. People who think there is something deeply cool about graveyards in autumn and summer lightning, and know that they just don't look right in summery pink leisure suits, probably didn't get that way through reading fiction. Although they may recognize themselves in fiction (as I did, as a child, in [Ray] Bradbury's story 'Homecoming'). It's a process of recognition."

Asked about *Sandman*'s conception, Neil says, "All I was trying to do was tell a story that mattered in monthly comics form. Anything beyond that was gravy."

Of all the characters in *Sandman*, the cute, friendly, and helpful gothish girl Death is the one most goths relate to or empathize with. Neil says, "I wanted to write the Death I wanted to meet. And I was tired of literary Deaths who carried the burden of angst about their job—she's been doing it for a long time. She's good at it."

The image for the character Death is based on photographs of goth supermodel Donna Ricci, who in her spare time owns an alternative modeling agency, and also runs a vampire nightclub. As Donna said to *Bite Me* magazine (issue No. 5) about modeling for Death, "I used to go to comic book stores and sign autographs and pose for pictures and traveled all over California." Neil told Donna she was a perfect match with the character in his mind.

Neil is an eclectic writer. Besides his comic series, he writes fiction, and screenplays for film and television. He has also written music. One of his most recent novels is the award-winning Alice-in-Unnervingland "children's" book *Coraline*. "I wrote *Coraline* for my daughters, both of whom have more than a streak of Wednesday Addams in them. (Holly, my oldest, announced she wanted to be a goth, when she was fourteen. 'Don't do that,' I said. 'Ah,' she said, with relish, 'you're trying to stifle my free expression.' 'No,' I said, 'it's just that, when you're together with all your goth friends, and they tell you how awful their parents are, when it's your turn to tell them how awful I am they'll just ask if you can get them my autograph, and that won't be much fun.')"

His novels include: *American Gods*, a funny yet serious confrontation of the American way of life; the delightful fairy tale *Stardust*; and the shadowy world beneath London of *Neverworld*. All of his work is amusing, biting, and . . . dark. "Why do I love darkness so much? Ogden Nash put it best: 'Where there's a monster, there's a miracle.' I love the magic you can find in dark places. Most of my next novel for children is set in a graveyard, after all." That would be *The Graveyard Book*.

The † Section fondly mentioned Edward Gorey over and over, for his incredible cartoon drawings. (see Chapter 11)

Other extremely popular comics are the delightfully disturbed and misunderstood *Johnny the Homicidal Maniac* (aka *JTHM*), *I Feel Sick!* and *Squee*, all by San Jose's darkly talented comicmeister Jhonen Vasquez. Also mentioned again and again were the wonderfully wicked *Oh My Goth* and *Humans Suck*, both by American Renaissance man Voltaire, who is also a singer/musician with CDs to his credit.

On the gothic comic short list is the quirky Internet goth strip *Writhe and Shine* by Robert Tritthardt, who, when not writing comics, like his comic protagonist Writhe, DJs at local clubs. Asked if he believes goths everywhere can relate to his comic set in New Orleans, Robert says, "Yes, they relate. They have told me so. The most common e-mails I get say 'It's like that here in my city too!' and 'Are you writing a story about me?!' Goths around the world can relate to *Writhe and Shine* because it's about them. Well, more appropriately it's about me and my experiences in the subculture, but my experiences are not unique. The scene is the same in every city. The music may be a little different and people might have cooler clothes, but all the people are exactly alike. So I focus on New Orleans because that's where I am right now. It also helps because everyone thinks that New Orleans is the Gothic Capital of the World. Probably because of those vampire books. It does have its unique charm, and I like drawing street scenes."

Robert began his comic career with a strip in college about an alien. "When I moved to New Orleans I really wanted to start drawing again. I also wanted to show people that I was more than just some girl's boyfriend. . . . I wanted people to know me for me and not for who I was associated with. So I made up this character based on me. I called him Deadboy at first, thinking that he was going to be a zombie. But I decided to write something that was real, as in no monsters or magic. I based all the characters on people I knew at the time, but the characters eventually began to develop into their own entities. Since I was used to drawing four-panel comic strips, that's what I started with. I made up this story and did about ten strips. It took me a few months because I had to work at a real job, I had no drawing table (I used to sit in the bathroom with a plank of wood balanced on top of a milk crate), and the place where I lived wasn't air conditioned. Sometimes I drew at a coffee shop called Kaldi's, but it closed down. In April 1999, we hosted Convergence 5. I produced about 300 ashcan comic books of all the *Writhe and Shine* strips and handed them out in people's goodie bags. I think people really liked them (even though it was some terrible artwork). So I kept going from there. I eventually got tired of the comic strip format and decided to tackle an actual comic book. Right now I have over 150 comic strips and I am working on book #2."

Writhe and Shine comic book #1, distributed by Cold Cut Distribution, is sold out, but Robert thinks, "You might get lucky and find one at your local comic store." He produces other work under the umbrella name Über Comics. His future plans? "A *Writhe and Shine* animated cartoon. I just need to find the time and money. . . ."

Other comics popular with Goths include: *The Crow* (James O'Barr); *Gloom-Cookie* (Serena Valentino and Ted Naifeh)—see the cover of *Elegy* magazine; *Donna Mia, Hellraiser, Purgatori,* and *Lenore* (Roman Dirge).

sporting goths

Goth and sports would not seem to be on the same team. Many of *The † Section* said the sports they enjoy are "dancing and sex." Goths often have bad childhood experiences with enforced sports, especially team sports, or in some cases, encounters with aggressive jocks. It's not surprising that an overwhelming majority are not interested in sports. *TankBoy* thinks "sports contribute nothing to society but date rape." *Cemetery Crow* says, "I believe your whole environment is where you should train, not in miserable cattle ranges for abused office sitters."

tea, high and low

The Duchess of Bedford (1788–1861), one of Queen Victoria's ladies-in-waiting, complained of a "sinking feeling" in the late afternoon. Back then in England, only breakfast and a dinner late in the evening were served. So the Duchess invented afternoon tea, to which she invited friends, around five P.M., and it kept them going. The Queen approved, and a tradition was born.

Food at these teas included crustless sandwiches composed of such ingredients as peeled and thinly sliced English cucumbers with butter and spiced with salt and pepper, and shrimp or fish paté. Also on hand were toasted bread with a variety of jams, scones, and crumpets served with Devonshire cream, assorted pastries, fruit compote, or traditional English trifle. These sandwiches, by the way, invented by John Montagu, Fourth Earl of Sandwich, became known as the tea sandwich.

Presentation is everything, and the Duchess no doubt hauled out the silver tea service and bone china cups and saucers. Back then, it was the parlor maid who would bring the tea tray to the drawing room. The hostess would proceed to serve her guests in grand style, while the ladies spoke of gentle subjects, and gossiped outrageously.

The terms *high tea, low tea,* and *afternoon tea* are interchangeable now.

Scones Fit for a King or Queen of Darkness

2¼ cups all purpose flour
salt to taste
1½ tsp baking powder
2 tsp baking soda
2 cups raisins or currants
1 egg, beat it well
2 cup butter cut into small cubes
1 cup milk or buttermilk
black food coloring

Sift together all the dry ingredients. Cut butter into that mixture with two sharp daggers. If daggers are unavailable, use steak knives. Do this until it resembles the Epsom salts you'll need in your bath later to soothe your muscles after all this kitchen work. Add the milk or buttermilk, the raisins or currants, and a couple of drops of the black food coloring. Dough should be a bit sticky. Either wear latex gloves or dip your hands in flour and mould the dough into a ball. Knead it gently while you listen to the opening stanzas of the angels singing "This Corrosion." Flatten these balls to 1" thick. Cut circles using a wide shot glass. Now comes the artistic part: paint the circles with the egg that you've beaten. These creatures will bake somewhere between 11 and 16 minutes in a 425˚ F oven. They should be light golden-grey when you take them out. You need to eat them warm, with Devonshire cream, maybe some preserves, because when they get cold and hard they are only good for paperweights.

Faux Devonshire Cream

For real Devonshire cream, you have to boil unpasturized milk. It's easier to fly to England than to find unpasturized milk. Here's a good fake recipe.

3 ounces Philly cream cheese
1 tablespoon sugar or Splenda or even honey, if you're so inclined
13 grains of salt
1 cup of the heaviest cream you can find

Mix the first three ingredients together, then whip in the cream until it forms the stiff peaks you see on meringue. Put it in the refrigerator while you go have that Epsom salts bath.

High tea was not the tea of the aristocracy but actually a working-class tradition. The "high" part referred to sitting on high stools in a tea shop, or standing at a counter or buffet table. High tea was served generally around five or six P.M., and consisted of a substantial meal with hot dishes, hefty sandwiches, scones, heavy cakes, biscuits, and, of course, plenty of tea. High tea was a cross between afternoon tea and supper, and for many workers was the main meal of the day.

Most of the world's top hotels offer guests a pricey high or afternoon tea, serving the food on three-tiered silver trays. From time to time guests of such hotels will see a murder of goths descend en masse on the restaurant, dressed in their best Victorian velvets, satin corsets, and ruffled shirts, lifting the Royal Albert bone china cups with gloved, beringed fingers and blackened fingernails. The best hotels recognize such stylish extravaganzas as free entertainment for their guests.

Goths are more likely than the average person to own a silver teapot, and hosting an elegant afternoon tea at home makes a pleasant social event for friends. Served between three and five P.M., it also fits right in with the gothic timetable.

goth gardening

The quest for the black rose—that romantic symbol of eternal love of death—exhausts goths. How to find that rose with no hint of blue, purple, or deep red hidden at the base of the petals? David DeMarco of the Black Rose Floral Company delivers the bad and the good news about black roses. "Black roses have been around for centuries, unfortunately in myth only. Currently real, true black roses do not exist. We have heard a wide variety of stories, from rose breeders who are cross-breeding the darkest red roses over and over to come up with a marketable black rose, to stories of the industry sneaking out at night and ripping out rosebushes of people who had proclaimed they had a true black rose plant growing in their yard! Where the truth really lies, I'm not sure, but I do believe that cross-breeding must be going on. Why all the mystery, confusion, and aura about black roses? At least part of the answer is this: On the darkest red breeds of red roses, when the plant produces rosebuds, the buds appear to be black. They really do look like black roses, but once the bud matures and the rose blossoms, you see the true color in the inner petals."

Bat Plant Tacca
Photo by Hugues Leblanc

Distressing as this reality might be to goths, there is a happy alternative. The Black Rose Floral Company specializes in black-only rose arrangements and bouquets, which can be ordered online and delivered. They use fresh roses, dried, then dyed black, and also black silk roses. The company now has a warehouse, but they began in a garage six years ago, and when they opened, "We had no idea our products would be so popular in the gothic community, but they certainly have been." Goths make up about a quarter of their customers.

David admits that normal people buy black roses for entirely different reasons than goths do. "Most of our customers have specific reasons to order our products, such as to get revenge, or embarrass someone, or for a milestone birthday—our black rose wreaths are unique, and quite popular for the thirtieth, fortieth, fiftieth, etc. Goths, on the other hand, are much more likely to order one of our centerpieces, or a wrapped bouquet that they can put in a vase at home, or send to a fellow goth for a wider variety of everyday occasions."

When it comes to gardening, completely black blooms are rare, and consequently full of mystery. Some of the common and readily available black flowers include: Black Prince pansy, black viola, black sweet william, black tulip, penny black, black and white columbine, and ace of spades. Exotic black flowering plants are often found in exotic locations, and consequently are difficult to grow in most of the world—for instance, *Tacca chanterii*, also known as the Black Bat Plant because the flower's whispy petals resemble the wings of a bat. *Tacca chanterii* seeds must be sewn quickly after harvesting, and germination takes nine months!

Those in the know say a good way to focus on black in a garden is by using foliage like Hillside Black Beauty, and Black Negligee. One new blackish cultivar is James Compton. Other flowers and plants to consider are the iris Black Knight, with its blue understones, and the dark asters Prince and Lady in Black. Plants that grow blacker the more sunshine they are exposed to are Sambucus Black Beauty, and the ruffled-leafed heuchera Black Beauty. Black mondo grass, aka *Ophiopogon planescans* Black Knight, is colored dark gray and grows slowly, barely creeps, and makes a nice sensuous base in a garden. Good black grasses for container gardens are *Lysimachia nummularia aurea*, and Mondo grass. A trick with black plants is to avoid planting them under a shrub, where they will not be prominent but will end up looking like a shadow of the shrub, leaving a black hole. On the other hand, that too could be a cool effect!

cultivating the perfect goth garden

Many goths love to garden, and three who do discuss the flora in their lives. *C.B.*, one of *The † Section*, has been goth gardening for about seven years in her backyard in Buffalo, New York, and has won awards for her roses. *Rain*, one of the six goth parents, currently has a container garden in Columbus, Ohio, with nine years experience with her black thumb. *Martine*, a member of the goth band Masochistic Religion, has been goth gardening for about ten years, currently on the roof of her building in downtown Toronto.

C.B.: "Before getting cats, I planted mainly abortifacients and other poisonous plants (belladonna, Solomon's seal, and those herbs they tell you not to use while pregnant). Now, it's wormwood, hyssop, nicotiana, moonflowers, black tulips (alas! a rather dark purple), night-scented-stock, and roses. Lavaglut (lavaglow) is a striking dark-red floribunda rose. It is very cool to be able to get and track down plants that were in existence when your favorite author was alive. Smell the same flowers that Poe smelled! 'Old garden' roses bloom only once per year but can be quite old—even from the 1790s!—and are very special. Actually, I think white flowers are better for a 'goth garden,' because they glow under moonlight, and you can actually see them at the time most of us sit outside lounging around in our velvet finery. Moonflowers bloom only at night. Talk about a flower created just for goths!"

Rain: "I grow poppies and ivies. I used a row of black tulips in front of the house for a non-traditional look."

Martine: "A good goth garden design is not just about surface. It has some deeper meaning. It is poetry and architecture. I like dangerous beauty: delphiniums, monkshood, digitalis, belladonna. I like fragrance: shrub roses in white and red, plus a Blue Nile rose, oriental lilies. My garden is like an opiate; it transports me. I have black hollyhocks and pansies. I have a ginkgo tree I'm trying to keep short and horizontal. My favorite arrangement of the past has to be a four-by-eight-foot plot I called 'The Killing Fields,' in which morning glory and mexican bamboo were pitted against each other in a death match that would not be won this century. Also, the baby's breath in the lavatory bowl was a nice touch."

Goth gardeners tend to use unusual ornamentation in their gardens.

C.B.: has "an iron cross tombstone, date of death October 31, 1888! I only put it out on special occasions, due to the neighbors."

Rain: likes to include "ornaments like fairies, blue glass/wire butterflies with climbing ivy, and roses."

Martine: utilizes "barbed wire, police motorcycle fenders placed on either side of the stairs, melted baby doll heads on metal spikes atop the fence, to which were lashed hand-bleached beef femurs, smashed electric guitars, over and through which grew ivy. At the bottom of this garden

Morbid Curiosity

Assisting a Suicide
Auschwitz
Cadaver Lab
Cemetery Tours
Civil War Ghosts
Crack Babies
Creepy Dolls
Cross-Dressing
Danse Macabre
Exotic Dancing
Folsom Prison
Graveyard Monuments
Haunted Sanitarium
Heroin Withdrawal
Impersonating Death
Mad Cow Disease
Mormon Youth
Mortuary Scandal
Phantom Hounds
Pittsburgh
Police Photographs
Postmortem Baptism
Prison Visits
Rotting Skulls
Sacramento's Old City Cemetery
Spirit Possession
SPAM
Tarantula Breeding
Voodoo
Zombie Salmon

100% TRUE

Issue 2
1998
$4.95

Courtesy of Loren Rhodes, Automatism Press

was a galvanized metal Mastaba-style tomb $12 \times 8 \times 8$ feet. In the last garden there was a griffin holding a ball, a cast iron lamp, some stone urns, a stone lion, and a pond with a fountain in it."

The goth gardeners have suggestions for gothing up a garden, whether it's in a yard, in a container, in window boxes, on a rooftop, indoors, outdoors, or anywhere growth is possible.

C.B.: "Even if it dies, you can just leave the plant there, and that would be goth too."

Rain: "A lot of goths I know lean toward herb gardens, for home use. I've planted herbs in the past to use for cooking, but I know others who use them for home remedies."

Martine: "Get a photo of yourself in your garden. Regretably, neither my gardens nor myself show up on film. However, I believe that the Gothic Society [of Toronto] is in possession of several photos of me, beating Morpheus at croquet while very drunk on the absinthe I made from my gardening exploits. Absinthe is, of course, very good for you, and gives you human powers!"

raising the goth learning curve

Many people relax by reading magazines, and goths are no exception. Beyond the usual music and fashion publications, intelligent goths are constantly seeking information on obscure and arcane subjects and minutiae outside the realm of interest of the mainstream. For eight years, out of San Francisco, Loren Rhoads has been publishing the magazine *Morbid Curiosity,* which, she says, "focuses on the morbid aspects of real life, both as a catharsis for the writers and as a reality check for readers." These are personal-account articles, like "people who have battled cancer, or escaped murderous boyfriends, or survived urban violence." In addition, there are brushes with the supernatural, visits to odd and creepy places around the globe, medical catastrophes, suicide attempts, war horrors . . . anything a human being can experience and still survive. "The UK's terrific glossy magazine *Bizarre* calls *Morbid Curiosity* 'fascinating front-line journalism,' which I thought was high praise."

Loren obviously dearly loves her publication and the people who submit material to it, but there is a downside, one which led her to a story of her own. She has a constant correspondent, a man she finds frightening; he is imprisoned for knifing his roommates to death. "I tried to dissuade him from sending in his story, but finally he submitted it. It took a week before I could bring myself to read it. I believe there is enough cruelty in the world. I insist on a sense of humanity and compassion in the stories I publish. This guy had no empathy for the two human beings he removed from the planet. His greatest regret about the murders is that they landed him in prison. After I rejected the story, he sent me a Christmas card. He still wants to be friends. I'm afraid he'll show up on my doorstep."

In the goth world, there are several lovely publications which apply an especially exquisite touch to the artistic exploration of obscure subject matter, often resurrecting the past.

Courtesy of The Sentimentalist

Madeline Virbasius-Walsh is editor of *The Sentimentalist* out of New York City. She began the publication six years ago as a "small literary/art quarterly with a modern interpretation of some of my favorite fin de siècle literary and artistic journals [of the nineteenth century]." Originally this in-print Victorian's curio cabinet was published in black and white to "recall the spirit of those older, now infamous journals. Our focus was on contemporary underground/alternative artists, poets, musicians and writers who have a sort of turn-of-the-century aesthetic in their work. An old-world-meets-new kind of feeling."

The magazine includes features on European cities, fashion spreads of goth clothing designers, band and artist interviews (for example, Peter Murphy, David Bowie, and Rasputina), and reviews, and has had articles on goth-interest subjects like Art Nouveau jewelry, pre-Raphaelite fashion, absinthe, Victorian society, and the films of Klaus Kinski. Madeline says, "We also put some focus on obscure poets and artists who deserve exposure."

The Sentimentalist Web site has taken on a larger focus over time, and now frequently runs contests, with prizes like the latest *Mediaeval Baebes* CD. Madeline says "We plan to do more contests in the future."

Courtesy of Ver Sacrum

Another stylish magazine given to arcane subject matter is Pisa, Italy's *Ver Sacrum* (Sacred Worm), run by Luca de Santis, aka Christian Dex. This delightful publication began as a photocopied journal in 1993 and by 1995 went to print, and now runs online. Luca says he publishes online to allow more international contributions, but "We love the 'historical' [printed] version of *Ver Sacrum* too much to neglect it completely, so sooner or later it will be reborn from the ashes."

In addition to the usual aspects of goth such as fashion and music, every issue has "a monographic set of articles that analyze a specific topic from various points of view. We have dealt with vampirism, female images in decadent literature and art, the Black Plague, Gothic in literature and art, witchcraft, death rituals, horror theater, eroticism and perversion, and so on. Our goal is to analyze the gothic spirit, wherever it casts its dark shadow. To get in-depth to the root of gothic." For Luca personally, the magazine "has been a sort of escape into a spiritual and artistic world, compared to the disillusion and crudeness of everyday life."

Ver Sacrum (named for the nineteenth-century literary journal) also published the first book on the gothic in Italy, *Gothica*, which sold out quickly and received quantity and quality mainstream press. Another venture was a collaboration with the gothic fanzine *Neogothic*, wherein they organized "a real unplugged *Ataraxia* concert, held in a deserted village in the mountains near Bologna. You had to walk thirty minutes to get there. People came from all parts of Italy, bringing the candles and torches that lighted the event at night. The singer was so touched by the atmosphere, he cried. It was magic!"

URLs

gothic.net
www.gothic.net

Dark Culture magazine
www.darkculture.net

Grave Concerns e-zine
www.angelfire.com/ny2/graveconcerns/index.html

The Asylum Eclectica–Morbid Fact du Jour
www.asylumeclectica.com/morbid/

Cavalorn
www.newaeonbooks.com

Macross Ascendant
www.digitalangel.com

www.altgothic.com

Sangre Eterna
www.sangreterna.cl/

Neil Gaiman
www.neilgaiman.com/

Jhonen Vasquez
www.lambiek.net/vasquez_j.htm

Oh my Goth (Voltaire)
www.voltaire.net/omg.html

Marcel de Jong
www.marceldejong.com

Writhe and Shine
www.writheandshine.com

The Black Rose Company
www.sendblackroses.com/

Morbid Curiosity
www.charnel.com/automatism

The Sentimentalist
www.asthetik.com/sentimentalist

Ver Sacrum
www.versacrum.com

10

VISITING THE VAULTS

One Ticket to the Catacombs, Please!

cemetery picnics and other diversions

Goths have discovered what the status quo has not—cemeteries are just about the last places available to be alone in the city. They are perfect for quietly strolling, leisurely reading, drawing, singing, simply spending time with a loved one. Old-growth plants, like rose bushes that can date back to the Victorian era, grow in cemeteries and are perfect for taking cuttings.

When populations were still small enough that most people lived in rural settings and little villages, it was easy enough to bury the dead. The bodies of the lord of the land and his family went directly down to the crypts beneath the castle, where they rested eternally in stone coffins. Serfs who worked the land were simply buried on the land. Community was everything, in life and in death. But when people began migrating to cities, and the population of those cities expanded, funerals became a more difficult affair. At first, nobility and clergy could be placed beneath the floor of the cathedral—those closest to the holiest spots inside the church, like the altar, had either supported the church financially or had lived the most pious lives. Parishioners complained that the churches did not smell very good, and it's easy to understand why. The ordinary faithful were buried in the churchyard, and there too positioning proved crucial. Those buried close to the church on the east side had the advantage: The resur-

Types of Cemeteries

Church vaults: Inside a church, near statues or areas of intense worship, beneath the floor in subterranean rooms or vaults. Usually reserved for clergy or important persons.

Churchyard/Graveyard: Small, flat, organized, situated beside a church, may or may not be enclosed by a fence. Burials for church members and families.

Family plots: Located near a rural house or a farm. Private, family members only.

Forest: A large piece of land with cemetery buildings around a central hilly part, graves hidden in dense foliage, dirt paths, artistically disorganized or haphazard feel.

Garden: Medium-height stones, a few obelisks. Ornamental monuments clustered within designated lots, not necessarily aligned in rows. Trees often line the paved roads and cars can drive through.

Lawn: Resembles a suburban lawn, clipped grass, footpaths, low stones, or metal plates at ground level. Non-ornamental. One central roadway.

Park: Slightly hilly, trees old and random growth, can be wild with undergrowth, asymmetrical. Concrete, flagstone or dirt paths, similar to larger city parks.

Rural: Small, located in the country, usually in a field. Burials of area residents.

rected would be able to watch the sunrise on Judgment Day! The north corner of the graveyard was considered the Devil's domain, reserved for stillborns, bastards, and strangers.

By the Middle Ages, populations in cities had exploded. Wars, and nearly two centuries of plague—black and other types—culled populations dramatically, and burials became impossible to carry out. Enormous "bone pits" were dug and bodies dumped into these communal depositories on top of those who had died before them. It wasn't until the middle of the 1700s that death reached a crisis pitch, and something had to be done. Cemetery design came into vogue.

According to Katherine Ramsland, author of *Cemetery Stories*, garden cemeteries—the new designs of the late 1800s that resembled a British garden—"merged nature and art." Consequently, "The public was lured into the sanctuary of the dead."

Katherine goes on to say, "The extensive landscaping inspired many sculptors to display their talents. Tourists came in droves, and artists soon found themselves in demand."

The Victorians took to cemeteries (the word means *sleeping chamber*) . . . well, the way goths do. Weekend outings with the entire family were a common practice, a chance to socialize and "take in the air." They held picnics, admired the statuary on the graves and mausoleums of the rich and famous, contemplated poetry and the mysteries of life, paid their respects to deceased friends and family, and enjoyed a visit to the frequently adjoining arboretum.

Katherine believes goths are enamored because "[cemeteries] inspire us to ponder possibilities, and since most people avoid the subject [of death], goths can claim it as their own special arena."

Today, cemeteries are more for the dead, not the living. They have fallen out of favor as places to visit, apart from mourning, or for tapophiles (lovers of tombs)—and goths, who are often tapophiles.

Goths have been picnicking in cemeteries since . . . well, the beginning. Possibly the first recorded instructions for a goth picnic appeared in *The Web*, a print publication out of Chicago, put together by Heather Spear in the early 1990s. In one issue, a picnic is described at Gore Hill Cemetery, with an accompanying list of general suggestions for goth picnikers.

It was the Chinese, around 300 B.C., who appear to have made the first rubbings. They used permanent colored wax and dyes to reproduce information on parchment, basically laws, slogans, and messages carved into the stone of temples. Rubbings are a kind of missing link in human history that led from records in stone to records on paper—a bit of a forerunner of the printing press. Over the centuries, rubbers began to favor images, done on stone and metal. Many Asian countries display large rubbings they call *batiks* (not the same as the fabric known as batik). Rubbings can also be done on surfaces like architectural reliefs, and even on leaves. Many of the more commonly seen rubbings come from churches—Medieval knights and dames and popes are popular.

But gravestones produce the most intriguing rubbings. The flat stones of New England's cemeteries have long been favorite haunts of rubbers. The Fugit Hora (Time is Fleeting) light-bulb death's heads began as crude, cartoonlike images dug into slate by the Pilgrims in the 1600s and evolved to the more sophisticated designs of the 1800s before they finally disappeared.

Epitaphs themselves can be worth reproducing. One perennial favorite from the gravestone of John Wilson in Georgia reads: "I told you I was sick!"

Gravestone Artwear is a ten-year-old mother-and-daughter operation based in York Harbor, Maine. Paulette and her daughter Cassandra specialize in reproducing Colonial, Celtic, and Victorian gravestone carvings, on T-shirts, sorcerers' pouches, stationery, and velvet garments like cloaks, scarves, and dresses. They also sell natural-ingredient soaps shaped like New England tombstones, and kits to do tombstone rubbings.

It was Cassandra who inadvertently began this company by carving silk screens from gravestone rubbings, then printing the designs on posters and fabric as part of her art school portfolio. These were given to friends and sold at fairs, and soon she and her mother opened a workshop, with space for a retail shop. "Naturally, our items are dark in nature—no bright colors for us," Paulette says. "Black is our favorite non-color, and thus the word was out—visit this macabre shop where black is dominant." They decorated their shop with "gravestone rubbings we have done or acquired over thirty years. Our black dog joins us most days." And above Cassandra's production area is their prized possession, a ten-by-two-foot black sign with gold-leaf lettering advertising the Austin Embalming and Mortuary business. "It dates back to 1912. When we rented the space we didn't know that back then this is where the embalming took place. The

How to Hold a Goth Picnic in the Cemetery

Suggestions adapted from Chicago's original Gore Hill picnickers

Organize! Pick a date when no other major goth events are being held, or events in or near the cemetery. (You can't help spontaneous funerals! But it's certainly better to skirt the mourners rather than rush up to the open grave and ask "Can I peek at the corpse?")

Advertise! Make flyers and Web sites with: date, place, time, how radically to dress, and a phone number for info. It's good to be specific: bring a blanket to sit on; bring food (no, it's not obvious); water (don't drink from the water used to refresh flowers on graves); sunscreen and sun umbrellas; insect repellent; something warm if it turns cool at nights.

Hypothesize! Distribute four times the number of flyers as you want attendees. Bigger=more attention. This has a negative effect, in that you don't want annoying elements to show up. On the other hand, if people don't know you're having a picnic, they won't come, will they?

Utilize! Pick a discreet spot, preferably under the shade of a tree, keep the noise level down, clean up your trash.

Proselytize! If the police or cemetery authorities show up, be friendly. People have the right to congregate in a cemetery for peaceful purposes, and you can even tell them you are reenacting the Victorian tradition. But you sould avoid identifying yourself as a member of a witches coven, don't mention that your brother is starting a teenage vampire cult, don't discuss your love of death and decay.

Deversify! While in the cemetery, there is plenty to do besides eat and get drunk. One annual picnic in Montréal, run by Cemetery Crow, allows him to do group photographs. Another activity is gravestone rubbings.

funeral parlor was three doors down the street and caskets were made about ¼ quarter mile away and brought to our location by horse-drawn carriage."

Paulette and Cassandra are in love with gravestones. "Our research has taken us all over New England, and even on a trip to Ireland to research ancient high crosses. Gravestone carving was the first American stone sculpture in the New World, and old burying grounds and Victorian cemeteries are museums without walls."

About 30 percent of Gravestone Artwear customers are goth. "And one of our stitchers is a beautiful, very stylish goth young adult who has a five-year-old daughter. We gave her some extra velvet fabric and she created mother/daughter matching dresses and cloaks. These two looked so fabulous that tourists in our summer coastal resort town had them posing for photos. We were so proud! They even stopped traffic!"

Goths visiting New England will be delighted to learn about the nighttime "Ghostly Tour throughout the summer, which departs our shop each evening at 8 P.M. (except Sunday), for the old burying ground in our village."

wicked holidays

Paris

Many of the world's most exquisite cemeteries were created out of necessity. Paris had its Cimetière des Innocents, a mass gravesite filled with plague victims, among others, located about where Les Halles is now. This was consecrated but contaminated ground, with crumbling stone walls used as a barrier between living and dead. At the Cimetière des Innocents so many corpses were heaped one upon another that not only did bones often fall over the walls and onto the streets, but disease-causing seepage that included adopcere (body fat that turns into a soaplike substance) came through at ground level to accost passersby. The stench must have been horrible.

In 1786, Paris decided to close down the Cimetière des Innocents and move the remains of about seventeen million people twenty-five meters underground, into the quarries over which the city was built around the tenth century, tunnels that had existed when the Romans held this part of the world. The massive tunnel system beneath Paris holds what is now the world-famous Catacombs of Paris.

Only a small section of the Catacombs is open to the public. Wandering the deep-in-the-earth corridors crammed with bones and skulls, many artistically arranged by the laborers who carted the remains below ground, is a spiritual and silencing experience for most goths.

Today, Paris has many small cemeteries and three major ones. All of its cemeteries are home to stray felines. Cemetery visitors feed them, and locals set out covered boxes for the cats to sleep in during inclement weather. One cemetery in Nancy, France—northeast of Paris and near Alsace—contains an actual cat condo, which houses hundreds of felines, fed and housed by the city government.

Cimetière du Père Lachaise—which receives over one million visitors a year—is now easily accessible by Métro, but back in the 1600s this area was far outside Paris proper, surrounded by a high-criminal area. (The city of Paris, at that time, like most European cities, was enclosed by fortification walls.) In the seventeenth century the Jesuits used the land for a hospice. Then it became a meeting place under the guidance of Père Lachaise (Father Lachaise), confessor of Louis XIV. In 1803 Napoleon, Prefect of Paris, bought the land to be used as a cemetery, and its history of death began. This planet contains many wonderful cemeteries, but perhaps none are as exquisite as Père Lachaise. Gorgeous rows of narrow crypts that resemble gothic telephone booths line quiet stone walkways. Many famous dead lie buried throughout the hills and lowlands within the cemetery's walls, and each grave has a story: The naked Egyptian Art Deco sculpture of the outrageous English homosexual author Oscar Wilde, created by Jacob Epstein, had the penis cut off (it has since been reattached). The tomb of the Italian painter and sculptor Amedeo Modigliani can be found here, along with the tomb of his lover, who, overwhelmed by grief, killed herself days after he died of meningitis. The grave of the beloved French author Colette is always blanketed with flowers. Other famous dead include Charles Nodier—an early French writer of vampire tales; Honoré de Balzac, who liked to "bury" the characters in his stories at Père Lachaise; brilliant, asthmatic French author Marcel Proust; composer Frédéric Chopin; French torch singer Edith Piaf; the playwright Molière; Jim Morrison of the Doors . . . the list goes on and on. Perhaps the statue here most familiar to goths is the tomb of French radical/revolutionary Vincent François Raspail. A sculpture of a life-size shrouded "weeper"—purported to be his wife—clings to the window.

Cimetière du Père Lachaise
Photo by Hugues Leblanc

Your mortal existence
was brief and adverse.
The blind masses accuse
you of excess desire,
Babble about a thousand
frivolous objects,
And refuse you even the
homage of a thought.
But vegetating with the mistake
they completely
Die, a thousand times better
still their fate.

The Catacombs of Paris, Italian poem from the section
for the Remains of St. Nicolas des Champs (1804)

Madame X "[Tends to] seek out local cemeteries wherever I go. I have visited native burial sites, catacombs all over the world, cemeteries in places like Transylvania, London, Rome, Madrid, Paris, Portugal, the Canary Islands, Mexico, Puerto Rico, Canada, and all over the US."

Malinda "The sculptures in cemeteries–I am fascinated by the way that people remember the dead. We all seek validation in life and wonder how we will be remembered. Cemeteries offer a peek into the possibilities of how those you leave behind will represent you to the living world."

Taoist admits he's lucky. "There is a beautiful cemetery near my home, at the Chapel of the Holy Ghost, a ruined church several hundred years old. Its cemetery is disused and there are lots of trees and some extremely ancient graves and tombs. I love it there."

WantonBlood "In a way [cemeteries] put life in perspective. I have never felt more alive than at some of the moments I spent there, with friends and people special to me. Cemeteries are like parks, well-groomed but in cooperation with nature."

Dead Can Dance used this deliciously morbid image on the cover of their CD *Within the Realm of a Dying Sun*. Père Lachaise is the Louvre of cemeteries, with everything France offers best—beauty and passionate history interwoven into an exquisite art of death.

The most tragically romantic cemetery story is that of the star-crossed Medieval lovers Abélard and Héloise, the oldest residents of Cimetière du Père Lachaise. Letters survive the couple, detailing a tempestuous history.

It was the twelfth century in France. Pierre Abélard was a handsome thirty-year-old student at the University of Paris, one of the new wave of learning institutions forming at that time. He was confident and challenging, and destined for great things. And he had never been in love—until he met Héloise.

The beautiful Héloise wandered the cloisters of a Paris cathedral. The niece of Canon Fulbert, Héloise was an anomaly for the times: unmarried, not a nun, she was allowed to study, and was known as a brilliant individual. Abélard boarded with Uncle Fulbert and, in exchange, provided instruction to Héloise.

Abélard and Héloise were perfectly suited—both attractive, intelligent, and possessed of a love of learning—but their ignited passions led to tragedy. Héloise was compromised in an era when a woman married a man or the church, and she had done neither. Abélard's lectures became uninspired, as his fascinations lay elsewhere. Rumors spread throughout Paris of an illicit joining.

Uncle Fulbert separated the couple, but soon Héloise got word to her beloved Abélard that she was pregnant. They fled to Abélard's family, where Héloise stayed until she delivered a son, Astrolabe. Abélard returned to Paris torn; to marry would legitimize the relationship but it would hamper his chances of a career as a church scholar. He wrote Uncle Fulbert that he would marry Héloise, "whom I had seduced," provided the union could remain secret.

Héloise believed her uncle would not be satisfied, and offered to sacrifice herself for the sake of Abélard's career by not marrying him. But ultimately they wed in secret, Uncle Fulbert in attendance, then parted, rarely seeing one another to perpetrate the myth that they were not involved. The baby remained with Abélard's family.

Héloise had been right about Uncle Fulbert—his pride was wounded, and he let the marriage be known publicly. To protect Abélard, Héloise denied the rumors, and Uncle Fulbert beat her. To protect her, Abélard sent Héloise to a convent at Argenteuil. He made the mistake of asking her to wear the vestments of the nuns, but not the veil—which indicated the taking of vows.

Further enraged, Uncle Fulbert hired two men who bribed Abélard's servants. They broke into his rooms in the dead of night and castrated him. With few choices left him, Abélard became a Dominican, entering the abbey of St. Denis. Before doing so, he convinced Héloise to wear the veil, against the wishes of her friends. She took the vows perhaps not so much for love of the Church as for love of Abélard.

Years passed. Abélard pursued theology and Héloise became a prioress, ultimately at an abbey at Paraclete established by Abélard. Eventually they resumed a relationship, but one far different from their early passions. Héloise for the remainder of her life was devoted to a man who could no longer be her husband. Abélard had won few friends in the religious-political climate, his career marked by controversy, and her support helped sustain him in times of bleakness.

When Abélard died in 1142, his body was brought to the Paraclete, where, upon her death, Héloise finally joined him for eternity. Four hundred years after their demise, the coffins of the star-crossed lovers were moved to Cimetière du Père Lachaise to rest in peace together, in perpetuity.

Cimetière de Montparnasse is home to the remains of Charles Baudelaire, author of *Les fleurs du mal* (The Flowers of Evil) (see Chapter 11) and other dark poetry, and translator of Edgar Allan Poe's works into French. This cemetery was created by joining three farms, and its stones date back to the early 1800s. It is a large flat expanse of graves and crypts, with lovely and unusual monuments, for instance, the life-size bronze sculpture of Charles Pigeon (inventor of a non-exploding gas lamp) and his wife in bed together, fully clothed. Mr. Pigeon is half rising from his bed, startled by the angel above. Also buried here are writers Simone de Beauvoir and Guy de Maupassant, as well as Camille Saint-Saëns composer of "Danse Macabre;" American actress Jean Seberg; and sculptor Constantin Brancusi, famous for the work *Le Baiser* (The Kiss).

Cimetière de Montmartre, the smallest of the large Parisian cemeteries, has an intimate feel. Located near the famous Pigalle (prostitution) district, it is multi-leveled, with the charm of Père Lachaise but a slightly darker en-

XjÜsĆcŘuĊifyX "They are beautiful places with many stories to tell, and it's really neat to try to imagine how people died, why they died, and what their lives were like. It's not always dark and depressing, but can be peaceful and interesting."

Arantèle

Photo by Cathy Brown

Highgate Cemetery
Photo by Stéphane Lord

vironment. Here lie the remains of painter Edgar Dégas and filmmaker Francois Truffaut. Because Montmartre is less visited, the boxes left by Parisians for the multitude of stray cats are kept inside the narrow crypts.

London

Many amazing cemeteries exist in England, but everyone's favorite is the now barely accessible Highgate.

Highgate Cemetery opened in the 1830s. Soon, so many were buried here that new ground to the East was bought, across Swain's Lane. Burials didn't take place in the eastern side until the 1860s. A tunnel beneath Swain's Lane connects the two halves, built mainly for pallbearers to walk coffins through.

Highgate over the years fell into abandonment to the point where, in the 1970s, a number of vampire hunters spotted the undead skulking through the grounds. Armed with stakes and garlic, they competed with Satanists who used the cemetery for rituals. More than one tomb was opened, more than one corpse disinterred; several pentacles were drawn on stones. The police came, court cases ensued, and at least one person was imprisoned, it now appears unjustly. Highgate Cemetery fell into desolation, the very condition goths appreciate most.

Ultimately, after changing hands a number of times, the historic cemetery was bought for $1—imagine!—by the Friends of Highgate, an organization that now conducts tours of only a small portion of the western side—the oldest part—of the cemetery. The eastern, less evocative half is wide open. But on the west, tourists are under the watchful eyes of elderly tour guides and are not permitted to leave the designated path to explore. Understandably, Friends of Highgate has a stake in preserving the cemetery. They make extraordinary efforts at removing the perpetually expanding wild growth, and do repairs to fallen stones and broken fences. Yet the fact that so much of Highgate is now unavailable to the public is a great misfortune, especially to goths, who adore and respect cemeteries. From what one is permitted to see, western Highgate inspires fantasies of what cemetery legends are composed of—walking corpses, ghosts of unrequited loves, graves that open and lure people to their doom . . .

About 170,000 people are buried at Highgate Cemetery. In the western cemetery, the circuitous winding paths led to it being dubbed "the most magical place in London." What delights visitors is the romantic decay, surrounded by an amazing forest of rambling hills and trees. One of the pleasures of this cemetery is strolling along the dirt paths and glimpsing old tombstones, angels, and sculptures half hidden in the foliage. Over the low rises, past centuries-old trees, sloping pathways appear, which are commonly called "Avenue of Death" and "Street of the Dead." A wide walk known as "Egyptian Avenue" leads to an anomaly, an enormous neo-Arabic construction built around a majestic cedar tree that predates the cemetery by about 150 years. This awe-inspiring monument to and for the dead—with fat pillars, a columbarium and twenty family catacombs within the inner and lower circles surrounded by a high retaining wall with low graves before it known as The Lebanon Circle—is situated at the cemetery's highest point.

Angelus

Highgate's famous dead include the Victorian writer Marian (born Mary Ann) Evans, forced by the era which sired her to write under the nom de plume George Eliot. Evans scandalized society by having an affair with a married man for twenty-seven years, living with him for twenty of those years, and then, when he died, she re-shocked her world by immediately marrying an old friend of the family. She was buried next to her lover, with her husband just a few graves up the slope.

Radclyffe Hall is another famous writer interred at Highgate. Hall, known as "John," smoked cigars and dressed in men's clothing. In 1901 she toured the New World in an old jalopy with her female cousin, a fierce one-eyed dog for protection, and a couple of six-shooters. Hall lived with her second female lover Una Troubridge for many years and it was Una into whose hands she placed the awesome responsibility for giving Hall the go-ahead to write *The Well of Loneliness*, which exposed their relationship to the world, and brought Hall mounds of scandal and negative literary criticism. The book was banned in England. Since then, *The Well of Loneliness* has gone on to sell millions of copies.

Other famous bones in Highgate include writer Charles Dickens, who left us a hideously realistic view of poverty in Victorian England, Elizabeth Madox Brown, wife and model of Pre-Raphaelite painter Ford Madox Brown, and Socialist Karl Marx.

But undoubtedly the most intriguing goth-interest graves at Highgate are those holding the remains of Pre-Raphaelite painter Dante Gabriel Rossetti, his sister Christina, and Elizabeth Siddal, Rossetti's tormented wife and the most famous and favored of the Pre-Raphaelite models. (see Chapter 11)

Elizabeth was discovered working in a milliner's shop near Piccadilly. Her mournful visual aesthetic struck the romantic Pre-Raphaelite Brotherhood of painters as the epitome of fragile womanhood, and she modeled for many of them, including the big three, William Holman Hunt, John Everett Millais, and Dante Gabriel Rossetti. To pose as Ophelia for Millais, Elisabeth was required to lie in an iron bathtub of tepid water, heated by candles underneath. She contracted pneumonia. It's thought this was the beginning of a lifetime of illness.

Rossetti fell madly, insanely in love with "Lizzy." She lived with him for a number of years, and although he was obsessed with her, he managed to avoid marrying her. Back then, a woman modeling for painters was considered not much better than a whore. An unmarried woman was bad enough, but one living in sin . . . Lizzy needed marriage to legitimize her. By the time Rossetti could bring himself to tie the knot, the relationship had deteriorated. Lizzy's ongoing ill health, his perpetual meanderings, and a miscarriage that seemed to break her spirit led the moody Lizzy to addiction and eventual death by overdose of laudanum.

Rossetti remained consumed by Lizzy until his own death, perhaps more so after her demise than when she was alive. As her body lay for viewing in the sitting room of their house in Highgate village, Rossetti tenderly placed into the coffin sheets of parchment with love poems he had written to her. The lid closed, and Lizzy took his romantic verse to her grave.

Seven years passed. Rossetti became increasingly addicted to alcohol and chloral (usually the chlorination of ethyl alcohol), among other things. His career as both a painter and a writer was on the skids. It was his literary agent who persuaded the reluctant Rossetti that the poems buried with Elizabeth—of which there were no copies—might be published and revive his career. Lizzy's exhumation took place after dark, when the public could not witness this grisly act. As a bonfire lit the eerie scene, and while the bells of St. Michael's Church chimed midnight, Lizzy's coffin was hauled to the surface. Rossetti, unable to face the macabre sight of his wife's corpse, hid at home. Reports from those present indicate that decomposition had not touched her. She had always been pale of complexion; now, only her auburn tresses were longer. Elizabeth Siddal looked as lovely as the day she had been buried.

The manuscripts were disinfected, published, and . . . met with lukewarm reviews. They did not garner the attention that Rossetti was led to expect. Until his death, he regretted removing them.

His life terminated in a haze of addiction and madness. He remained haunted by the ghost of his dead wife until the end.

Toronto

Toronto's largest cemetery is Mount Pleasant, home to the Massey Crypt, one of the most unusual and gorgeous pieces of cemetery architecture in the world. The building, constructed between 1890–1894 of large stones, is a mélange of complementery shapes, which include a tower with tiny stained glass windows. As astonishing as the outside is, it is through the crypt's metal and glass doors that the magic occurs. Inside at the back, the large altar is always adorned with an enormous bouquet of dying flowers. As the sun sets each day, the light pouring through the stained glass rises up the sides and back of the crypt casting the most breathtaking element of morbidity and decay onto the altar.

Massey Crypt interior, Toronto
Photo by Hugues Leblanc

Lovely as this large cemetery is, one of the smaller cemeteries of Toronto stands out. The Toronto Necropolis has headstones dating to the mid-1800s. The layout of this cemetery is singularly appealing. It lies at the end of a dead end, hidden from the residential neighborhood on three sides, and on the fourth slopes down a high embankment towards the Don River. Here there are no crypts, just stones, and a fascinating feeling of loneliness and antiquity that permeates the atmosphere.

Montréal

The bilingual city of Montréal (aka the France of North America) where a mountain dominates the terrain is home to three enormous graveyards. Mount Royal is the English cemetery, Shaar Hashomayim the Jewish cemetery, and Notre-Dame-des-Neiges the French cemetery, although English and French are buried in all three. Cimetière Notre-Dame-des-Neiges is the final resting place of tormented French Canadian poet Émile Nelligan, who spent most of his unhappy life in mental institutions, diagnosed as schizophrenic. His 160 poems are rich in symbolism and imagery and many speak of dreaming and death. In a city caught in a deep freeze between December and March every year, Nelligan's haunting despair as he writes of ice crystals forming on the windows, obliterating the outside world, is a peek into the mind of this afflicted soul.

Massey Crypt exterior, Toronto
Photo by Hugues Leblanc

Cimetière du Notre-Dame-des-Neiges is also famous for its gorgeous nineteenth-century crypts, with ornate filigree metallic grillwork doors

Cimetière du Notre-Dame-des-Neiges, Montréal, Québec
Photo by Hugues Leblanc

Danse Macabres, Clusone, Italy
Photo by Hugues Leblanc

that allow viewing of interiors. As replacement doors are installed, this unique glimpse into the past becomes less and less available. Still, there are crypts where one sees wood and metal coffins from the 1800s stacked, some adult size, some small enough for infants, adorned with elaborate hardware, accompanied by crypt furnishings like decaying kneeling chairs, dusty crucifixes attached to the walls, overturned flower vases and lanterns.

The Italian Alps

Danse Macabre is the name given to the fifteenth-century "plague-art" paintings and drawings done by anonymous artists found on cemetery and church walls. (see Chapter 11)

Italy is one of the few places remaining with early *Danse Macabre* artwork still extant. In 1485, Giacomo Borlone painted a *Danse Macabre* on the exterior of the Oratory of the Disciplinarians, a church for an order of flagellant brothers in Clusone, Italy. In 1519, Simone Baschenis painted his *Danse Macabre* on the outside of the cemetery chapel San Stephano in the village of Carisolo. Then, in 1539, he reproduced those images high on the walls of the church of St-Vigile in the village of Pinzolo, two kilometers away. These last two villages are in the Alps, not easily accessible, and require a pilgrimage of sorts.

Venice

Italy has no shortage of amazingly artistic graveyards, including San Michele Cemetery, founded in 1810, located on an island visible from Venice. This island was formerly a prison until France took over the region in the 1800s and Napoleon ordered the Venetians to ferry their dead through the canals to the island. The cemetery which takes up the entire island is run by Franciscan monks who tend the garden-like grounds.

Genoa

Perhaps the most important and lovely cemetery in Italy lies in Genoa. The enormous Il Cimitero di Stagliano dating from the eighteenth century is crammed with neoclassic porticos, Gothic chapels, and statuary. One sentimental statue reproduces the small, bent form of Teresa Campodonico. The poem carved below recounts how she sold her nuts in sunshine and rain to earn her daily bread, and also to propel her image into the future by way of this monument! The grave of Constance Lloyd is in the Protestant section. Lloyd, the wife of Oscar Wilde, died at the age of forty in 1898, less than a year after Wilde's release from prison. Shamed by his imprisonment, she changed her name and that of her two sons to Holland.

Palermo

Palermo on the island of Sicily is home to the Catacombe dei Cappuccini, located beneath the church Convento dei Cappuccino, built in 1623 on the remains of the original medieval church.

It all began in 1534 when the newly formed order of Capuchin monks arrived in Palermo. Their first cemetery was a well where the bodies of their dead were tossed one over the other—cappuccino coffee is named for the color of their robes. In 1599 those corpses were exhumed and discovered to be preserved. Later that year, a local priest decided to continue this accidental habit and intentionally mummified Brother Silvestro so he could pray to him. Soon other monks, and then the locals, wanted in on the action, and mummification came into vogue. Priests, professionals, and professors have their own section, as do children and women. One area is for virgins, so designated because of the metal headbands they wear.

The normal method of preservation was simply to place a corpse in one of the passageway cells called "strainers," composed of the local tufaceous (porous limestone) soil, which dried out the body in about eight months. Once dehydrated, the mummy was then dressed in the finery of the day and displayed along the walls of the catacomb, in a coffin, or placed reclining or standing in a niche, alone or as part of a tableau, wherever and however they had requested to be positioned for eternity. The practice continued until the late nineteenth century, when mummification was outlawed. By then nearly 1,000 mummies were on display at the Catacombe dei Cappuccini.

The mummies of Palermo—in various stages of decay—are fascinating, but they are not pretty. One imagines that George Romero saw them before shooting his now-classic zombie movie *Night of the Living Dead*. These mummies make an appearance in the opening shots of Werner Herzog's 1979 remake of the classic vampire silent film *Nosferatu the Vampyre*.

In the 1920s an exception was made and one additional mummy was permitted entry. Dr. Solafia of Palermo embalmed the best-preserved corpse in the catacombs, two-year-old Rosalia Lombardo; unfortunately he took the ingredients of his chemical concoction to his grave.

Mummies of the Catacombe dei Cappuccini
Photo by Hugues Leblanc

Guanajuato

Guanajuato is a dusty city five hours northeast of Mexico City through the mountains. The Panteon Municipal in Guanajuato is composed of several walled-off sections of simple whitewashed graves, and "drawers" in the walls that are also resting places for the dead. What makes this cemetery so fascinating is the adjacent Museo de las Momias (the Mummy Museum). On display are mummified bodies taken from the cemetery. The interred were exhumed when their descendants stopped paying for upkeep. Only about 2 percent—108—of the mummies at the museum are available for viewing in their wood and glass coffin-like cases. It is thought that the hot, dry climate results in mummification, but only bodies removed from aboveground crypts—not buried in the earth—seem to mummify.

Museo de las Momias, Guanajuato, Mexico
Photo by Hugues Leblanc

At the Museo de las Momias, a mummified fetus—the world's smallest mummy—sits next to its mother, who died pregnant. The fetus was discovered when the mother's mummified remains were disinterred. Also on display are children dressed in frilly christening outfits; the oldest mummy at the museum, a French doctor who came to the region and died 200 years ago; and a mummy called the Witch, who was probably a healer. Shreds of clothing cling to their leather-like flesh. Most are still wearing socks, if not shoes. Outside the museum, vendors sell twisted clear toffee called "mummy candy."

Mexico is also home to the two-day holiday el Dia de los Muertos (Day of the Dead). On November 1 and 2 each year it is thought that the souls of the departed return, briefly, and it is important to welcome them back. During this time, especially in the less urban regions, families clean graves, apply a fresh coat of whitewash, plant flowers, and burn copal resin incense. They even cook meals by the graveside, and sleep there, and pay the mariachi bands to sing a favorite tune of the deceased loved one. At home, altars are built, adorned with fruits, yellow marigolds (the "flowers of the dead"), bottles of tequila, perhaps a brand of cigar that the departed favored, a skull made of sugar and decorated with icing sugar and sequins with the deceased's name attached, and a small skeletal figure that represents the deceased, often in a humorous role. These tiny Day of the Dead skeletons are collected the world over as Mexican folk art. Water is also placed on the altar—the dead get thirsty during their travels. Anyone who has played the excellent George Lucas computer game *Grim Fandango* can catch the bizarrely humorous feel of this celebration, variations of which are also practiced in some South American countries.

World's smallest mummy, Museo de las Momias, Guanajuato, Mexico
Photo by Hugues Leblanc

St. Louis Cemetery #1, New
Orleans, Louisiana
Photo by Hugues Leblanc

St. Louis Cemetery #3, New
Orleans, Louisiana
Photo by Hugues Leblanc

New Orleans

Between New Orleans and Baton Rouge more than sixty graveyards exist. Forty of them are within the city limits of New Orleans, the "City of the Dead"—a favorite goth haunt. The unique mixture of French and Spanish architecture of the French Quarter spills over into the cemeteries. Even the newest, Meterie Cemetery, with its enormous whitewashed crypts and rows of rooftop angels appealing to heaven, reflects this tradition. But it is the oldest, most decrepit cemeteries here that enjoy tremendous goth appeal.

Saint Louis #1, at the foot of the French Quarter, is well-known and well-preserved. The voodoo priestess Marie Laveau has a tomb here, although it's unknown whether or not, as rumored, her bones have been secreted away by followers. Saint Louis #1 possesses charm. With all the upkeep available, frequent tours are conducted for those wary of tackling ghosts alone on grounds crammed with the high oven-like tombs, so close together their alleyways resemble those of Cimetière du Père Lachaise. It's easy to feel like a child in this cemetery, dwarfed by these huge "oven crypts."

New Orleans is cursed/blessed with a low water table, meaning that below-ground burials are rare. During floods, more than one coffin with a body has been found floating in rivers and even in the Mississippi River. Consequently, cremation of an unusual nature has always been the popular choice in New Orleans. "Oven crypts" are usually designed to hold two bodies, upper and lower, like sleeping berths on a train. Space is rented for a year and a day. During that time, the heat and humidity of this Delta city works to cremate the flesh. If another family member dies before the year and a day are up, the new corpse is stored temporarily in a brick wall of niches used for that purpose. Once the designated time lapses, the bones within the oven are shoved to the back, the most recently departed is interred, and the crypt walled up for at least another year and a day. In this manner, family members' ashes are mixed together for eternity, which might be comforting or horrifying, depending on how one views one's relations.

Equally well-traveled as Saint Louis #1 is Lafayette #1, an historic cemetery—Anne Rice's favorite, apparently, and within walking distance from her home—in the Garden District, a more upscale area of town.

But the most often visited cemeteries are not necessarily the most inter-

esting, at least to goths. Saint Louis #2 is right behind #1, but this is a high-crime neighborhood, and not everyone is brave enough to venture inside walls that hide much from the view from the few passersby. These crypts enjoy little in the way of upkeep, but the disrepair has a charm of its own. The ornate fences surrounding the crypts are broken and rusted, and bricks composing the ovens are frequently crumbling or missing entirely, leaving holes large enough to peer into, and in some, to see bones. It's the same with Lafayette 2 and 3, and with the two Washington cemeteries, the Odd-fellows Cemetery, and so on. It's easy to see the unpreserved past as it has come down to the present, and corrosion adds a charm that upkeep denies.

St. Roc is a little gem of a cemetery, protected by a guardhouse. Here there will likely be few visitors at the same time. Dumpsters accumulate empty tall glass votive candleholders, and more dead roses than can be carted off. The cemetery surrounds a small chapel, full of lighted votive candles, and crutches affixed to the wall—St. Roc apparently healed the lame.

New Orleans is also famous for voodoo, or vodoun, the West African–Caribbean religion transported to the United States by way of the black slaves kidnapped and brought over to work on Southern plantations. Voodoo is a religion. It borrows from Catholicism, but incorporates poly-deities. Candles are burned, magic bags of herbs, stones, and perhaps human hair or fingernail clippings are worn around the neck for protection, spells can be cast to entice love or money or success, and sometimes bad spells can be placed on others—the intended victim of one of the most popular evil spells is the philandering mate, or even that mate's lover.

ENCOUNTERS WITH DEATH

A COMPENDIUM OF ANTHROPOMORPHIC
PERSONIFICATIONS OF DEATH FROM
HISTORICAL TO PRESENT DAY PHENOMENON

By LEILAH WENDELL

Courtesy of Leilah Wendell

Voodoo ceremonies involve music and dancing that can produce a tranced state among some participants, and when the spirits enter them, they might speak in tongues in much the same way Pentecostals do. Little outsider information is available about voodoo, and it is mainly media hype that has brought the religion to the fore. Particularly because of the ability to create zombies (see Chapter 12), B and some A movies have taken the concept and run with it. True practitioners of the faith in New Orleans can be found at the Voodoo Spiritual Temple. They declare that most of what people associate with the voodoo religion is utter nonsense at best, and disrespectful at worst.

The spin on cemeteries and death in New Orleans crystallizes at Westgate, which for many goths fills a need. The Westgate is the gate of the four directions that opens to the west, to death. For the past twenty-three years, Leilah Wendell and Daniel Kemp have been documenting encounters with anthropomorphic death entities by way of the Azrael Project. Westgate, their black-and-purple house on Magazine Street, is home to artwork and writings, and a meeting place for people who have met Azrael, the Angel of Death, in any of his myriad forms.

Leilah, who is perhaps the most frequent visitor to cemeteries in New Orleans, believes meeting the Angel of Death is a common experience. "We have all 'met' him at one time or another as we pass through many lives. It is that many choose *not* to remember."

Her first visual encounter with Azrael occurred when she was four years old. "I saw him 'float' down from an attic entry and down the hall to my room. I was terrified! He came towards me, sat beside me; I turned towards the wall, shaking. I felt a hand on my shoulder. The next thing I knew it was several hours later, and I oddly had full recollection of *what* he was and I never feared him after that point. I don't know to this day why, or what transpired during those 'lost' hours, but I 'woke up' remembering a whole lot of things a four-year-old kid should not know." Since that initial meeting, Leilah has had many encounters, including crawling into crypts and sleeping with corpses to invoke Azrael, which she documents in her books.

Such necromantic love is difficult for many people to understand, but not for most goths. Goths comprise about 30 percent of her visitors. "I think a lot of the ideals and images and emotions in my works many goths can identify with. The feeling of isolation, loneliness, melancholy, the aforementioned affinity of darker things, death. My style of writing often harkens back to the earlier styles of literature, i.e., 'purple prose' of some of their favorite writers." Leilah, who wore black long before there was anything remotely called "goth," says she has ". . . never considered myself a part of any named subculture." Still, she believes that her interests gel with most goths because "many goths have also had either an affinity or some type of inner connection with that energy on some level, which is why they are 'goth' in the first place." For Leilah, meeting like-minded individuals is "like finding family."

Leilah describes her relationship with Azrael in this way: "I am here in service to him and to humanity as a whole. I do this solely out of my love for him and my hope for 'them,' that by example of our love, humankind will eventually reconcile with their own deaths as well as with him." She sees the relationship as "two halves of one whole, one foot in this world, one in the next . . . always together, always apart, yet we share emotions, understandings. We are empathic dualities, yet we are one . . . completely in love."

She has often been asked if her encounters are "real." "For those who have never had an encounter or a relationship with the Angel of Death, they may never understand, but that's okay, one day they will remember. For those who have, it is cathartic for them to be able to finally express these things without fear of being called 'psychotic.' These things are very real. Ask anyone who has experienced him. For those who have faith, no proof is necessary, for those who doubt, no proof is sufficient."

Chicago

In a city of fifty cemeteries Chicago's 350-acre Rosehill Cemetery—the largest—stands out because of its famous haunted chapel.

The Rosehill Cemetery Company's 1913 promotional booklet says the cemetery was named for the white roses growing in abundance on the hills. But another story insists the cemetery was named because of a mapmaker's error. The area was originally called Roe's Hill, after a nearby tavern keeper.

Whatever the truth, opposite the Middle Lake a widow built a Romanesque chapel in 1913 dedicated to her husband Horatio N. May. The May Chapel can hold 250 mourners, although in its history it has been closed to mourners more than it has been open. Adjoining the chapel is the receiving vault. A grassy mound covers the exterior of the vault, which

Edgar Allan Poe's grave and
monument, Baltimore, Maryland

Photo by Hugues Leblanc

contains 300 crypts available to anyone wishing to defer interment "for any reason."

Like the tales of how the cemetery got its name, there are several stories about the May Crypt, and the strange goings-on there. One is that in the 1970s a Satanic group used the chapel for rituals. But its bleak history stretches back even further. The land had been used for burials since the 1700s, long before Rosehill Cemetery came into existence. The May Chapel was constructed over a preexisting cave that became a crypt. During the 1800s, bodies were stored in winter in the subterranean crypts until the ground thawed and they could be given a proper burial. But rumor has it, come the spring, not all of the deceased were brought aboveground. Burying people twice seemed like a waste of money to the powers that then were, who decided to just leave many of the bodies there. Mourners were directed to fake graves.

Since that time, frequently when the chapel has been open to the public for funeral services, paranormal occurrences have been observed, the source of which seems to emanate from these belowground vaults. Lights flicker on and off in the chapel, caskets shake and lids fly open, statues and candleholders fall over, moans and screams are heard, as well as footsteps running on the hardwood floors. Currently the chapel is closed to the public. There is even talk of walling it up. But peering down the skylights on the grassy mound one can catch a glimpse of crypts below, the openings sealed but unidentified. Do these hold the bodies not given a proper burial? Souls not resting in peace? Many Chicagoans think so.

Another haunted cemetery in Chicago is the small White Cemetery in Barrington, north of Chicago. Red or white orbs of light have been observed here many times. Orbs of light, as the psychically inclined tell us, are souls of the departed caught on the physical plane. As well as lights, cars have reportedly disappeared, and even a house vanished, all adjacent to the graveyard.

Baltimore

The controversy rages on: Just who is it who is buried in Poe's grave?

Edgar Allan Poe (see Chapter 11), considered the originator of the short story, left us a wealth of macabre fiction and grim essays. His life was fraught with financial hardship and emotional pain, his work largely unappreciated until long after his demise. All this plus a weak constitution drove him to alcohol for solace. He married his cousin, creating scandal, and when she died he never recovered from the grief. His own tragic life ended at the age of forty.

The stories he penned are shrouded in the bizarre, but then, so is his death.

Poe, indigent, died on the morning of October 7, 1849 in an out-of-the-way hospital. His body lay in state for three days in the rotunda of the college adjoining the hospital, where friends, family, and strangers paid respects. At least fifty women arrived to receive a lock of his hair as a memento. Relatives paid for an oak coffin, and Poe, who always dressed in black, was buried in black.

On October 9—a cold, rainy, cheerless day—his body was carried to Westminster, burying ground of the First Presbyterian Church. He was interred to the right of his grandfather, General Poe, in a lead-lined coffin with a brass plate at the foot of it. A temporary marker with the number 8 scrawled on it was placed at the head of his grave. Poe's headstone had not yet been transported to the cemetery from the marble yard near the Baltimore and Ohio Railroad tracks where it was cut and carved when a train jumped the tracks and crushed it.

In 1875, schoolchildren donated money for a stone monument that was placed in a corner of the cemetery yard, where it still stands. Poe's body was exhumed and moved to this new grave site. Or was it?

Eleven years earlier, in 1864, the headstones of the cemetery were all turned from facing the east gate to facing the west gate, reason unknown. Apparently no one told the grave diggers of 1875, who only knew that Poe had been buried to the right of his grandfather. But Poe, because of the movement of the headstones, was now on the left. Who was on the right? Private Philip Mosher, Jr. The coffin that was dug up—twelve feet to the right of General Poe—was not the lead-lined oak Edgar Allan had been buried in, but mahogany, with no plate. Records state that Private Mosher had been buried in a mahogany coffin. There were other discrepancies, including the excellent condition of the teeth, again pointing to the occupant as the younger and more affluent Private Mosher.

The body exhumed to the right of General Poe was reburied under the new monument, and joined by the remains of Virginia Poe.

Since 1949, this grave identified as belonging to Edgar Allan Poe has been visited every year in the early hours on his birthday, January 19. Rumor has it an elderly gentleman draped in black using a silver-tipped cane for support

Lightbulb head tombstone,
New England
Photo by Hugues Leblanc

kneels at the foot of the grave for a toast of Martel cognac, then leaves behind the half-empty bottle and three red roses when he departs.

Rhode Island

At the end of the nineteenth century, consumption ran rampant. In a small farmhouse just outside Exeter, Rhode Island, Mary Brown died in 1883. Her daughter Mary Olive died in 1884. Then another daughter, Mercy, died in 1892. George Brown, his young son Edwin and three daughters remained. When young Edwin took sick, the family decided that he did not have consumption, but was being attacked by a vampire. They dug up the three females. Mary and Mary Olive had decomposed to bone. But Mercy's body, buried only two months, was still fresh. They cut out her liver, and her heart, which still dripped blood, and burned them on a rock in the cemetery behind Chestnut Hill Baptist Church. The ashes were dissolved in medicine given Edwin by his doctor. But Edwin died two months later. Mercy, the only one of the Brown women dug up with blood still in her veins, was deemed the vampire. The locals say that violation of her grave has caused her spirit to haunt the graveyard at night ever since.

Prague

Seventy kilometers outside Prague near Kuntá Hora lies the sleepy village of Sedlec. Since 1141 the tiny town is home to the *hrbitou*, or cemetery of the Cistercian Monastery. It wasn't until 1278 when Abbot Heidenreich returned from Jerusalem with a jug of dirt dug from Golgotha, the hill where Christ was reputedly crucified, that the cemetery became consecrated ground. Pretty soon all of Europe was dying to be buried there.

In the middle of the cemetery stands the fourteenth-century Church of All Saints, with its copper cupolas atop twin spires. The crypt in the basement was used to store old bones dug out of the cemetery to make room for new burials. In 1511 a blind monk gathered the excess bones that had been overflowing the basement crypt for more than 200 years and placed them into the church proper. It took until 1870 to hire a wood-carver named Frantisek Rint, who arranged what amounted to 40,000 sets of bones into "pleasing designs."

Stark white bones. Everywhere. Daisy chains of skulls draping the arches, crossed bones dangling here and there, a pyramid of bones with tarnished silver crosses hanging above, bones arranged to form chalices, an enormous eight-armed chandelier suspended from the ceiling made entirely of bones. The church lights the candles in the bone chandelier on All Saints' Day, November 2, the same day Mexico celebrates its Day of the Dead.

Vienna

The Viennese are said to be obsessed with death. Awash in cemeteries, Vienna is also home to the Bestattungsmuseum, aka, the Undertakers' Museum. *The Big Book of Death* by Bronwyn Carlton (DC Comics, Paradox Press, 1995) depicts a goth girl, in cartoon format, touring the museum and providing a history of Austrian funeral customs. The outside of the building is nondescript. Inside are offices, the museum located in the back rooms where everything comes to life, so to speak. On display are coffins, casket coverings, needleworked shrouds, velvet curtains and silk funerary footwear, ornate casket hardware, toy worm-eaten corpses and painted floral skulls, and the elaborate funeral uniforms of powerful men and the drapings for their horses. Also displayed are a variety of contraptions invented through the ages to allow the false dead to ring for help from below ground in the event they had accidently been buried alive. Being Vienna, there is a strong emphasis on composers: Beethoven's death notice, Schubert's death certificate, and Haydn's death masks. An enormous variety of macabre objects are displayed, including an antique hearse. Tours are conducted, in English as well as other languages, by a dapper gentleman, one of Vienna's leading undertakers.

Houston

Houston, Texas is home of the National Museum of Funeral History, open for ten years. On display are thousands of artifacts, including an ornate 1860 German "Glaswagen" Funeral Coach, antique motorized hearses, the original John F. Kennedy eternal flame (it was replaced in 1992), and many caskets, including one entirely of glass made in the 1800s. As well, a variety of mourning pictures line the walls, and plenty of early embalming equipment is exhibited.

Lithuania

Six miles north of Siulivi in Lithuania is a hill piled high with crosses, rosaries, and other religious objects, more than 50,000 of them! This area, originally a stronghold against the Knights of the Teutonic Order, became

Hill of Crosses, Lithuania
Photo by Hugues Leblanc

a receptacle for crosses in 1831, to protest the deportation of residents to Siberia. Many attempts were made by the Soviets when they occupied this land to destroy the hill—the last attempt in the early 1970s. Hundreds of crosses came down under the Russian bulldozers, followed the next morning by a thousand magically appearing to replace them. Considered not a cemetery but more a mausoleum, this is a holy place. A Lithuanian postage stamp from 1990 commemorates The Hill of Crosses.

As the traditional crosses decay, they fall and create new soil onto which more crosses are added, piling up, making the view as far as the eye can see overwhelmingly thick with crosses of wood, metal, stone, glass, clay, enamel, woven fibers. There is no pattern, only the anarchy of controlled rebellion mingled with faith on a hill that symbolizes resistance to assimilation, something goths can appreciate.

other goth vacation fascinations

When on vacation, many of *The † Section* head for churches, castles, museums, antique shops, and old libraries, like *Daevina, Emily Bronte, Nimue, the Crow, Paola,* and *museumbitch*, who says "Museums, archives, historical sites. I'm especially interested in bog bodies, and there are two museums in this area of Sweden." And *Nadia* likes "Stonehenge, Avebury Ring, Stanton Drew. Feeds the romance in my soul."

Shopping is a holiday for a lot of *The † Section*, for example, *Calhoun, Medea, Samael, Shekinah, Silver Moon, Slavel, SUZANNE,* and *White Raven.* They will visit not just goth shops but a spectrum, from antique stores to thrift stores and flea markets.

Naturally goth clubs and other gothy spots are big on the to-do list, as well as gatherings like Convergence. *Taoist* says, "When I went to Goa, I went straight for the Hindu temples and the chocolate plantations. But if I'm in a city, e.g., San Diego, I'll check out the goth clubs."

Madame X and *RaVeN* like spooky holidays that include ghost tours and haunted houses. And just getting out in nature does it for *DJ Caluna*, *Jola*, *RaVeN*, and *XjUsTcRuCifyX*. *Arantèle* "Found in New Brunswick a wonderful old priest's house converted into an inn with the yard leading to the sea and to a cemetery."

Euro restaurant and bar critic Mandy Slater discusses two goth-interest establishments in Belgium:

"Halloween Café (part of La Brasserie de l'Etrange) is a horror-themed restaurant and bar, one hundred meters from the famous Manneken Pis in Brussels. This large, lively restaurant and bar is beatifically decorated with paintings, gargoyle sculptures, pumpkins, and fountains. Waiters dressed as monks serve horror-themed food, and if you're really lucky, you might be visited by a monster, vampire or witch while munching on your tasty Belgian fare! Tables are named, such as Fu Manchu and Dracula. While a little on the touristy side, Halloween is well worth a visit.

"*Le Cerceuil* (the Coffin) is located just off the Grand Place. This vampire bar is one of the oldest of its kind [horror themed] in Europe. Music can be classical or roam through the range of goth. Lucky Belgian goths sit at tables made from coffins and sip their cocktails from a skull."

North American goths do not need to go so far afield for creepy dining. New York City boasts the haunted Jekyll and Hyde Restaurant Bar in Greenwich Village, where wall artwork like Dreadmina the Vampire and Tobias the Werewolf animate as diners consume the Cannibal's three-meat pizza, and sip their beer from a mold green two-foot-high glass!

Other hot spots include:

Bodyworlds—based in Germany (a roving anatomical exhibit of real human bodies (seen in the German movie *Anatomie*)
www.koerperwelten.de/index2.htm

The Catacombs of Paris—Paris, France (hundreds of years of bones, artistically arranged)
www.members.tripod.com/~Motomom/index-3.html

Dracula Theme Park—Sighisoara, Romania (the name says it all)

Jewish Cemetery in Prague—Prague, Czech Republic (oldest and only cemetery left intact by the Nazis)
www.rabunda.com/qtvr/cemetery.html

Madame Tussaud's Wax Museum–London, England (check out the chamber of horrors and Marie Antoinette's death mask)
www.dimkin.df.ru/mt/

Medieval Criminal Museum Collection–San Gimignano, Italy (a traveling exhibit for the criminologist within)
www.torturamuseum.com/

Museum of Death–Hollywood, California (Hollywood macabre, serial killer oddities, crime scene photos, skulls, coffins, artwork, mortician tools, body bags, you name it!)
www.museumofdeath.com/

Mütter Museum–Philadelphia, Pennsylvania (Victorian medical oddities, and lots of bones, including the famous two-headed skeleton)
www.collphyphil.org/muttpg1.shtml

Pitt Rivers Museum–Oxford, England (excellent anthropology museum, shrunken heads, talismans, mechanical toys)
www.prm.ox.ac.uk/

The Salem Witch Museum–Salem, Massachusetts (history of those nasty witch trials!)
www.salemwitchmuseum.com/

Songran Niyomsane Forensic Medicine Museum–Bangkok, Thailand (what it sounds like)
www.corkscrew-balloon.com/misc/siquey.html

Torture Museum–Amsterdam, Netherlands (where much of that torture equipment from the Inquisition ended up)
www.arise.demon.co.uk/photos/holland-torturemuseum.html

Tower of London–London, England (endless imprisonment, and the crown jewels, too!)
www.toweroflondontour.com/

Vienna Vampire Museum–Vienna, Austria (obvious)
www.hollenthon.com/other.html

Voodoo Museum–New Orleans, Louisiana (voodoo artifacts and history)
www.voodoomuseum.com/

URLs

Gravestone Artwear
www.gravestoneartwear.com

Gravestone epitaphs
www.made2smile.com/funpages/epitaph/

Virtual tour of the Catacombs of Paris
www.triggur.org/cata/

Danse Macabre of Italy
www.sympatico.ca/tapholov/

Graveyards of Chicago
www.graveyards.com/

Museo de las Momias
www.sympatico.ca/nancy.kilpatrick/

www.whatsonwhen.com/events/viewevent.asp?id=33892

Capuchin Mummies of Palermo
www.members.tripod.com/~Motomom/index-3.html

The Bone Chapel outside Prague
www.ludd.luth.se/users/silver/p/Sedlec/kutna01.html

The Hill of Crosses–Lithuania
www.catholic-shrines.com/page23.html

Westgate–New Orleans
www.westgatenecromantic.com

Voodoo Spiritual Temple–New Orleans
www.w3.iac.net/~moonweb/NOSVT/NOSVTMain.html

National Museum of Funeral History
www.nmfh.org/Index.html

11

SUBSCRIBING TO THE DARK ARTS

Pardon me, but why aren't your teeth in my neck?

art of the Gothic

The world of stained glass and sculpture enjoyed a Gothic period for over two centuries, beginning around the thirteenth. Statuary up to that period had been restricted by the building that housed it, almost always a religious building. A square temple with square stone in the wall inside the temple required a traditional sculpture carved from memory right into that stone. Gothic sculptors carved their statues outside the building, then brought them into the cathedrals, which gave them more freedom to create. As opposed to the simple crosses, depictions of Christ, and alpha and omega symbols that were the subject matter of stained glass until the 1100s, Gothic stained glass emulated nature, simulating flowers, trees, and animals. To traditionalists, this was tantamount to sacrilege, and it's easy to see why. For example, a few centuries down the road, when the Italians could finally bring themselves to recognize Gothic art, they labeled it "Goth" (as in the original Goths of Europe), or crude, at least until the Italian Renaissance came along, at which point they embraced the more natural and romantic concepts if not actual Gothic designs. Much of Europe had the same reaction.

The Gothic period of visual art greatly influenced all art in the periods that followed it. The Renaissance drew heavily from Gothic sentiment.

WILLIAM BLAKE'S LEVELS OF CONSCIOUSNESS TO REACH ART

Level 1: Blame. The lowest common denominator. Nobody takes responsibility. Everybody viciously accuses others of being the source of their problems.

Level 2: Conflict. People debate openly and fairly, arguing their respective side without blaming the others. Holding onto tension without cracking.

Level 3: Love. Opposites attract. Conflicts are resolved through respect and understanding.

Level 4: Art. Borne of the merging of opposites. Creation. The baby born of an ova and a sperm, the painting or novel bursting into existence when the deadlock of two opposing ideas results in a third, creative sollution.

"Annabel Lee"

(last stanza)

"For the moon never beams without
bringing me dreams
Of the beautiful Annabel Lee;
And the stars never rise but
I feel the bright eyes
Of the beautiful Annabel Lee;
And so, all the night-tide,
I lie down by the side
Of my darling, my darling, my life
and my bride,
In the sepulcher there by the sea,
In her tomb by the sounding sea.

—Edgar Allan Poe

Before Gothic, everything was dark—that's why they called it the Dark Ages. But by the late eighteenth century, everybody had had enough straightforward logic, and wanted something to stir the emotions. Gothic brought light and ornamentation, and the public applauded it!

Literature had its turn at Gothic Revival. Romantic writers from the mid-1800s pursued themes of death, moonlight, and lost love. The wealthy and the newly emerging literate middle class devoured all those wonderful stories written during that period by writers such as Horace Walpole, Matthew Lewis, and Anne Radcliffe, as well as the penny dreadfuls, enormous volumes of chilling tales often serialized in newspapers. Such stories featured helpless damsels-in-distress, isolated at crumbling Gothic manors, under the control of cruel, stern, mysterious but handsome guardians. Ah, the moors on a misty full-mooned night! Wolves howling in the distance, and the crash of the tormented surf bashing against the virgin white cliffs . . . what an atmosphere of impending danger! Delicious high melodrama.

Modern Gothic romances hit their stride in the 1970s and 1980s with Harlequin—the world's largest publisher of romance novels—giving them their own line, including the famous "bodice rippers." Readers are devoted to this type of fiction.

languid literature

Long dead writers:

Edgar Allan Poe's real life flies in the face of any romanticized version of viewing existence. His tale is heart-wrenching. He was a man of extraordinary talent, whose ability to create pathos with words reduces readers to immense sadness, to crippling despair, or chills them to the icy bone with dread. And yet fate seems to have decreed that he would suffer insult upon injury, and suffer greatly all of his days, and beyond (see Chapter 10).

Edgar Allan Poe was born in 1809, and died in 1849. The forty years he spent on this earth were laced with torment. Given the level of internal suffering, his output was staggering; he published dozens of works of short fiction and poetry, and many philosophical essays.

The events of Poe's life can be summarized but not really felt—his despair goes beyond what most of us have lived. His mother died of tuberculosis when he was just two years old. He then lived with his foster parents

John and Frances. Frances died when he was twenty, also of TB. When John died five years later, leaving an estate valued at three quarters of a million (mid-1800s) dollars, he bequeathed Edgar Allan not a dime, relegating him to poverty. Poe married his first cousin Virginia, whom he deeply adored. Seven years later his beloved began to cough up blood, and she, too, quickly succumbed to TB. Her death crushed his spirit and he plunged into alcoholism and spiraling despair. If ever a man was born with a dark star above his head, it was Edgar Allan Poe.

One of Poe's most evocative poems is "Annabel Lee," published in 1849, the year of his demise. It speaks of a love so deep that death itself cannot break the spell of that passion, which resides in the one who remains, a theme that resonates with most goths, for whom love is crucial. Poe's love of Virginia forced him to face the finality of her death, and perhaps hastened his own.

Poe's work is widely known and translated. Many of his stories have been turned into movies, some from the 1970s and 1980s starring that delightfully macabre personality, the late, great actor Vincent Price.

But Poe's best-known work is, of course, his evocative poem, "The Raven," published in 1845, four years before his death. It is a poem that allows this darkest of all winged creatures to personify the madness and portend the death that lingers but a hairsbreadth away from us all.

"The Raven"
(last stanza)

And the raven, never flitting,
still is sitting, still is sitting
On the pallid bust of Pallas just
above my chamber door;
And his eyes have all the seeming
of a demon's that is dreaming,
And the lamp-light o'er him
streaming throws his
shadow on the floor;
And my soul from out that shadow
that lies floating on the floor
Shall be lifted—nevermore!

—Edgar Allan Poe

"ENIVREY-VOUS" (Get Drunk) from Les Petits Poèmes en Prose

by Charles Baudelaire, translation by Caro Soles

It is essential to be drunk all the time. That's it! The great imperative! To avoid feeling the appalling weight of Time breaking your shoulders, bending you to the ground, get drunk and stay that way.
But on what? On wine, poetry, goodness, please yourself. But get drunk.
And if now and then you wake up on the steps of a palace, on the green grass of a ditch, in the gloomy loneliness of your own room, your drunken state gone or disappearing, ask the wind, the waves, the stars, the birds, the clock, ask everything that runs by, everything that groans or rolls or sings, everything that speaks, ask what time it is; and the wind, the waves, the stars, the birds, the clock will answer you: "It's time to get drunk! Don't be martyred slaves to Time, get drunk! Endlessly drunk! On wine, virtue, poetry, please yourself!"

Charles Baudelaire (1821–1867) is another goth favorite. Poet, essayist, and literary and art critic, his best-known collection is *Les Fleurs du Mal* (Flowers of Evil), considered the most infamous book of poetry in French literature. During his lifetime, Baudelaire was charged with offenses to religion and public morality for thirteen of the 100 poems in that collection. The court ordered that six poems be removed from the book on the grounds of obscenity. In an age filled with rules and regulations of conduct, with the main emphasis on preparation in this life for the next by way of the Church, Baudelaire reflected the budding individualism that would emerge fully some 100 years after his demise. Much of his poetry reveals a deep introspective search for God, but it seems he was unable to find any religious belief system to sustain him. In some circles his name is still synonymous with depravity, morbidity, and obscenity.

When he discovered Poe, Baudelaire felt the two had an almost preternatural connection. He became obsessed with the American and, two years before Poe's death, began translating his work into French. These translations would provide Baudelaire with a steady source of income throughout his life. He also translated sections of British essayist Thomas De Quincey's *Confessions of an English Opium-Eater*.

Baudelaire fell from wealth to financial disaster. For much of his life he was emotionally and financially dependent on his mother. After he was expelled from college, he spent time in Paris's Latin Quarter, frittering away his inheritance in two years and racking up huge debts that would hang over him until he died. A habitual smoker of hashish and opium, he also regularly drank absinthe. His poem *"Enivrey-vous"* ("Get Drunk") expresses his licentious philosophy, and is a cleverly worded sarcasm aimed at Parisian politically correct society of the day.

Moods of isolation and despair tormented Baudelaire: he termed them his "moods of spleen." The love of his life was a mulatto woman named Jeanne Duvan, with whom he was obsessed for twenty years, and who inspired some of his most anguished and sensual love poetry. He died embittered at age forty-six of venereal disease, leaving a body of work that at the time of his demise was mostly unpublished, his contribution to literature ignored. It is only upon his death that the world began to recognize Baudelaire as one of the great French poets of the nineteenth century. Above his burial site at Cimetière du Montparnasse in Paris is a sculpture of Baudelaire, looking down on and contemplating his own grave.

"Les Litanies de Satan" is one of Baudelaire's most dramatic and best-known verses. Scandalous in its day, the stanzas sing the praises of the Prince of Darkness, with the repetitive chant: Satan, have mercy on my long distress!

In 1982, Diamanda Galas released her first album, *The Litanies of Satan*. The Canadian goth band Masochistic Religion has a CD titled *The Litanies of Satan*, dedicated to Baudelaire and putting his text to music.

Poe and Baudelaire are writers who led lives of not-so-quiet desperation. Consequently it is not surprising that another author goths appreciate is the witty and pithy Oscar Fingal O'Flahertie Wills Wilde (1854–1900), whose homosexual love—particularly an affair with a young aristocrat—clashed sharply with the values of Victorian England and landed him in jail, breaking his spirit.

Oscar Wilde left us many gems, and more than one goth can no doubt relate to this one: "I never travel without my diary. One should always have something sensational to read."

Other dead writers popular among goths are: Emily Brontë, Charles Brockden Brown, Lord Byron, Lewis Carroll, Charlotte Brontë, Samuel Taylor Coleridge, The Marquis de Sade, Charles Dickens, Emily Dickinson, Sir Arthur Conan Doyle, John Donne, Fyodor Dostoyevsky, Lord Dunsany, Sheridan le Fanu, Johann Wolfgang von Goethe, Henry James, Franz Kafka, John Keats, Guy de Maupassant, John Milton, Frederich Nietzsche, William Shakespeare, Mary Shelley, Bram Stoker, Algernon Swinburne, Ugo Tarchetti, and Sir Robert Walpole. Dante Alighieri and his levels of Hell receives an honorable mention.

Recently dead writers:

Perhaps no other late writer of darkly strange fiction has had the impact of Howard Phillips Lovecraft. His short stories reflect his strange interior worlds, just behind the seam that divides reality, where powerful, demonic beings dwell, gods of darkness eager to enter the realm of the living and engulf us.

Lovecraft, born August 20, 1890, was a precocious child, reciting poetry at the age of two, reading at three, and writing by the time he was six years old. At the age of sixteen he penned regular columns on astronomy for various newspapers. But he was a lonely boy, moody, often suffering illnesses with a psychological basis. His father died of paresis, a neurosyphilis. An unhealthy relationship with his mother contributed to his loneliness.

It was his grandfather who introduced him to weird Gothic tales. His grandfather died when H.P. was fourteen and soon afterward mismanagement plunged the family into financial difficulties, resulting in the loss of the family home. Lovecraft contemplated suicide; he suffered a nervous breakdown that left him unable to graduate from high school. He became a hermit, studying astronomy and writing poetry, and reading old pulp magazines with their lurid horror fiction. Eventually he began to write stories of madness and death.

Three years after his mother's death in 1921, he met and married Sonia Haft Greene, who owned a hat shop on New York's Fifth Avenue. But the hat shop went bankrupt. Then Lovecraft turned down a good job editing a pulp magazine. Finally, Sonia's health forced her into a sanitarium. At thirty-four, with no job experience, H.P. could not find work. He lived alone, and became depressed, writing even bleaker fiction. In 1929 his marriage ended in divorce, and he moved back to Providence.

Ironically, toward the end of his life things improved for a while. He traveled a lot, and he had acquired a number of good friends through correspondence. He nurtured the careers of several young writers who enjoyed fame if not fortune, in particular Fritz Leiber and Robert Bloch, author of the classic *Psycho*. But the final three years of his life returned him to extreme financial hardship—his writing had altered and became unsalable. He also suffered from cancer of the intestines, which eventually killed him.

It was only after his death that his work was collected by friends into book form. The publishing company Arkham House was set up specifically to bring the work of H.P. Lovecraft to the world. He died March 15, 1937 at the age of forty-six, and is buried in the cemetery at Swan Point, Providence, Rhode Island.

Taoist sums up Lovecraft's goth appeal: "He created an entire mythos which he brought to life in immense detail. I love the way he builds up the sense of impending doom and the way he uses madness as a tool to unsettle the reader."

Other recently dead writers that goths enjoy include: William Burroughs, Edward Gorey, Anton Lavey, Edna St. Vincent Millay, and J.R.R. Tolkein.

Undead writers:

Not all of Anne Rice's readers are goth, but all goths, it seems, have read Anne Rice. Katherine Ramsland, friend and biographer of Anne Rice, says this about the author's popularity:

"*Interview with the Vampire* tapped into unspoken social archetypes about secrecy, need, angst, and the desire to have an open alternative lifestyle that captured a large audience right away. Then it was nine years before she offered the sequel, *The Vampire Lestat*, and that brought her audience back. However, it was a very different type of book, more of a story than a metaphor, and people were now used to her breakthrough concept of doing everything from the vampire's point of view. They knew her characters and wanted more. She wasn't the first to do so, but she did so with the largest audience."

Underground queen Poppy Z. Brite holds just about the same caché as Anne Rice with goth readers. Poppy penned many exquisitely written short stories before bursting to prominence with her spectatular first novel *Lost Souls*, a kind of modern underground culture, gay vampire musical road trip. She followed this up with two more novels of modern macabre, *Drawing Blood* and *Exquisite Corpse*.

Poppy Z. Brite (her birth name) says, "You know, technically I'm not sure I have [ever considered herself goth]. Back in my late teens and early twenties, I had never heard the term 'goth'—the phrase we used was 'deathrocker' or sometimes just 'deather.' Even if you concede that it's essentially the same thing, I always felt like more of an observer than a participant in the subculture—I didn't have a group of friends who dressed the way I did or listened to the same music. By the time I knew what a goth was, and certainly by the time I had goth fans, I'd probably lost touch with too much of the scene to qualify as one."

Regardless of whether or not she is goth, Poppy's work touches goths in a special way. "I think I've written a few things that show a knowledge of the subculture without co-opting it or pandering to it. As I say, I don't know that I was ever really a part of any goth scene, but I've certainly been closer to it than some authors who try to write about it because they think it's spooky, edgy, or whatever. I think that sort of silliness reached its apex with an article that appeared in the HWA [Horror Writers Association] newsletter—'How to Write Goth Characters,' seemingly for people who'd never met a goth or wanted to. I can't imagine why anyone would wish to write about a subculture they felt no personal attraction to, but unfortunately it has happened."

It is *Lost Souls*, which Poppy published at the age of twenty-five, that strikes a chord with most goths. But she admits, "Trust me, there are plenty of people who don't like *Lost Souls*. If you don't believe it, just check out the Amazon.com reader reviews. Gauntlet Press just published a tenth-anniversary edition of the novel."

Poppy has this to say in her forward to the recent limited-edition reprint: "I'm attempting here to put *Lost Souls* to bed. I don't want to bury it entirely, because every writer likes to think his work will stay in print and continue to be read for as long as possible. But I'd also like my readers to accompany me as I move on to other things. The publication of this limited edition happens to mark the end of an era for me. Between 1992 and 1999 I published four novels, all of which are pretty deeply rooted in the horror genre. I spent 2000 and 2001 writing two novels [*The Value of X* and *Liquor*] which cannot be called horror by any stretch of the imagination, and that seems to be the direction in which I'm continuing to move. I have no idea whether these novels will be as well received as my horror work, but as I've tried to explain many times, I don't really have a choice in the matter. The one thing I've always felt 100 percent sure of is that the work won't be any good unless I follow my own obsessions, rather than attempting to 'write to market.'"

Poppy's fierce individuality as a human being and as a writer are attractive to goths. She discusses a situation that gives tremendous insight into the values of this unique spirit. "A couple of years ago I published a book called *Plastic Jesus*. As I often do with new releases, I auctioned off a few of the advance reading copies on eBay. One of the purchasers made a special request: He wanted me to inscribe it 'Death is easy,' the twins' song-chant from chapters four and thirty-one of *Lost Souls*. He said this phrase had special meaning to him, and he hoped I would write it in his book along with my autograph. I agonized over this for days. I bothered my husband and my friends: 'What if he's, like, dying of AIDS? What if he just wants a little false comfort and I refuse to give it to him? Okay, even if he's not dying, he just paid seventy-five dollars for this book; maybe I'm an asshole for not writing anything he wants in it.' Ultimately, though, I could not do it. I would have had no problem inscribing a copy of *Lost Souls* in such a way, but I could not make myself write those words in *Plastic Jesus*. Between the writing of the two books I had learned that death is *not* easy; it's hard. Hard for the person doing the dying, hard for the people who must watch and stay behind. That's part of what *Plastic Jesus* is about: the first scene has a character dying messily and in extreme pain, and many of the subsequent scenes are about the way his life and death affected those around him. Death can be quick; death can be merciful; but I no longer believe that there is anything easy about it. I e-mailed the young man and explained all this, offering to let him rescind his bid if he wished. He was very gracious about it, telling me to inscribe his book any way I liked, but I could not have changed my mind no matter how he had reacted. Probably I made far too much of this, but it did make me feel as though I'd come a long way and gotten a lot older since I wrote *Lost Souls*. My husband, whom I've been with for thirteen years and who lives with my characters nearly as intimately as I do, never knew Steve and Ghost and the others as well as he knows my more recent characters; I was almost finished with them by the time we met. I no longer live in the American South (some people think Louisiana is part of the American South, but those of us who live here know it's really a Third World country that has more in common with the Caribbean than with any part of the United States). I no longer listen to any of the music I so cherished in this story, with the exception of Tom Waits—it's great music, but evocative to the point of qualifying as time travel, which I hardly ever wish to engage in. I don't drink Chartreuse or spend a lot of time in the French Quarter. I don't think death is easy."

modern gothic writers on their art

Sèphera Girón, a goth, and a writer with several horror novels to her credit, talks with the top-four goth writers in the world about being goth, and about their work.

Storm Constantine is an award-winning goth favorite. She lives in Great Britain and has been publishing novels, short stories, and collections since the mid-1980s. Her popular novels are richly textured in the language of the fantastic. Her most recent novel is *The Wraiths of Will and Pleasure* (Book 1 of the *Wraeththu Chronicles*).

Caitlín Kiernan, born in Ireland, now living in the United States, burst onto the book world in the late 1990s. Her debut novel, *Silk*, set in the goth subculture, was a wild success, and she has written both fiction and comic books, including *The Dreaming*. Currently she is working on a new novel, *Low Red Moon*.

Nancy Kilpatrick, born in the United States, now living in Canada, has published twenty-six books since the early 1990s, including novels, collections, and anthologies she has edited. Her popular contemporary *Power of the Blood* vampire world has a large goth following. Her most recent work of fiction is the horror novel *Eternal City*.

Freda Warrington lives in England. She has been publishing novels rich in language, imagery, and history since the mid-1980s, and has a large goth fan club. She has just finished the novel *The Court of the Midnight King*, based on Richard III, for Earthlight.

Sèphera asks: "Do you consider yourself goth?"

Storm: "It's tempting to say [I've been goth] 'all my life'—as I've always been into the dark and mysterious side of things, with a penchant for exotic clothes and magic. However, from a cultural point of view I evolved from being a Punk into being a goth at the end of the 1970s and early 1980s. In the UK, goth evolved from something that was called 'Positive Punk.' I'm still not sure why it was called that, but it was when bands like Bauhaus and Killing Joke started bringing out 'darker' music and the look people adopted had a certain—shall we say—voodoo ambience! I was always involved with bands, though not as a musician. I was an artist or designer before I became seriously involved in writing, and I used to design cassette covers and posters for bands."

Caitlín: "I didn't actually encounter the 'g'-word until college, about ten or eleven years ago, but, even then, it was really not much more than a comfortable label for a way that I'd felt and dressed and thought since high school. And the discovery that there were a lot of like-minded people, that was an important part for me. Discovering that there were entire genres of music focusing on similar aesthetic concerns, that was really wonderful."

Nancy: "I think I awoke one day to find myself goth in the early 1990s, this out of what I have always been—a dark, alienated soul, struggling to find my way. It seems a kind of movement developed while I was napping where others like me came out of the woodwork. People began to call me goth, I began to answer yes to the question: Are you? I've worn black most of my life, always visited cemeteries wherever I went, and have had a love of moody and tormented literature, film, and music. I've been nothing less than thrilled to find others such as myself."

Freda: "I'm not a hard-line goth . . . more towards the Pre-Raphaelite end of the spectrum! I'm not sure, it kind of evolved in the early nineties from my customary long red hair and velvety clothes to something darker. The first time I took a deep breath and dyed my hair black, I realized it actually suited me!"

Sèphera: "Who or what has inspired your writing?"

Storm: "I think, for me, it was a happy coincidence that a youth culture arose that so closely reflected my own worldview. For most people, I expect, the 'symbols' of goth were more of a fashion statement than anything else, but over the years I've noticed that people who've stuck with it as a movement have mostly ventured into Pagan territory. Most goths I meet are into magic or some form of alternative spirituality. This certainly wasn't there in the beginning, although one thing that identified goth (and I think was carried over from Punk) was that everyone was into being creative. If you weren't in a band, you were an artist, or a writer. The art might simply have been how you adorned your own body, and there were some very flamboyant examples out there! This whole scene influenced my early books, in particular the *Wraeththu* trilogy, which was greatly inspired by what I saw around me. Looking back, I'm really grateful I was young during those early goth years, because nowadays it appears to be a much more exclusive or fringe movement. I know it is still thriving, but at one time, it seemed that everyone was into it. Then, of course, the Dance culture took over and the part-timers moved on. No doubt modern kids into Dance think it's just as great as I thought our scene was, but to me the rave scene is impoverished by comparison. That's probably just my age showing!"

Caitlín: "I wouldn't say that I think anyone's ever born into goth. It's something I discovered within myself, a cumulative product of environment, various morbid curiosities, and antiquarianisms that unfolded as the years went by. I became fascinated with fantasy, especially dark fantasy, and weird fiction as a teenager, and that helped feed these fascinations. The trappings and ceremonies of Catholicism were also probably a factor, as was my family's belief in ghosts and hauntings. The veil that a lot of people seem determined to keep drawn between the rational and the irrational was very thin when I was a child, and sometimes it was brushed aside altogether."

Nancy: "I've always been quiet, a loner, struggling to make connections to people, generally stunned by the amount of useless babble and noise around me, and the shallow realm that the masses seem to prefer to live in and from which they relate. I've naturally been attracted to the fringes, where there's a chance to breathe. I remember being taken to an actual leftover beatnik coffeehouse in Philadelphia called the Artists' Hut when I was a kid and longing to be part of that exotic black-clad world which, by the time I was old enough to go to a club on my own, had dissolved into a psychedelic paradise—which was all right because that's where I first heard the Doors singing "The End." That darkness which inspired me is to me the precursor of goth, although it took a while for the outfits to move towards the shroud-like and Victorian attire I favor."

Freda: "I've always been allergic to the mainstream and liked the more alternative, underground, mysterious side of life, in literature, music, art, and everything. When I was at school in the seventies my friends and I loathed the ghastly pop of that era. We were into Alice Cooper and David Bowie! And I've loved the Hammer films and vampire and ghost stories since I was a child. These have obviously helped shape the imaginative landscape of my writing. *A Taste of Blood Wine* evolved from my longing to write a vampire novel in which the vampire (Karl) did not end up being staked, and in which his 'victim' (Charlotte) evolved from being victim to lover; actually passed through the vale of danger and came to know this perilous creature intimately. To do so, Charlotte has to make some terrifying and amoral choices. Fascinating ground that novels such as *Dracula* tended to shy away from, keeping things within a conventional Christian framework. The erotic subtext is there but very repressed. This was the sort of thing that Gothic literature led me to want to explore. To shine a light onto those dark things in the cobwebs!"

Sèphera: "All writers face obstacles, but being goth and being a writer must have presented special problems."

Storm: "Being goth has presented certain difficulties for me over the years. In particular, I felt that my appearance didn't go down too well in the established SF/fantasy scene when I first got published and started going to conventions, etc. For the most part, this was no doubt due to misunderstanding, but I do believe that some people didn't take me seriously and probably still don't! For all its technical flaws (so easy to see fifteen years on), I'm aware that the original *Wraeththu* novel, *Enchantments of Flesh and Spirit* did break ground when it came out. In 1987, (when it was first published in the UK), few writers had addressed issues of gender and sexuality in fantasy/SF fiction. There were a few notable exceptions, but on the whole it was a fairly prim scene. I don't think my first publishers knew quite how to promote me, so as a consequence—didn't."

Caitlín: "Yes, I think being goth has made things much more difficult at times. I'm not going to spend a lot of time bellyaching about success, because I think I've done so much better than I ever thought I would. But I know it has kept me at arm's length from a lot of readers, very close-minded people who see my byline and say, 'Oh no, not Caitlín Kiernan. Not that *goth*. How can anyone take that darkety-dark drivel seriously?' It's very difficult knowing that you're being judged a priori, the way people in the past have dismissed black writers and women writers, Jewish writers and gay writers. This was a big problem with *The Dreaming*, one that came as a surprise since one reason I was offered the gig in the first place was *because* I was goth. I'm very proud of most of my work on the series, as well as the work I continue to do for Vertigo, but I've had to deal with a lot of criticism that amounted to no more than people complaining about 'sissy goths' and stories that were 'too dark.'"

Nancy: "I think it's difficult just being alive, and if you add any extremism onto that, well, there are even more problems in your life. Following the rules almost always gets people the superficial rewards. If you are not born middle-class or wealthy, as I was not, if you have a penchant for darkness instead of light, as I do, if you are compelled to be a writer in a world where thought-provoking and emotional writing is considered barely tolerable and an unnecessary evil, well, you're going to have a rough time of it, as I have had. It's been a struggle, writing about darkness, being considered amoral in many ways because frequently I take the position of not judging my characters, which makes them seem immoral to the mainstream."

Freda: "Not at all, I never even thought about it! I'm just me. It's interesting though that developing a stronger, more gothic image has helped my public profile as a writer. I'm not the sort of person anyone would look at twice in everyday life, but by 'gothing up' I can make people look at me and remember me. I can turn their attention on or off according to the way I'm dressed. Gosh, it's only clothes and makeup, but it gives me a little bit of power I never had before! I don't think my writing will ever be truly mainstream, I think it's too quirky."

Sèphera: "Do you have any wisdom you'd like to impart to would-be writers, to fans, or to goths?"

Storm: "Fans are very important, because without them no writer would have an audience, so I have the greatest gratitude to and respect for mine. I'm lucky in that I have quite a close association with the core of my fan base—the people who have designed Web sites about my work or who write fan fiction based in worlds I've created. I'm holding a convention for them in England in October 2003 [Grissecon 1]."

Caitlín: "Stay spooky, dress better than everyone else, and chew with your mouth closed."

Nancy: "I'm so grateful that goth exists—or I would have had to invent it! Goths are the most interesting, intelligent, and creative people on this earth. I appreciate that my work appeals to such people, that I can call goths 'family' in the most positive meaning of the word. May the power of darkness continue to permeate our souls!"

Freda: "If you enjoy a book pass the word on to your friends. Publishers tell us that word-of-mouth is what really sells books, and that keeps them in print longer and means there will be more books published of the sort you like to read. And writers can keep on writing! And apart from that, thanks for reading my work. When people write or e-mail to tell me they've got so much out of one of my novels, it makes it all worthwhile. I really appreciate it."

Other undead authors goths admire include: Clive Baker, J.G. Ballard, Ray Bradbury, Italo Calvino, Clint Catalyst, Nick Cave, Nancy Collins, Charles de Lint, Umberto Eco, Harlan Ellison, Sèphera Girón, Tanya Huff, Barbara Hambly, Verschwende Deine Jugend (German New Wave and Punk scene), Stephen King, Tanith Lee, China Miéville, Octavio Paz, Terry Prachett, Thomas Roche, David Schow, Peter Underwood, Colin Wilson, and Mehitobel Wilson.

bards

Poets, that most misunderstood of species, are almost all goth by definition.

Rain Graves is coauthor of *The Gossamer Eye*, among the other poetry, fiction, and nonfiction she has published since 1997. She lives in San Francisco, and is the poetry editor for gothic.net. "I consider myself a lot of things—goth is definitely one of them. Given that most goths are defined by appearance, I should preface to say that on any given day I don't necessarily look or feel 'goth.' I teach and perform Argentine tango—so there are days I look like something out of a turn-of-the-century brothel in South America. There are days I'm corporate, and days I just go to the post office in ratty sweats. I'd say it would be more accurate to define me as Lon Chaney's daughter than anything else."

Rain believes that what makes a poem goth is that it "Tends to be of dark subject matter, angsty, sad, or macabre—from cemeteries to lovers to BDSM bloodplay. It's a fine line between what one might call 'goth' and just 'dark.' Dark poetry encompasses anything and everything a horror novel, dark fantasy novel, or science fiction novel might. Sonnets about Cthulhu. A love letter to Hannibal Lechter. The sadness one feels bending over the grave of their father, or mother, or child. These are things the literary world might dismiss as disgusting or outrageous subject matter, even though it may be written just as well as Tennyson or Keats. Dark poetry goes all the way back to them. It's been around in morbid fascination and revered for centuries but tucked away in that vein of 'literature' that cannot be touched in modern poetical times."

Like most poets, most writers, Rain derives inspiration from "People I meet, places I go, things I do, what I read. It could be the way a flower wilts in a dandelion patch, the way an old man is bent as he smiles, or a sudden impulse to catalogue someone else's beauty. Music, visual stimulation, and sometimes drink—it all lends to this in both good and bad ways. I have to 'feel' something before I can write it." Her favorite poets include "Malaysian writer A.M. Muffaz, Chilean Pablo Neruda, who wrote some chilling war poetry, Neil Gaiman, Canadian dark poet Sandra Kasturi, New York writer Linda Addison, Charlee Jacobs, Daphne Gottlieb. One can never forget Dante. "Manifestation of the Animals" by Ernest Bozzano. And Angus Griswold, a misguided Scottish writer, wrote some really gross dark poetry about sheep . . . but I digress."

Courtesy of The City Morgue. Photo by Larry Bradby

piercing periodicals

Magazines and periodicals come and go in the goth world. Many of the larger goth magazines are sprinkled throughout this book, catering to music, literature, fashion, and obscura. *The City Morgue* is a small publication, and reveals a lot of what little goth zines are about.

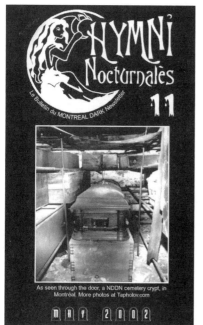

Courtesy of *Hymni Nocturnalès*. Photo by
Hugues Leblanc

Damion Boulden wanted to start a magazine because he thought
it would be a good way to get his art published, and to meet new
people. "We also wanted to give back something to the people to
enjoy, and to showcase local talent. This idea is, if there was no
place for Damion to showcase, then possibly no one else had an
outlet either."

The City Morgue is located in Alexandria, Virginia. Like many
labors of love, this magazine operates by collective, which includes
Damion—art/photo editor/layout; Joshua Hoover—ad/market-
ing manager; Carrie Hoover—article editor; Kris Kochevar—
business manager/copy editor; Christophe Maso—fiction editor.
Their first issue was born February 2002. Joshua says, "We try to
take a little of each area of goth and even branch out into non-goth
topics, since the majority of our content is based on people submit-
ting their work to us. We don't place restrictions requiring it to be
goth. We like to allow others to explore other genres, but we try to
maintain a goth theme. Initially we wanted to highlight local talent,
but realized if we wanted to branch out, we shouldn't limit ourselves to the
DC area for submissions. We now highlight artists nationwide and
abroad. A quarter of our print run is sent to the UK." He goes on to say
"We give a voice to the muted artist. We bring more than pretty pictured
models and fashion to life, or 'beautiful people.'"

Another small goth publication is the formerly black-and-white *Hymni
Nocturnalès,* a 90-percent French language zine out of Montréal, now a
Web publication. Their first issue appeared June 2001 and they have pub-
lished monthly since.

Michel Poulin de Courval, editor-in-chief of *Hymni Nocturnalès* says
that the collective began the publication in order "To promote the cultural
and artistic scene of nocturnal Québec. Any subject, artistic, musical, or
cultural that has a link with the night can be included. It's a place for expression of the dark side of goth artists, authors, painters, photographers,
or any fan of lunar inspiration. We want to gather as many artists as we
can in Québec around the same passion."

Hymni Nocturnalès features short prose, poems, papers on anthropo-
logical subjects, local and international news, CD and concert reviews,
any nighttime goth topics. "We're hoping to make the zine self-sustaining.
We'd like to expand our network beyond the zine to include other cultur-

al and artistic media to better promote the talents of local creative goths."

exquisite art

Ars Moriendi, illustrations of the art of dying, emerged in the fifteenth century when Europe was awash with plague. In these illustrations, the dying person encounters priests, demons, angels, friends, all of whom argue the merits of heaven or hell, trying to sway the soon-to-be-departed towards one realm or the other.

More than a century later, when the Cimetière des Innocents in Paris was destroyed, along with it went the walls. On those walls originated amazing and macabre artwork, accompanied by poetry attributed to Jean Gerson, all of which has come to be called *Danse Macabre* in French, the Dance of death in English, and *Totentanz* in German.

Danse Macabre, Basel, Switzerland
Courtesy of Hugues Leblanc

Danse Macabre artwork, and the poetic story often accompanying each illustration, is a dialogue and a dance between human beings and skeletons representing death. The skeletons, due to primitive medical knowledge, are not always anatomically correct. Sometimes they appear friendly, sometimes angry, rarely sad, occasionally menacing. They are engaged in energetic debate that has a seductive undertone because the job of the skeletons is to move the living along into their world.

The soon-to-cease-living human beings represent a spectrum of society: lawyer, doctor, priest, farmer, laborer, and so on. Death entices, cajoles, argues, all in an attempt to dance the mortal to his or her demise. In the end, of course, Death succeeds. *Danse Macabre* is a memento mori (remember, you must die). The dance is irrespective of persons. The theme clearly reminds us that each one of us will die, eventually, from the wealthiest corporate mogul to the poorest homeless person, the exercise fanatic to the terminally-ill patient, the newborn and the centenarian, men, women, hermaphrodites, and transgendered alike, all will reach a level playing field in the end.

Fortunately, a few copies based on the original *Danse Macabre* artwork at the Cimetière des Innocents were made on church walls in France and other European cities. Unfortunately only a handful remain.

Publisher Guyot Marchand in 1486 used Gerson's poem, and illustrations by an anonymous artist who replicated the twenty-three tableauxs from the walls of the Cimetière des Innocents based on woodcuts done the year before by Hans Holbein the Younger. Holbein's woodcuts have become the template for *Danse Macabre* that has come down to us through the ages, reproduced most often in books. All of the people depicted in the original *Danse Macabre* were male.

In France at that time, the *Danse Macabre* frescoes at La Chaise-Dieu were the only ones commonly known to include women. Then another set of frescoes of females (and males) with skeletons, *The Dance of Basel,* was discovered in Switzerland in 1480 when a Dominican convent of sisters was evacuated. The macabre dance of Kleinbasel reveals female figures conversing with death. The nunnery was demolished but fortunately an exact copy had been made across the Danube at a monastery, preserving the female Dance of Death. Here, death can even be amusing.

Another *Danse Macabre des Femmes* (Dance of Death of Women) found in a lavishly illuminated late-medieval manuscript, is based on a fifteenth-century French poem by Martial of Auvergne that describes thirty-six women, called to dance with skeletons.

Death in skeletal form varies in its depiction, depending on the country from which it originates. German images are a bit more grisly, showing some flesh remaining, and a few tufts of hair. Elsewhere, figures appear more stark, the drawings primitive. Still others are sophisticated. Some dances show several skeletons and several people together.

Between the seventeenth and the twentieth centuries, artists in Germany, England, Italy, Belgium, the Netherlands, the United States, and elsewhere have produced artwork utilizing the same type of imagery, of a skeleton patiently bringing the living toward dissolution. Notable is Thomas Chambra's illustrations of the eighteenth century.

Another extensive Dance of Death appeared in England at the end of the nineteenth century when noted humorist and political satirist and artist Thomas Rowlandson produced two volumes of wry poetry and tinted sketches of skeletons in dialogue with (usually) resistant Englishmen and women.

Danse Macabre is also the name of a famous symphonic poem for orchestra, reminiscent of bony skeletons dancing in graveyards. Camille Saint-Saëns, born in 1835, was the composer, and his macabre work was thought to be influenced by his readings of the bubonic plague of the fourteenth century.

The founder of a California theatrical troupe researched the *Danse Macabre* woodcuts, fascinated by the instruments many of the skeletons are seen with in the drawings, and replicated those musical instruments, then formed the Bone Band, which also draws its influences from Mexico's Day of the Dead festivities.

For over thirty years the grinning skull with roses motif—an early death's image—has been symbolic of the rock band the Grateful Dead.

The goth-Industrial metal border-crossing band Danse Macabre uses the name, and one of their most famous songs is "Totentanz," German for "dead dance."

California artist Beatrice Coron has produced a modern *Danse Macabre* of paper cuttings and dialogues based on the original works, in a limited edition of three copies!

There's a goth message board called Danse Macabre; bestselling horror author Stephen King wrote his thoughts and experiences with the world of horror in the book entitled *Danse Macabre*; the role-playing game set in 1356 Paris is called Danse Macabre; there exists a 3-D comic called *Danse Macabre*; and the entire country of Mexico devotes two days a year to their living version of *Danse Macabre: el Dia de los Muertos* (the Day of the Dead) (see Chapter 10), during which human beings dance alongside skeletons through the streets, reflecting the eternal connection between the living and those who have passed before them through the veil to another realm.

the Pre-Raphaelites

Pre-Raphaelite art and goth are linked at the soul level. Pre-Raphaelite paintings, from the mid- to late-1800s, were typically executed in delicate colors with a kind of inner radiance to the work. The subject matter involves brooding faces, sometimes trance-like and full of moodiness. Sensitive men and dreamy, languid women full of half-requited or suicidal passions portray moments of mythological stories and legends that had often been told through poetry. The highly romantic bittersweet images that the Pre-Raphaelite painters are famous for evoke emotion in the viewer—what the painters intended.

In 1848 England, the Pre-Raphaelite Brotherhood was founded—a group of young painters who changed painting forever. Three of the originals were John Everett Millais, William Holman Hunt, and Dante Gabriel Rossetti. An unconventional lot, they flew in the face of rules and what was expected of painters then, and managed to turn the world of painting of the day upside-down. Millais described the then-favored style of painting as "Drooping branches of brown trees over a night-like sky, or a column with a curtain unnaturally arranged."

The Pre-Raphaelite painters worked with light, attempting to capture a natural feeling by painting on a wet white background, a technique derived from fresco painting. As Gay Daly describes in her book *Pre-Raphaelites in Love*, their methods departed radically from what was fashionable in the art world at that time, where painting was done on a dry canvas coated with asphaltum, a tarry brown compound that muted colors. The Pre-Raphaelites decided that the previous three centuries of art were lacking in aesthetics and jumped back in time, pre-Renaissance, prior to the painter Raphael, in order to capture the spirit of the early Italian artists. They wanted to return to a direct connection to nature. They craved that inner light.

They achieved their goal, but not without a tremendous amount of rejection by the established order. Back then, the Royal Academy was the only game in town for painters. The curse of death was either to not have a painting selected for exhibition there, or to be hung so high up the wall toward the vaulted ceiling that no one could see your work. It took years for these three innovators to be shown at eye level.

What captures most people immediately about Pre-Raphaelite art is the use of vibrant, almost burning color, color that—combined with the bittersweet emotions captured on the faces of the subjects and the intense, often dark, mood—stirs the emotions and moves the soul.

Perhaps the most well-known painting is by John William Waterhouse, not one of the original Pre-Raphaelites, but of the second wave, who came thirty years later. His *The Lady of Shalott*, painted in 1888, depicts what many goths consider to be the most poignant heartbreaking sadness. This classical image is based on the beautiful and moody poem by Alfred, Lord Tennyson written in 1832. (see Chapter 5).

As amazing as the Pre-Raphaelite paintings are, they could not have been accomplished without the help of the women who modeled for them. Many of those women were shopgirls or ladies of the night, whom the Pre-Raphaelite painters discovered and became obsessed with.

Elizabeth Siddal, found working in a hat shop, is the most well-known, and perhaps the most pathetic of the models. Siddal and Rossetti eventually married, but only after years of a tumultuous relationship. Siddal produced some artwork in her own right in the Pre-Raphaelite style, for which she received positive critical review. Lizzie's life was full of illness and insecurity. The only child she conceived was stillborn. She died of laudanum poisoning. Rossetti stood over her body for four days after her death crying "Lizzie, Lizzie, come back to me."

The Pre-Raphaelites were innovators, outré artists, given to experimentation in both their work and their lifestyles. More than one model had an affair with more than one artist. Their complicated relationships, based on mixing passion and beauty, resulted in wild and tempestuous involvements. A shared aesthetic in art extended to relationships. Reading about their lives is about as close to a goth soap opera as one can get.

modern gothic art

One modern gothic favorite is the late Edward Gorey, writer of idiosyncratic little books illustrated with his humorously stark black-and-white artwork evoking Victorian society. Gorey managed to illustrate in words and pictures a wicked bend in reality, creating slightly odd and unnervingly off-kilter images.

Edward St. John Gorey was born on February 22, 1925, in Chicago. He was not part of the nineteenth century, nor did he travel outside the United States. He spent most of his life on Cape Cod, alone, an eccentric, occasionally traveling to New York City to see the ballet. He was, apparently, a highly opinionated man, bizarre, living a lifestyle that definitely reflected another era, one in which eccentricity was encouraged if not valued. His love of the arts was particular, and ranged from classical ballet to *The X-Files* and *Buffy the Vampire Slayer*.

The Victorian mode of expression he favored in his artwork and the

PRE-RAPHAELITE MODELS AND THEIR LOVES

Fanny Cornforth: (Lady of the night, long-term affair with the married Rossetti)

Jane Burden: (Unhappily married to Pre-Raphaelite arts-and-crafts artist William Morris, long-term affair with Rossetti, affair with Blunt). Morris appeared in many Pre-Raphaelite paintings, including Rossetti's Proserpine.

Georgiana Macdonald: (Painted in her own right. Wife of Edward Burne-Jones, who had affairs during his marriage to Maria Zambaco, Frances Horner, and Helen Mary Gaskell)

Annie Miller: (Barmaid/lady of the night, affairs with Rossetti, Hunt, and Lord Ranelagh whom she eventually married)

Fanny Miller: (Dubious background, married Hunt, died in childbirth)

Christina Rossetti: (Poet and sister to Rossetti)

Effie Ruskin: (Married art critic John Ruskin, affair with Millais, scandalous divorce from Ruskin and marriage to Millais)

Elizabeth Siddal: (Married Dante Gabriel Rossetti. Achieved critical acclaim as a painter in her own right)

Edith Waugh: (Second wife to Holman Hunt)

Maria Zambaco: (Affair with the married Edward Burne-Jones)

French bons mots sprinkled throughout his written work are not from his direct experience with Victorian England or France, although he did study French. Gorey—and goths relate to him partially for this reason—loved a time and place not his own. He brought another century to life in both his art and in his lifestyle.

The subject matter of Gorey's books and art is familiar. We've read his demented little poetic snippets and highly cryptic phrases that accompany his fine black-and-white drawings of dismal and helpless beings stuck in A Situation. His artwork extended beyond the interiors and covers of his own books to be included in the work of others as well.

Edward Gorey is even more popular posthumously than during his lifetime. Now all manner of products bearing Edward Gorey's hapless full-moonfaced characters is available: *Deranged Cousins* calendars, *Neglected Murderesses* date books, address books depicting the *Man in the Long Raccoon Coat*, Christmas cards featuring various Victorians carting their fruitcakes to an ice hole to be dropped in. (Gorey hated fruitcake and joked that there were only a few fruitcakes in the world, never eaten, repackaged each Christmas and given as gifts.) There are CD covers, rubber stamps, mouse pads, posters, and on and on. PBS commissioned Gorey to design a little coffin as a giveaway that has become a valuable collectible. The Funeral Consumers Alliance commissioned a T-shirt design, two designs for coffee mugs, as well as the cover sketch on the booklet and another sketch on the refrigerator magnet included in the package of their "Before I Go, You Should Know" end-of-life planning kit. One mug features the twenty-six adorable children of his *Gashleycrumb Tinies* world, accompanied by the cadaverous stovepipe-hatted funeral director holding a large, black umbrella haphazardly over their cherubic heads.

Perhaps Gorey's most famous work, and one for which he won awards, is the theater poster (and sets) he created for the 1977 Broadway production of *Dracula* starring Frank Langella. It is a perfect example of the artist's charmingly macabre style—the fragile heroine adorned in gauzy fabric, draped across the lavish bed while the dark, bewinged vampire gazes down upon her with not-quite-obvious ill intent.

Certainly it is the darkside of life that Gorey presented to us, the world goths understand only too well. Often his women and children possess a waif-like fragility, a born-victim quality. He drew ballerinas. His men wore running shoes, and long fur coats (as did Gorey himself). Beyond his humans, Gorey portrayed cats—he had a houseful. But some of his characters were like gargoyles in that they were neither this nor that— most popular is the strange and pointy-faced, scarf-and-Keds-wearing creature featured in *The Doubtful Guest*.

Edward Gorey declared that he had no wish to live on into the twenty-first century. He died April 13, 2000, of a heart attack. Thank God his work exists. Almost every one of *The †* *Section* mentioned Gorey and, to quote *ariana*, "We would be lesser mortals without him."

Another popular modern artist is British photographer Simon Marsden. Simon, fifty-three years old, lives in the countryside of England. His amazing photographs have seen print in seven books. The haunting other-worldly style and the dark subject matter he pursues—from decrepit ruins to nature's bleakness to the lost elements of previously communist East Germany and the darkly romantic sites in Venice—ensure that his work is beloved by goths around the world.

Simon says he had no idea what he wanted to do in life until he became interested in photography but: "My father gave me a camera on my twenty-first birthday."

He claims he was ". . . brought up in a haunted house in the remote English countryside, and my father had a large library of books on the supernatural. I am beginning to realize that I have always been interested in the Gothic period, the architecture, the romance, perhaps the highest point in the history of man's artistic achievements."

Besides a sharp eye for subject matter and angle, what makes his photographs so eerily beautiful is technique. He uses black-and-white infrared film, which turns day into night. The result is a photo that resembles an etching. "My pictures have always been dark and mysterious, no matter what the subject matter," but he recognizes that "some people seem frightened by the images."

Simon photographs with an honorable objective in mind. "I simply want to inspire the viewer not to take everything around him or her at face value; to show that what we are conditioned to believe is 'reality' may not be all it seems, if only we take the time to inquire."

One of his favorite moments involves a goth. "During an exhibition for the book *Visions of Poe* in a London gallery, I spent an afternoon in the gallery on the opening day where I noticed a very gothic-looking lady spending a very long time looking at the pictures. After about an hour she left without saying a word, returning ten minutes later with a beautiful bunch of white lilies which she presented to me on behalf of herself and all like-minded people, as a thank you for presenting such a beautiful and moving show-book."

His most recent work is *The Twilight Hour*, photographs illustrating extracts from masters of the supernatural with Celtic ancestry, which includes Bram Stoker, Edgar Allan Poe, and Sheridan le Fanu. He has also just released a seventy-minute film on the same subject called *Simon Marsden's The Twilight Hour*.

Other artists, past to present, special to goths are: Lorraine Albright, Diane Arbus; Jason Beam; Ambrose Bierce; William Blake; Hieronymus Bosch; Sandro Botticelli; Walter Crane; Salvador Dalí; Leonardo da Vinci; Edgar Degas; Gustave Doré; Albrecht Dürer; (Romaine de Tirtoff) Erté; M.C. Escher; Brian Froud; H.R. Giger; Jenny Holtzer; David Horton; Paul Klee; Gustav Klimt; Ivan Le; Robert Mapplethorpe; Franz Marc; René Magritte; John Martinez; Dave McKean; Michaelangelo Buonarroti; Claude Monet; Henry Moore; Alphonse Mucha; Theirry Mugler; Edvard Munch; Kay Neilsen; Georgia O'Keefe; Yoko Ono; Michael Parkes; Pablo Picasso; Floria Sigismondi; Vincent van Gogh; Andy Warhol, and Joel Peter Whitkin.

The most beloved contemporary artist among goths universally is, not surprisingly, Tim Burton. Burton is best known for his movies, with goth favorites being: *Beetle Juice; Ed Wood; Edward Scissorhands; Sleepy Hollow* and the wonderful grimly clever animation *The Nightmare Before Christmas*. Yet Burton did not begin his career in film; he started work as a cartoonist, and an animator for Walt Disney Studios.

Tim Burton was born in conformist, middle-of-the-road Burbank, California in 1958. In an online interview with Gavin Smith, he said, "When you grow up in a blank, unemotional environment . . . the impulse to create and do stuff, especially movies, is a desire to create things that you are lacking in your life." A quiet and moody boy who loved horror films, he drew from an early age. As a youth, he made a couple of Super-8 movies, one a wolf tale, another called *The Island of Doctor Agor*.

He said in the same interview that he was drawn toward filmmaking because it forced him to relate to people. "When you look at all the people who work in films, they're all kind of loser types." But working on a film, "All of a sudden you find yourself in an environment where you have to speak to hundreds of people during a day."

Burton won a scholarship and attended the California Institute for the Arts in 1979 and 1980, a school founded by Walt Disney. He ended up working for Disney, but much of the "happy" animation he did left him depressed. He longed for work that let in the darkness which, of course, Disney Studios was not known for then. But it was in 1982, while working for Disney, that he had the opportunity to create the very gothic five-minute short *Vincent*, a tribute to one of his idols, Vincent Price, which Price narrated. He also wrote and directed the twenty-nine-minute live-action *Frankenweenie* in 1984, a remake of *Frankenstein* where the monster is a dog. Disney deemed the latter an unsuitable product and the film did not see video release until 1992. Ironically, it premiered on the Disney Channel! Both of these films can be viewed on *The Nightmare Before Christmas* DVD.

Tim Burton has a passionate love of myths and fairy tales and the derth of such in the United States has led him to try to create a few. *Edward Scissorhands*—intrinsically goth—is one attempt. He told Smith, "The people I have known who have been individuals have always been tortured. There's this love-hate thing in the [U.S.]; they get preyed upon and devoured." Another element in the film comes from Burton's psyche. He admits to being a Punk-music junkie in his youth, and he frequented clubs but he could never bring himself to speak with anyone. *Edward Scissorhands* captures that sense of the outsider, of alienation, of strong emotions with no way to verbally communicate them to another person.

Burton has said he is fascinated with dualities, and most of his films reflect that. Perhaps this is why he has been such an incredible success in Hollywood and yet at the same time embraced by goths.

tV witb bite

"Six participants were chosen at random from a murder of goths at Toronto's Velvet Underground bar. Representing S.S.U. (Shapeshifter University): Liisa Ladouceur, a writer; Baron Marcus, a Microsoft Access developer as well as frontman for the band Vampire Beach Babes; and

Drawing by Hugues Leblanc

Renee, a student of biomechanical engineering. Representing B.S.C. (Bloodsucker College): Singuala, door girl at an unnamed New York gothic club; Peter Mansfield, gothic zinester; and Stephanie Quinlan, moderator of the Toronto Dark Writers' Group. And let us not forget the stunning Ola, our Vanna White in black."

These are the words of Canadian writer and Book TV head honcho Daniel Richler, who produced *Reach for the Crypt*, the first goth game show for TV. Daniel acts as host, tossing out questions about the King of the Undead himself, Dracula. The correct answers are confirmed by Dracula specialist Elisabeth Miller. "It's dressed up as the 'several thousandth' episode," Daniel says, "as if it were a show doomed to air eternally with the two teams forever stuck 'neck and neck' [*arf arf*], at fourteen hundred and thirty eight points apiece. [The points are years accumulated on the teams' respective gravestones; the aim is to catch up with the present Year of Our Lord, thus to be released from the agony of undeath and to die, at last, in peace. But of course the episode ends with the same score it started with.]

"My principal interest," Daniel confides, "was to demonstrate that those weird, shrouded kids you see squinting against the sun aren't only fashion victims; that they are the most literate of the pop tribes, in my view. *RFTC* was inspired first and foremost by Dr. Miller's *Dracula: Sense and Nonsense*. But it was also an opportunity to talk about writers of gothic interest such as Sheridan le Fanu, Andrei Codrescu, Oscar Wilde, et al. In the end I think the teams acquit themselves very well, demonstrating a healthy mix of obsession and bullshit detection, especially since half the show was booby-trapped."

Daniel authored the Punk coming-of-age novel *Kicking Tomorrow* in 1992. Does he consider himself goth? "I'd feel like a pretender if I called myself a goth. I look pretty bad in a fishnet shirt and corset collar, for a start. I also think that saying 'I'm goth' sounds like you're trying too hard; like being eccentric, it's something that's better said of you by others. Nonetheless, I developed a gothic sensibility quite early. I was also aware at the time that my mother bore a striking resemblance to Morticia Addams. Later on my father wrote some movies and I remember him sending me a letter from Hollywood that bore the *The Omen*'s six-six-six logo on the envelope; he wrote me that all the research you'll ever need is contained in Revelations. Latterly, my interest in modern goths stemmed from a glancing reportorial acquaintance with the guys in Bauhaus, and from a more sustained relationship with some Hungarian *Grufti*—the goths notorious for keeping up that country's world-ranking suicide performance. Come to think of it, I don't see how it's possible to a have a 'sustained' relationship with suicides. . . ."

Reach for the Crypt has aired in Canada, and is making the rounds and may see the light of the moon on a TV screen near you.

Many of *The † Section* does not watch much or any TV. And when they do watch, most claim they don't like it. *DUSK* says, "What's available? So let's say [I watch] nothing." More than one of *The † Section* watches "the news!" *Vile* admits. And *Cemetery Crow* says, "The news. I love it. Don't ask me why!" *VampirMike* says he "watches it all, because it's fun to see the crazy people."

sinister cinema

Theda Bara and Rudolph Valentino, Hollywood silent screen stars around the 1920s, were both early prototypes of the goth look. Theda snagged the term "vamp," with her sultry and seductive look, and became the precursor for female vampires in silent films. Valentino exuded the charm and charisma of the darkly romantic and exquisitely handsome lover, full of passion and not afraid to express it.

In 1922 the German filmmaker F. W. Murnau tried to buy the film rights to Bram Stoker's novel *Dracula*. Stoker's widow, Florence, refused to sell. Undaunted, the thirty-four-year-old Murnau made the film anyway. To get around the copyright issue, he called his movie *Nosferatu*, and named the vampire Count Orlok, played so disturbingly by actor Max Schreck. He was sued for copyright infringement anyway. Florence asked the court to order all copies of the black-and-white silent film destroyed by fire. But, of course, mysteriously, copies survived, or we wouldn't be able to see the movie today.

Murnau went on to make other films, including *Faust*. He died in 1931 in Santa Barbara, California, when his car went off the road on a stretch of coastline. His fourteen-year-old Filipino houseboy Garcia Stevenson was driving. The book *Hollywood Babylon* recounts a rumor that Murnau was pleasuring his houseboy at the time of the accident.

In 1979 German filmmaker Werner Herzog directed the gorgeous remake, called *Nosferatu the Vampyre*, starring the late Klaus Kinski as the hideous Orlok, and Isabelle Adjani as his exquisitely beautiful nemesis,

Lucy Harker. Set to the lonely and terrifying music of Richard Wagner, almost every goth who sees this film has been swept away by the dark magic of Herzog's cinematic poetry.

The superb 2001 movie *Shadow of the Vampire*, directed by E. Elias Merhige and starring Villem Dafoe and John Malkovich, is an intriguing fantasy of the filming of the original *Nosferatu*.

One modern cinema vamp with super goth appeal is Elvira, aka, Cassandra Peterson, who says, "Do I consider myself a goth? I consider myself the Queen of Goths! I hate to sound too egotistical, but I feel very much like Elvira is somewhat of a forerunner of the goth movement. When I started doing the character, people looked at me like [I was] some kind of a freak just because my nails were black! Now Beverly Hills wives paint their nails black. It's great that all the misfits and freaks of the world, like myself, have their own special club to belong to."

Elvira got her start on TV. "I first hosted late-night horror movies on TV in L.A., then was able to syndicate the show across the country and eventually wrote and sold a movie idea involving the character [*Elvira, Mistress of the Dark*] and actually got it made. It only took thirteen years to get another movie made!" [*Elvira's Haunted Hills* (2001)]

The slinky, witty Elvira who sports the ultimate in an hourglass figure, came about, like so many cool things in life, by accident. Cassandra says, "I actually didn't have any role models for Elvira. I got the part in 1981 when the director at a local L.A. TV station was looking for someone to host old horror movies and saw me doing improv with the Groundlings, a popular improvisational comedy group in L.A. (along with Phil Hartman and Paul "Pee-wee Herman" Reubens). Once I got the part, the station told me I needed a 'scary' look, since, after all, I *was* hosting horror movies. Their only stipulation was that I dress all in black.

"My best friend at the time, Robert Redding, designed the 'look.' He borrowed the hairstyle from Ronnie Spector of the sixties girl group the Ronettes, the makeup from a book about Japanese Kabuki theater, and the dress . . . well, he just designed it as low-cut and form-fitting as possible, since, as we all know, sex sells.

"Vampira, of fifties horror-hosting fame, later sued me for allegedly ripping her off, but it was thrown out of court. If anything, I subconsciously got input for my character from Morticia Addams, since I grew up worshiping *The Addams Family* TV show."

She sees her most recent movie, *Elvira's Haunted Hills*, as a goth staple. "I think it's a perfect movie for the goth crowd because its roots are in the old gothic-horror films of the sixties from AIP, Hammer, and Roger Corman. It also costars Richard O'Brien, the writer, creator and costar of *The Rocky Horror Picture Show*, and of course, it stars . . . Elvira!"

Goth favorite directors and filmmakers include: Dario Argento, John Carpenter, David Cronenberg, Werner Herzog, David Lynch, Quentin Tarantino, and Guillermo Del Toro.

high- and lowbrow art

In 1897 France, a type of theater became popular known as *Le Grand Guignol*, and its grisly reign lasted for sixty years. Taking bites out of the ancient Greek playwright Aeschylus, and elements of medieval, Elizabethan, and Jacobean dramas as well as the dark emotions of Gothic melodrama, Le Grand Guignol went further in its outrageous approach to violence than all of those, and became the sinister granddaddy of modern horror.

In its day, it did blatantly what theater had not done before—throats were slit, eyeballs gouged out, limbs severed. Fake blood spurted freely from the stage, chopped limbs dropped to the floor, gore splattered the audience—all this was early FX, but not the Hollywood type. Terror and cruelty were its backbone, black humor the underbelly. In its heydays actors fought for parts in these shows, and the theater of *le Grand Guignol* drew to the theater hordes of tourists and Parisian regulars—called *Guignolers*—all hoping to be shocked, hell-bent on a dose of ultra-reality of the perverse kind. This is the basis for the Theatre of the Vampires that Anne Rice so cleverly wrote about in *Interview With the Vampire*, whose star performer, the vampire Armand, was alluringly played on the screen by Antonio Banderas.

Live theater, dance, and opera often appeal to goths, especially performances involving darker subject matter, like the undead.

Dracula, on Broadway and on tour, with its decadent Edward Gorey sets, starred Frank Langella, who brought that production to film with Kate Nelligan as Mina Harker. This modern version showed the audience more overt eroticism than previous retellings of Stoker's classic.

The opera *Der Vampyr* by Heinrich Marschner, the nineteenth-century German composer, has never been staged outside Germany. The story is based on the short story "The Vampire," started by English poet Lord Byron. His personal physician, John Polidori, pulled the fragment from the trash, completed the tale, and published it under his own name.

The Canadian Broadcasting Corporation (CBC) produced a television adaptation of the Royal Winnipeg Ballet performance of *Dracula*, directed by Guy Madden, who specializes in films with a 1930s German-decadence look. The filmed ballet morphed into a film directed by Madden: *Dracula: Pages From a Virgin's Diary*, a quirky old-cinema-style movie full of wit and touches of surrealism, staring Wei Qiang-Zhang as Dracula.

Nosferatu was transformed into an opera, staged in various parts of North America in 1991, written by Randolph Peters—demand for tickets for the world premier was unprecedented.

Dracul, An Eternal Love Story, was staged by Mainstage Productions for the first time in California in 1997, with an accompanying CD, and a novel based on the production written by Nancy Kilpatrick.

One popular European opera was *The Last Vampire Show*, staged initially in Vienna in 1997.

Other goth favorites include the musical *Phantom of the Opera*; the play *Dr. Jekyll and Mr. Hyde*; the stage musical and film *The Rocky Horror Picture Show*; the ballet *Frankenstein*; the sideshow *Carnival Diablo;* and the stage play and film *Marat/Sade*.

URLs
Poppy Z. Brite
www.poppyzbrite.com/

Storm Constantine
www.stormconstantine.com

Caitlín Kiernan
www.caitlin-r-kiernan.com

Nancy Kilpatrick
www.nancykilpatrick.com

Freda Warrington
www.members.aol.com/FredaMike/index.html

Rain Graves
www.raingraves.com

Danse Macabre
www.geocities.com/ppollefeys/dance.htm

The Bone Band
www.gregoland.com/bones/

Beatrice Coron: artist creating modern Danse Macabre
www.beatricecoron.com/dansemacabre.html

Funeral Consumers Alliance
www.funerals.org/bookstore/index.htm

The Strange Case of Edward Gorey
by Alexander Theroux Fantagraphics Books
www.fantagraphics.com/

Paul Joyce
www.pbjoyce.co.uk/

Simon Marsden Archive
www.marsdenarchive.com/

Hugues Leblanc's macabre photos
www.tapholov.com

Stéphane Lord's Dark Fairies
www.necrobabes.org/darkfairies/main2.htm

My Pet Skeleton
www.mypetskeleton.com/

Monolith Graphics
www.monolithgraphics.com/

The City Morgue
www.thecitymorgue.com

Hymni Nocturnalès
www.hymninocturnales.com

Tim Burton
www.minadream.com/timburton/home.htm

Elvira
www.elvira.com

THE PRETERNATURAL
IS CALLING

Pay the exorcist, or get repossessed!

psychic phenomenon

When the supernatural, psychic, or paranormal experience enters a room, anything beyond normal dreaming, and that déjà vu we all experience makes its presence felt, goths are on it, tuning their ESP antennae. Many goths have stories to tell.

Amanda: "On December 9, 1997, I sat at the piano and wrote a song titled 'In Heaven.' The song and most of the lyrics came out within twenty minutes. I shook my head and thought, 'Okay . . . In Heaven . . . whatever!' It wasn't until six weeks later that my mother called to tell me my dear friend Michael had passed away on December 9, 1997. The song has been dedicated to him, since it was his presence that inspired that gift to me as he traveled onto the next world."

ariana: "I am a tarot reader and have had a few odd experiences. I have definitely communicated with my dead grandmother. I have also communicated with the 'spirits' of loved ones that my clients ask me about."

Azazelle: "My house may have a ghost. There are many times when we have seen or felt a presence here—thinking that someone has come up behind you, talking to them, and when there's no answer, turning to find no one there. And the person you thought you were talking to is clear off in another part of the house. Once we saw a book fly off the shelf for no ap-

The Lady Para-Norma
Artwork by Vincent Marcone

parent reason. Once I thought my cat Monster was behind the door I was trying to open because I felt resistance, but he wasn't there. An owner of this house got run over by a car just around the corner. Sometimes we think it might be her. In a different house I once owned there were definitely cold spots, and once I heard breathing at the end of the bed when no one was there. It's just sort of mundane strangeness."

C.B.: "About a year ago I was in a restaurant that was closed for the evening. It was quiet and dark. A very weird chill. My friend told me later a male ghost is rumored to inhabit the place. It wasn't threatening, just a very odd feeling, one which I haven't felt since."

Individuation: "I've been 'in tune' since I was about five. I've felt, seen and heard 'ghosts' for lack of a better term. I really, really, really hated it. It's scary. Growing up, there were three places in my parents' house that really freaked me out. I had to run past them. In my early twenties my father and I were talking about the supernatural after watching a film on TV and he told me about experiences he'd had in the house. He'd seen a small boy in pajamas (I only have sisters) in three different spots. The same three that always terrified me. Apparently a small boy passed away due to illness in the house before they bought it. Lots of other things have happened, but I'd prefer not to talk about them."

Medea: "I have a ghost in my house who smokes. (No one else does, but you can smell it.) She died of emphysema while living here."

Miss Lynx: "I used to be really uncomfortable with cemeteries, up until the funeral of a close friend several years ago, who had been heavily into Santeria. The funeral was done Santeria style, with drumming, dancing, and random possession of people by the Orishas (spirits/deities). I ended up possessed by Oya, who is among other things, Mistress of the Cemetery. When I gazed around the cemetery in the afterglow of the ritual, I thought it was the most beautiful place I'd ever seen. Also, I've been practicing Wicca for over twenty years, with occasional forays into Santeria, chaos magic, and other magical paths, and I've had one hell of a lot of supernatural experiences. I've seen someone possessed by the Orisha Chango set himself on fire without being burned. I've seen someone deathly allergic to peppers eat them while possessed without being harmed. I've done quite a lot of magical rituals that have gotten results, including one intensive healing ritual on someone in hospital where I could see the results of what I was doing on the digital displays of the machines the patient was hooked up to. I've been in a coven where we did a lot of exorcisms and 'ghostbusting.' One time, in a house we were working on, I looked in a mirror and saw my normal reflection, but the flesh melting off my bones, leaving only a skull. It completely creeped me out!"

Nevermore: "I love the stunning sculpture and landscaping of local cemeteries when I'm traveling. I often photograph local cemeteries, and take my video camera at night. I got footage of a floating orb. It was at night, and as I zoomed the camera closer, it seemed to move away. During the day I was walking around the cemetery and saw an older headstone with two stone pots, one on either side. I looked in and saw plain white pebbles in both. I continued walking for awhile and then went back past that stone. When I looked in the pots again, the pebbles in the pot on the right had what looked like dried blood all over them. There was no one else in the cemetery; I have no idea how the blood or whatever got there. To this day, it's still there."

Vena Cava: "Elmwood Cemetery, in Memphis. I originally went with a tour, then again by myself one quiet Saturday morning with my camera. Though I was supposedly alone, I saw human-shaped shadows walking a foot above the grass, with no human to cast them, and heard footsteps on the walkway behind me that stopped when I stopped, but no one was there. No one had mentioned the place being haunted. They weren't scary ghosts—I felt curiosity and loneliness. Hardly anyone goes there anymore. I like to go now so they have someone to visit them. Also, in a former apartment I was writing a warlock story and one night the room filled with the strong odor of sewage. I investigated, but the plumbing was all right. Then I had a very strong impression of something huge and dark hovering behind me. I prayed for God to send whatever it was away, and after a few words of prayer, it was gone. Next, my neighbor and his girlfriend moved into that room. I'd left a large sorrowful angel picture on the wall. He placed his monster toys and action figures on shelves and a few

Ten ways to slow down, perhaps even stop a vampire

(courtesy Dr. Jeanne K. Youngson, president, the Vampire Empire)

1. Drive a nail through its forehead.

2. Cut out its heart and slice it in twain.

3. Smear it with the fat of a pig killed on St. Ignatius' Day.

4. Put a clove of garlic, a stone, or a lemon in its mouth.

5. Sprinkle its body with holy water.

6. Drive a stake through its heart.

7. Give it a knitted sock to unravel.

8. Bury it face downward.

9. Take away its shroud.

10. Blow up its tomb.

Sire Cédric

Photo by Andy Julia

days later came running up to me to say, 'Why say I can decorate however I want if you're going to mess with my things?' I didn't know what he was talking about but when I followed him to his room, all the action figures were turned to face that painting. Then, in the days that followed, things began disappearing from where they had been placed, only to reappear a few seconds later somewhere else. Sometimes I would say, half jokingly, 'Okay, give it back!' Bing! There the item would be. It creeped me out. His girlfriend heard someone 'walking' in the hall, and refused to stay in the room alone. We three would sit in my room watching TV and hear his little motion-detector figures go off, one after the other, in a row, as if someone was walking in front of them. The presence continued to drive us crazy and we three sat together and concentrated *GO AWAY!* Next morning my lamp shade I'd left in their room was ripped to shreds as if by claws, and my keys were bent double! After that, we never heard from it again. I've had many other experiences."

Sally: "I talked with a transparent man in my bedroom when I was less than three years old, and remember it well. I met Alexander, our ghost in Atlanta, which guests saw as well. To get to sleep as a child, I used to 'chat' with knocking conversations on the wall with invisible respondents. I passed through a cold area on the staircase of an old house that made me cry for no reason—the house is known as haunted."

Shekinah: "In our old house, which was getting on a hundred years old, I used to feel like I was being watched all the time, especially when alone. Not in a threatening way, more like an invisible friend. We did find a gravestone in the backyard."

XjUsTcRuCifyX: "I feel the dead. I feel cold spots quite a lot, but they calm me—I think it is someone I know who died. I must sleep under covers because the cold spots make me very uncomfortable so I protect myself from them. I saw the ghost of a horse come to me six months before my favorite horse died. It might seem trivial, but the horse I saw died of cancer. Immediately I called the barn to see if anything was wrong. My horse was sick, and they didn't find out until a few months later what it was. He was put out of his misery shortly after that."

Dracula and friends

Vampires have appeared in the mythology of just about every culture since the beginning of recorded history. *The Epic of Gilgamesh* in 2500 B.C.

talks about the Death Bringer, one who preys upon human beings, forcing death upon them, and the vampire has grown in popularity ever since.

Often the vampire is a formerly living human being who is now not quite dead, rather, undead as they say. Traditionally the undead stalk the living, often those who were close in life. In the European tradition, the nosferatu drinks human blood. But in other cultures the cherished source of nourishment is energy, time, dreams, the soul itself. In Katherine V. Forrest's story "Oh Captain, My Captain," a vampire lives off vaginal secretions.

Vampires possess a number of bewildering traits: they can fly; hop (China); walk through walls; appear in dreams (Japan); possess the strength of ten men; transform into animals like a bat (South America and Mexico); or a wolf (Balkans). They are able to control the elements, control animals, mesmerize human beings. They do not get sick and they do not grow old and, more important, they do not die of natural causes. They can be ugly and caught in the process of decay, but more often appear beautiful, even perfect physically, which only adds to their allure. In parts of India it is believed crows, whose diet includes carrion, can be controlled by the Undead. In Ceylon, female vampires can survive entirely on elephant blood. In Iceland, vampires shape-shift into dragons, birds, wolves, bears, and horses.

Traditionally, their weaknesses are few but severely limiting: sunlight often burns them, as does fire; a wooden stake through the heart—especially made of hawthorn—will destroy them and cutting off the head for good measure isn't a bad idea; they are repelled by garlic and wolfsbane; they do not cast a shadow; they are terrified of mirrors because they cannot see their own image; they cannot cross running water; they cannot enter a dwelling unless invited. In China, a priest's prayer pasted to the forehead stops the undead cold. Vampires are usually compelled to drink blood, most of the time human, although sometimes they can survive on animal blood. But one thing is clear: vampires are the predators, we mere humans their prey.

Dr. Elizabeth Miller, scholar and chapter president of the Transylvanian Society of Dracula, is an expert on the novel that started a chain reaction. She has authored three nonfiction books about her favorite subject, the most recent *Dracula: Sense and Nonsense*. "First published in 1897, *Dracula*, by Irish author Bram Stoker, has never been out of print. It has

Top 10 Infamous Vampires

(courtesy of Dr. Jeanne K. Youngson, president, The Vampire Empire)

1. **Russia:** Upierczi–so bad it can dry the dew off plants
2. **Romania:** Nosferat–makes husbands impotent
3. **Bavaria:** Nachehrer–ties cows together by their tails
4. **Moravia:** Vampire–likes to skulk around naked
5. **Serbia:** Mulo–boils ladies he fancies in a huge vat
6. **Dalmatia:** Kuzlak–tosses pots and pans around the kitchen
7. **Albania:** Sampiro–dresses in a shroud and stilettos
8. **Crete:** Catacano–can't stop laughing
9. **Ashantiland:** Asanbosam–normal except he has books for feet
10. **Portugal:** Bruxsa–only enjoys the blood of children

Sire Cédric

Photo by Andy Julia

THE † SECTION ON VAMPIRES

Azazelle "Vampires make good fiction. People living a delusion are not ones I'd want to hang out with."

C.B. "I'm not one, and don't know any. But there are lots of people out there who are psychic vampires, and they drain your energy and live off your misery."

Cemetery Crow "I'm not one for sure. I've never met anyone who thought they were a vampire, but I've met people who hoped a vampire would come into their life. And I do know a lot of psychic vampires; their personality makes them very dependent on others. Psychic vampires are like children, or like wolves without pack leaders."

Jetgirl "I don't think I'm a vampire, though I look pretty damn good for 457 years! Vampires are so much a part of my life, I can't even consider not being interested in them. They are interested in me as well."

Johnny Formaldehyde "I don't believe in blood-drinking undead creatures. There are blood fetishists, which is something that doesn't appeal to me in the least, but to each his own."

Miss Lynx "Morons who think they are a vampire are the biggest bane of the goth subculture. Aside from people who think they look good in heavy makeup, and don't."

been reissued in over three hundred editions, including dozens in foreign languages. Though today the title character is universally recognized, the book did not become an instant success upon publication. Initial sales were moderate and reviews mixed. In fact, in his own day, Stoker was known much more widely as a theater manager than as a novelist.

"It was not until the 1920s, several years after Stoker's death, that the book became a hit. A successful stage production on Broadway in the 1920s, followed by the Universal Studio's highly successful *Dracula* (Bela Lugosi, 1931), made Dracula a household word. Since then, the novel has spawned hundreds of films and works of fiction, as well as a considerable output of scholarly studies. Today, Count Dracula is arguably the most widely recognized of all literary characters. The figure of Dracula has pervaded just about every aspect of Western culture: from cereal boxes to video games and comic books, from *Sesame Street* to ballets and musicals."

Elizabeth isn't sure if the author was fully aware of the archetypal energy he worked with. "Whether Stoker realized it or not, through his novel he tapped into hidden fears, anxieties, and desires, while creating a character who epitomizes the ostracized 'other'—be it cultural, racial or sexual. These factors help explain the continuing popularity of *Dracula* more than one hundred years after its publication."

Dracula's popularity has ebbed and flowed and then around 1976 surged into the modern psyche, mainly because of three novels published that year: *Salem's Lot* by Stephen King, *Hotel Transylvania* by Chelsea Quinn Yarbro, and *Interview With the Vampire* by Anne Rice. Since then, more and more vampire fiction and nonfiction books are in our collective face, and thousands of vampire movies have been made. Just about everyone has read *Dracula*. And whatever else they read, virtually all goths have read some vampire books, and they have strong author allegience.

Two intriguing books of documentation of vampire myths and stories were written by Alphonsus Joseph-Mary Augustus Montague Summers, a Protestant minister turned Catholic priest. He dressed like an eighteenth-century cleric, with the addition of a long, sweeping cape, and the silver-tipped cane he carried, depicting Leda being ravished by Zeus in the form of a swan. His hairstyle—one of his own design—is now fashionable with goths—two knots on the side of the head.

Summers wrote several other books of interest to goths: *History of Demonology and Witchcraft, The Gothic Quest: a History of the Gothic Novel, A*

Gothic Bibliography, and he also reprinted *The Discovery of Witches* by the infamous Matthew Hopkins, and undertook the first English translation of the fifteenth-century treatise on witchcraft, *Malleus Maleficarum.*

In much the same manner as goths, Summers saw himself as a refugee from another century, in his case, the eighteenth. He chronicled not so much legends and mythology, but what he saw as the terrifying reality of vampires. He wrote a pair of dense tomes on the vampire in Gothic literary style: *The Vampire in Europe* (1929), and the massive *The Vampire: His Kith and Kin* (1928). Both books are long out of print but can still be found through antiquarian bookshops. Summers's work, and that of the French seventeenth-century priest Dom Augustin Calmet who came before him and which he used as source material, are the authors upon whom modern vampire scholars base most of their ideas.

In her book *Piercing the Darkness,* Katherine Ramsland delved into the vampire subculture and has this to say about vampires and goths: "I found that many goths resented being associated with vampires, and rightly so. They have their own identity, but there is an overlap in fashion, the desire for connections to the riches of darkness, and often in poetry and music. Some goths see the mythological vampire as an icon of darkness and mystery, but don't identify themselves as vampires, whereas people in the vampire subculture may adopt goth fashion and music—perhaps even some of that perspective—but they don't accept the more passive, wraithlike qualities of goth culture. They do mingle at parties, but the pure types in each subculture tend not to want to be identified as belonging to the other. Yet there are no clear-cut definitions for members of either."

A few of *The † Section* see themselves as vampires, or possible vampires. Several know people who consider themselves vampires, or are at least into drinking blood or blood sports. And while almost all of *The † Section* love vampries, most don't believe the traditional vampire exists in reality, although many have encountered what is known as psychic vampires—people who drain another person's energy. But you don't have to be goth to have met a psychic vampire!

vampires unlimited

Modern vampires keep creating more of their kind, and the spawn have taken strange forms of late: Count Chocula cereal, Mexico's Vampiro brand tomato-based vegetable juice, New Orleans's Vampire Hot Sauce

Vena Cava "If I knew anyone who was a vampire I'd hound them constantly to bring me across. I keep a mirror in my purse for testing purposes."

Taoist "I'm interested in vampires as a myth; they embody a lot of the things that goth is all about. Beauty, romanticism in death, and all that."

VampirMike "I'm realistic. I can dream I'm a vampire but I can't be one. I live like a vampire and it's a lifestyle. If I thought I was really a vampire, the devil would have me and I'd kill people like a Satanist. I'm normal, and I know the difference between reality and dreams."

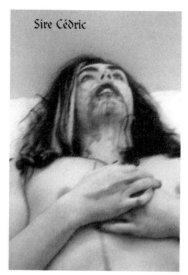

Sire Cédric

Photo by Andy Julia

(from Little Cajun Outpost). The United States has Elvira (see Chapter 11), and in Brazil LizVamp (daughter of horror movie genre's Coffin Joe) is that country's vampire queen—she was even the poster girl of the 2002 blood bank drive.

In the Western world, all vampires seem to stem from the old-school tradition that brought us Vlad Tepesh, aka, Vlad the Impaler, a fifteenth-century Transylvanian prince and *viviode* (warlord) who became one of the inspirations for Stoker's *Dracula*. That tradition is part of medieval class structure, and it was the aristocracy that became vampire, the rest of the population their victims.

The first piece of short vampire fiction in English was based on a page and a half written in 1819 at the seashore by the infamous poet Lord George Noel Gordon Byron. His personal physician John Polidori lifted the snippet Byron tossed out and finished the tale, creating the story "The Vampire," about a European aristocrat who seduces and murders, vampire-style, the sister of his traveling companion, for the sheer pleasure of it. Rumor has it that Polidori based his decadant vampire on Lord Byron!

The first vampire novel in English was the nearly 1,000-page tome *Varney the Vampire, or The Feast of Blood*, probably penned by Thomas Preskett Prest (author of *Sweeney Todd, the Demon Barber of Fleet Street*, and other macabre works), but possibly Malcolm James Rymer (authorship in dispute). This penny dreadful appeared as weekly newspaper installments, and then was gathered together into a book in 1847, the year Bram Stoker was born. Sir Francis Varney, the major character, forever sealed the Western concept of the undead. He is a guilt-ridden vampire, an aristocrat by birth, who just can't stop himself from drinking the blood of voluptuous young virgins in their bedchambers. Eventually Sir Varney, unable to bear the emotional pain any longer, tosses himself into fiery Mt. Vesuvius, ending his unnatural existence, and the three quarters of a million-word novel.

The French excelled at vampire stories. Charles Nodier, who is interred in Paris's famous Cimetière du Père Lachaise (see Chapter 10), wrote several. Guy de Maupassant—considered the best French short story writer—penned "The Horla" in 1887, a tale told in classic diary format of a protagonist stalked by a malevolent energy that actualizes and drives him insane. De Maupassant wrote this story six years before he died in an asylum from syphilis, where he was placed after a suicide attempt. Charles Baudelaire (see Chapter 11) wrote the banned poems "Le Vampire" and "Les Métamorphoses du Vampire."

One short story of note is "Carmilla, The Female Vampire," a soft lesbian vampire tale written by Irishman Joseph Sheridan le Fanu in 1872. It is entirely possible that this story is loosely based on the life of Countess Erzsebet Bathory, a distant cousin of Vlad Dracula, who lived in Hungary in the seventeenth-century and became known as "the Female Dracula."

the blood countess

Erzsebet Bathory had a normal aristocratic upbringing. But she was a problem child, given to fits of rage and violence, and loved to torture small animals and insects. At fifteen, she married Count Ferenc Nadasdy, who spent most of his time away from home. Countess Bathory had a couple of cohorts, including her servant Dorka, thought to be a witch, who also enjoyed sadism as her main source of entertainment. Over the years, the Countess fell into the practice of torturing her servant girls by pressing red-hot keys or coins into their hands, and burning their faces with a hot iron fireplace poker. She stuck needles into the flesh beneath the fingernails. Once, she forced open a maid's mouth until the flesh tore. In winter, she had girls play naked in the snow, dousing them with water until ice formed and they died of hypothermia. In summer, she coated their bodies with honey and left them outdoors for twenty-four hours to suffer insect bites and stings.

Then the Countess, who had always been beautiful and used that power, began to age. One fateful day she slapped the girl who had been brushing her hair not to her liking. A cut in the girl's lip produced blood, which splattered onto Erzsebet's face. She rubbed the blood into her skin, and tasted it. "You look younger," Dorka cried. The Countess gazed into a mirror and said, "It's a miracle."

Reenacting this miracle resulted in incredible suffering. The Countess beat and tortured servant girls until they bled, washing in their blood to renew her youth, which became a daily requirement. Eventually she left the castle for Vienna and there had built by a German clockmaker a mechanized precursor of the iron maiden, which she called the iron virgin. She decorated her life-sized sarcophagus with painted blue eyes, real human teeth, and hair. The suspended vertical contraption opened like a mummy case. Victims were placed within, and the door that contained spikes was shut, forcing the spikes into the body, which bled into a tub as the girl died a painful and prolonged death. The street in Vienna where so many girls died at the Countess's hands is now known as Blood Alley.

As signs of aging increased, Countess Bathory determined that she needed the superior blood of virgins of noble birth to rejuvenate her. She began biting, then killing, young girls unwittingly sent to her by their families for service among royalty. Rumors of the disappearances of the wealthy reached the ears of the Hungarian emperor, who sent a committee to Castle Bathory to investigate. They discovered a detailed diary of names and dates, and 650 graves. A trial ensued; court records still exist. Because of her high station, the Countess could not be executed. Instead, she was walled up in the tower of her castle, food and water slipped through an opening. She survived for three years in solitary confinement, never seeing the sun, not speaking to anyone or hearing a sound from the outside world. After her death, and until this day, locals believe she rises from her grave, seeking the blood of young virgins.

la Comtesse du Sang de France

France had its own version of a blood countess, who lived in the Château de Deux-Forts in the twelfth century. *La Comtesse* found a red spot on her belly that her physician deemed to be leprosy. She didn't like his diagnosis and threats led the medical man to prescribe bathing in fresh human blood.

This she did, murdering children for their vitae, until the court at Auvergne put a stop to it. The doctor was hanged, and the Comtesse drawn and quartered. A stone cross stands today, called *la Croix de Mal Mort* (the Cross of the Female Death).

peter Kürten, the vampire of Düsseldorf

There are many "real-life vampires" in history, some of whom have been fictionalized in books, plays, and movies. One that stands out is Germany's vampire of Düsseldorf. The highlights of his story are told by Euro-horror specialist Marcelle Perks, who is writing a book on this killer.

"Peter Kürten, the vampire of Düsseldorf (1883–1932), was born into a violent and impoverished family of thirteen children that lived in one room. His alcoholic father committed incest with his sister. Kürten began at the age of nine to cut the heads off swans to drink their blood. Around this time, an older man introduced him to masturbation, and dog torture. By the age of ten he drowned a school friend in the River Rhine. During his teenage years he was jailed repeatedly for petty crimes (stealing food or clothes), and, while serving a two-year sentence, whiled away the hours fantasizing about killing hundreds of people. Later he confessed: 'I derived the sort of pleasure from these visions that other people would get from thinking about a naked woman.' He even broke prison rules to get himself placed into solitary confinement in order to indulge in these fantasies.

"On May twenty-fifth, 1913, eight-year-old Christine Klein was found raped with her throat cut. Later Kürten admitted, 'In a room above an inn at Köln-Mulheim, I discovered a child asleep. Her head was facing the window. I seized it with my left hand and strangled her for about a minute and a half.' Then he cut her throat. The whole thing took just three minutes.

"His murderous career was temporarily curtailed when he was imprisoned for desertion during World War One. In 1921 he was released and attempted to change. In 1925 he became a trade unionist and married an older prostitute. Whilst cultivating a respectable image (he was always meticulous and neat), he secretly murdered lovers, prostitutes, and strangers. Unlike most serial killers, he would murder anyone: men, women, children, and animals.

"By 1929 Düsseldorf was in an uproar and the idea of a real-life vampire had taken hold of the populous. Unemployed Maria Budlick arrived in the city in May 1930 to find work and was initially accosted by a man who tried to waylay her. Another man intervened—ironically, he was Peter Kürten. They had a sandwich at his house, and on the way to a hostel he put a hand to her throat and demanded sex. She consented, and he allowed her to go free. Maria did not contact the police, but described the incident in a letter, which was misdelivered and opened by someone who informed the police. Later, Maria unwillingly led police to the outside of number seventy-one, Mettmannerstrasse.

"When Kürten found out about this, he took his wife out for a meal and confessed everything. Worried about being destitute in her old age, Frau Kürten suggested they commit suicide together. Kürten advised her to report him to the police so she could claim the reward. His loyalty towards his wife confounded everyone who was involved in his capture.

"Kürten was tried for nine murders and seven attempted murders, but he confessed, in excruciating detail, to sixty-eight crimes. Suave and so-phisticated in court, he remained calm, despite being on display in a shoulder-high cage surrounded by [evidence such as] his murder tools and victims' body parts.

"In July 1932 his death sentence was carried out by guillotine. His last words were: 'Tell me, after my head has been chopped off, will I still be able to hear, at least for a moment, the sound of my own blood gushing from the stump on my neck? That would be the pleasure to end all pleasures.' "

the Vampire of foster, Rhode Island

New England in the eighteenth and nineteenth centuries was a hotbed of vampiric activity. For example, in 1827, nineteen-year-old Nancy Young died of consumption in Foster, Rhode Island. Her father, Captain Levi Young, was a religious man. When one by one his remaining children became ill, rumors sprouted throughout the town that Nancy must be a vampire, returning from the dead to infect the living. As is the custom in almost all vampire legends, the undead prefer to prey upon their relatives first.

Captain Young apparently believed the rumors and felt there was only one course of action that made sense. Two months after her death, he invited the neighbors to gather at the cemetery while Nancy's body was exhumed and burned on a wooden pyre. The remaining Young family inhaled the fumes, in the belief that this would cure the sickness that plagued their line. Sadly, it did not.

The story of Nancy Young is one of a dozen vampire tales that come out of New England, eleven of which involve tuberculosis, a disease that ran rampant between the eighteenth and nineteenth centuries. In the early 1990s, Paul S. Sledzik and Nicholas Bellantoni wrote a paper for *The American Journal of Physical Anthropology* (No. 94) reprinted on the Internet, discussing what was found when the remains of twenty-nine individuals in Walton Cemetery were exhumed, a rural farm family burial ground in Griswold, Connecticut, used for burials between 1690 and 1750. The remains of one complete skeleton of a male in his fifties indicated a severe case of pulmonary tuberculosis. The other interesting thing about his bones is that they had been rearranged, the skull and femora in a "skull and crossbones" position on top of the ribs and vertebrae. The authors discuss the usual method of dispatching a corpse thought to be a vampire in early New England, which involved destroying the heart. "In this case, taphonomically, the physical arrangement of the skeletal remains in the grave indicates that no soft tissue had been present at the time of rearrangement; no heart remained in the body. We hypothesize that, in the absence of a heart to be burned, the apotropaic remedy was to place the bones in a 'skull and crossbones' arrangement. In support of this hypothesis, we note that decapitation was a common European method of dispatching a dead vampire, and that the Celts and Neolithic Egyptians were known to separate the head from the body, supposedly to prevent the dead from doing harm.[Barber, 1988]."

The world is full of real-life vampires, and one site, Shroudeater, run by Amsterdam vampire expert Rob Brautigam, documents real-life and mythological encounters with vampires from around the world.

Many publications exist that focus on the vampire. One, out of Glasgow, Scotland, with a large goth readership, is *Bite Me*. Most of the models used in the publication dress goth.

Model Donna Ricci (modeled for death on the *Sandman* cover)
Copyright by Arlene Russo

Arlene Russo, publisher and editor of *Bite Me*, says that the centenary of Stoker's *Dracula* (1997) changed her life. "I traveled to the world's biggest *Dracula* convention, in Los Angeles, and met a host of interesting characters, including actress Ingrid Pitt and other Hammer film stars, and also the son of Bela Lugosi. It was there I decided my mission was to come back home and produce a vampire magazine, uniting fans from around the world. Someone suggested I apply for a grant and I thought 'What chance have I got, there's nothing to lose.' I received a woman's grant so my humble fanzine was forced to become a magazine. *Bite Me* launched July 1999 at a cinema in Glasgow, with a special screening of *Blade*. The Scottish news covered it!"

Since then, Arlene has "traveled to Transylvania on several occasions. Got stranded in a forest there during a blizzard. That was both scary and exciting!"

frankenstein, or the modern prometheus

One summer in 1816, the British poets Percy Bysshe Shelley, Lord Byron, Shelley's lover Mary Wollstonecraft (Shelley was married at the time to someone else), her half-sister Claire Clairmont, and Byron's personal physician, John Polidori, took a little vacation to Geneva. Mary had met Percy when she was just fifteen, and fell in love. Uncharacteristic of girls

Gollum
Artwork by Vincent Marcone

of their day, Mary and Claire had run off to Europe several times with Shelley.

It was a warm but rainy evening, keeping the party indoors. Despite plenty of laudanum—a tincture of diluted opium—the vacationers became a bit bored. Lord Byron challenged them all to write a ghost story over the weekend. Byron himself produced a fragment, later completed and published by Polidori under his own name. Shelley produced nothing much. But Mary Wollstonecraft had a dream, one that became the basis of the novel *Frankenstein*. A wonderful depiction of the weekend's events has been created by Ken Russell in his film *Gothic*.

In her novel, unlike in most of the film versions of the book, Mary's creature is a pathetic being. Dr. Victor Frankenstein fashioned the creature from the flesh of recently executed criminals dug up by grave robbers—a common practice then, when doctors needed corpses for medical experiments. His creation is physically hideous but sentient, possessing mixed morality. It is driven by instincts and emotions beyond its control, often fueled by the rejection it experiences from human beings who cannot tolerate being in the presence of something so primitive and hideous, and composed of the body parts of the dead. There are many touching scenes in the novel that show this being, caught between intelligence and emotion, struggling to take the high road, yet crushed again and again by its baser instincts until it commits murder.

That same year, Shelley's wife Harriet Westbrook committed suicide by drowning, and the poet married Mary, then twenty-one years old, and achieving a modicum of fame herself with the publication of *Frankenstein*.

But life was far from blissful for Mary and her romantic poet husband. The young child of Claire and Lord Byron died of typhus in a convent. Mary's other half-sister Fanny Imlay committed suicide. Two of Mary's children died in Italy. After she gave birth to their only surviving child—also named Percy—the nuclear family moved to Italy. One fateful day in 1822, Percy Shelley went fishing with two companions. An unexpected storm capsized the boat and all three drowned. Ten days later Lord Byron, with Capt. Edward Trelawny—a fan of Shelley's who had only met him six months before—tried to retrieve the body, which had washed up on the beach at Massa, only to discover that quarantine regulations were in effect. Trelawny buried Shelley in the sand but soon after exhumed his body and burned it in a portable crematorium he had built for that purpose. During the cremation, the body burst open, exposing the heart. Trelawny grabbed the smoldering organ, scorching his hands in the process. Naturally Mary Shelley wanted her husband's heart, and eventually Trelawny gave it up. But he took the ashes to Rome and purchased adjoining cemetery plots, one for the poet, and one for himself!

Mary Wollstonecraft Shelley died in 1851 at the age of fifty-three of a brain tumor.

My Mummy
Artwork by Vincent Marcone

lycanthrophy

In the first century A.D., the Roman poet Virgil wrote of a sorcerer who took poisonous herbs to turn himself into a werewolf. The *wer* part of *werewolf* comes from the Old English word meaning *man*.

In the mythology of many lands, there seems to be two types of werewolves. Voluntary werewolves were considered to be people who made a pact with the devil. Involuntary werewolves were those whose actions inadvertently caused a nasty transformation. For instance, in Sicily, a child born during a new moon would surely grow up to be an involuntary werewolf. In Germany, folktales told of a mountain brook where the water turned one into a werewolf. In Serbia, those who drank water from a wolf's footprint would turn. In Greece, epileptics were thought to be werewolves. And in Armenia, an adulterous woman would be visited by the devil, who would fornicate with her, then give her a wolf's skin to wear for seven years, after which she could return to human form.

The last British wolf died in 1743. They managed to survive in Ireland until 1773. Few wolves remain in Europe today, and in places like Italy, only about 250 have survived, forced to give up their instinctual pack hunting because of encroaching civilization. Most European countries consider wolves an endangered species. In Norway it is illegal to kill a wolf, unless a farmer is protecting livestock. The organization Grupo Lobo, founded in Spain and Portugal in 1985, protects the wolves along their border. Germany has a strong wolf conservation group, created when the wolves began returning.

Today's European wolf, on the edge of extinction, is the descendant of

Willow
Artwork by Vincent Marcone

the wolves on which the medieval werewolf legends are based. European wolves that existed up to the 1700s and 1800s were not the small, timid, doglike creatures we see today, but, according to reports, were larger, with more hair, and far more fierce. They lived in the wilderness and were not so intimidated by the smaller populations of human beings dwelling on the continent then.

Guy Endore's tour de force novel *The Werewolf of Paris* is one of the most intriguing werewolf books to be published, alive with Gallic manners and mores of the nineteenth century. Endore based his book on newspaper accounts of *le loup-garou* Sergeant Bertrand, as recorded by Sabine Baring-Gould in his 1865 *Book of Werewolves*. The actual events took place in 1848, in the cemeteries of Paris, where at night graves were rifled. Baring-Gould writes: "The deeds were not those of medical students, for the bodies had not been carried off, but were found lying about the tombs in fragments." The initial thinking was that a wolf had done this, but human footprints belied that idea. Close watch was kept at the cemeteries and the following year a trap was sprung, setting off a gun. Guards rushed to the scene, in time to watch, "a dark figure in a military mantle leap the wall, and disappear in the gloom." Blood and the fragment of a blue cloth were found, and Bertrand was eventually tracked down. Endore fictionalizes the accounts.

ghouls

It is in a work dating from at least the tenth century—*The Book of the Thousand Nights and One Night*—where ghouls first surfaced in daylight. The late Brian McNaughton told us, "The ghoul derives from their [Arabic] folklore as 'a spirit or demon that haunts graveyards and feeds on the dead.'"

The ghouls featured in the Arabic classic are all lusty flesh-and-blood creatures. One story is of a wife who only realizes her husband is a ghoul when she finds a pile of severed heads he's stashed away. In another tale, a husband is cuckolded by a ghoul, who lures his young bride away from the marital bed for midnight trysts.

Brian McNaughton's novelette *The Throne of Bones*—which won both the World Fantasy Award and the International Horror Guild award—chronicals the antics of a multigenerational family of ghouls. Brian said about his seminal work, "My own ghouls are former humans who have been transformed into ghouls either by contagion, genetic predisposition, or morbid preoccupations—depending on which of my fictional experts you believe. They are somewhat more than human in that they have the ability to recall the memories and even mimic the personae of the people they eat."

Brian believed that "families with dark secrets have long been a staple of Gothic fiction. What darker secret can you have than that Grandpa was a ghoul?"

zombies

Haiti is the home country of zombies. A voodoo *bokor* (practitioner of black magic or petro voodoo—usually a male) places a spell on a human being, accompanied by a poisonous potion that brings about a state that imitates death in the imbiber. For all intents and purposes, the zombified person is dead, and frequently buried in a shallow grave, or aboveground. Three days later the person is "resurrected" in a state of walking catatonia and traditionally used as slave labor on a plantation. The will of the human being has been stolen, through poison.

White Zombie made in 1932 and directed by Victor Halperin, was one of the first movies about zombies. This classic stars Bela Lugosi as the overseer of a sugar mill who turns his workers into zombies. It set up the link between management control and labor, and formed the concept of the zombie. *Revolt of the Zombies*, by the same director, made in 1936, is about zombified Cambodian soldiers. A third early zombie movie, also from 1936 and directed by Michael Curtiz, is *The Walking Dead*. But Pittsburgh, Pennsylvania filmmaker George Romero did more for zombies than anyone on the planet. His classic horror trilogy *Night of the Living Dead, Dawn of the Dead*, and *Day of the Dead* took an old monster and revived it for a

HOW TO MAKE A ZOMBIE

1 shot of light rum
¼ shot Cream de almond
1 shot Sweet and sour
    hot Triple sec
1–2 shots orange juice (you can use
    other fruit juices or combos)
1 shot rum over 100 proof

Take a small sip of the rum and put the shot glass of rum aside. Shake the rest of these ingredients together with some ice slivers. Use a strainer and pour into a tall glass filled with ice cubes–Zombies have a low body temp, so these babies should be cold! Gently pour the rest of that mega proof rum into the tall glass–it will just rest there quietly at the top, like the dead. If you're not afraid of #2 red dye, add a cherry. Drink this, look in the mirror, and voilá! You will see a zombie.

new audience, and created a mythology in the United States. Suddenly, the traditional Haitian poisonous brew was irrelevant. Now, microbes from outer space, or . . . something . . . infected the dead, bringing them back to life. And the dead were hungry. Their diet: living flesh.

Author and explorer Wade Davis, who has degrees in anthropology and biology and a PhD in ethnobotany, wrote two definitive books on Haitian zombies, *The Ethnobiology of the Haitian Zombie,* and in 1986 the bestselling *The Serpent and the Rainbow.* In 1988 Wes Craven directed a film based on the latter, a highly sensationalized version of Davis's experiences in Haiti.

A pair of researchers who wrote a paper for the international medical journal *The Lancet* studied three Haitian zombies—identified as such by family and neighbors—and concluded that one suffered catatonic schizophrenia, which made him mute and immobile, another brain damage and epilepsy possibly owed to oxygen starvation of the brain, and the third suffered a severe learning disability, possibly owed to fetal-alcohol syndrome.

Whether or not actual zombies exist, the metaphorical state does. It can have a variety of interpretations, and Clive Barker nailed one when he was quoted in the introduction to the anthology set in Romero's zombie world *Book of the Dead* (1989), edited by John Skipp and Craig Spector. Clive said this: "Zombies are the liberal nightmare. Here you have the masses, whom you would love to love, appearing at your front door with their faces falling off; and you're trying to be as humane as you possibly can, but they are, after all, eating the cat.

tools of the supernatural trade

Psychic and other paranormal, supernatural, or preternatural experiences frequently require tools to allow the spirit world to connect to the physical one: Crystal balls, divination rods and pendulums, astrological charts, and tarot cards. Leilah Wendell of Westgate (see Chapter 9) designed a tarot deck called the Gothic Tarot, which she sells from her Web site.

talking boards

One intriguing prop whose divination powers are accessible by all is the talking board, commonly called a Ouija board.

It was 1848 when two sisters, Kate and Margaret Fox of Hydesville,

New York contacted the spirit of a dead peddler. This led to personal fame for the Fox girls, and the birth of spiritualism across North America and Europe that flourished through the remainder of the nineteenth century and into the twentieth. Special churches dedicated to contacting those on the "other side" sprang up, and inviting a medium to your party became all the rage.

At first this was done by way of talking tables. The medium and the participants would sit at a small table with fingers resting lightly on the edge, ask a question, and wait for the table to rotate, then for the legs to "knock" out the letters of the alphabet. That long and tiresome process led to the invention of the planchette, a piece of wood usually pointed at one end, with a small hole for a pencil that allowed for "automatic writing." But automatic writing was often difficult to read. Consequently, apparatus was dispensed with for a time and mental channeling via a tranced state came into vogue. Then—briefly—bulky, impossible contraptions with pulleys and wheels called "dial plates" appeared. Obvious drawback—they couldn't be easily transported.

The patent for a talking board was granted in 1891 in the United States to Elijah Bond, and assigned to two men from Baltimore. One of those men, Charles Kennard, called the board Ouija (*WE-ja*), after, he said, the Egyptian word for *good luck*—which it is not, but that's marketing for you. He set up Kennard Novelty Company and began manufacturing the boards. The first boards were made of solid wood, held together at the back by wooden braces. A hostile takeover in 1892 forced Kennard out of the business. His successor, William Fuld, changed the name to Ouija Novelty Company, which soon became the William Fuld Novelty Company, and boards were mass-produced and sold by the millions. Fuld claimed he had invented the Ouija board, calling it *Oui* (French for *yes*) and *Ja* (German for *yes*). His children sold the company to Parker Brothers in the 1960s. Parker Brothers initiated the slogan for the Ouija: "It's only a game—isn't it?"

Talking boards tap into the spirit realm, with letters that can spell out words, and the words *Yes* and *No,* and *Goodbye* for when the spirit has said enough. There are often pictures of a sun on one side, moon on the other, perhaps a pentagram, a witch, a cat. One early board features a swastika—the word derived from the Sanskrit meaning *so be it* or *amen.* (An ancient symbol used in many religions down the ages, the swastika has been associated with magic, but its use is possibly ruined forever thanks to Nazi Führer Adolf Hitler adopting it as the emblem of the Third Reich.)

Boards come with a wood or plastic planchette that sits on the surface, often a triangle with a small viewing window. Players rest the tips of their fingers on the planchette. A question is asked, and then the planchette mysteriously moves around the board. It will stop over Yes or No for simple answers, and over individual letters that must be spelled out to form words or sentences for more detailed responses. Boards are usually rectangular in shape, but there are round and square boards. In the early years, they were made of solid wood, but since have been constructed of plywood, glass, plastic, copper, and even cardboard.

Talking boards reflect their era. William Fuld's Ouija in the early 1900s was known as the Egyptian Luck Board. Other turn-of-the-century boards include: Mystifying Oracle; Throne Board; Wireless-Messenger from 1898 with instructions in seven languages on the back; I-D-O PSYCHO-I-D-O-GRAPH from 1919, a psycho-graphic board packed with images; Electric Mystifying Oracle, an early board with an Art Deco design; Psyche, and Mitche Manitou from the 1920s.

The 1930s and 1940s produced many fascinating boards that deviated from the original visual designs by adding unusual images and color. These include: Swami; Rajah; Mystic Soothsayer; and the Black Magic Talking Board with lettering in the shape of bones.

The boards made in the 1960s and 1970s reflect the hippie era: Guiding Star Board; Mystic Genii; Predicta; Finger of Fate; a round board the size of a grapefruit; Ziriya; the pre-AIDS Psychic Sex Board; a talking table board from England that attaches to a table—the fine print identifies it as psychic investigators' research equipment; ka-Bala, a roulette wheel–type board with a black die; a black seeing-eye ball with answers that could be had via alternative means such as tarot or astrology.

The 1980s saw Pen-G, a folding board that can also be used with a pendulum; and the Midas Board from Canada, packed with digits, good for picking lottery numbers.

Other great names and visuals are Witchery Board; Father Time; Weeja Queen; We-Ja Girl and Crystal Gazer—two boards from the same unidentified company; the Olympia ESP Board, which comes with a 45-vinyl record of *Music to Play ESP By*; Witchboard; Portals to the Beyond custom boards with a devil face on the board; Yogee; Wizard; Mystic Quiz, the smallest board for playing at 7" × 12"; Mystola, the board for romantic questions; Cardinal's Swami with its detailed Victorian circus-style alphabet; Asterial Ouija Board; Telepah; and Mystic Glow.

There are glow-in-the-dark boards, bilingual boards, tiny boards for dollhouses, and odd items like Ouija Board mouse pads, the 1940s Mystic Tray,

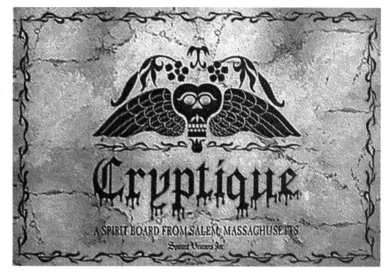

Courtesy of Cryptique, photo by Mary Taeger and Christian Day

and the Star Gazer Talking Board, the last two doubling as serving trays. And besides the mass-produced boards, there are many examples of hand-painted one-of-a-kind boards.

In 1999 Parker Brothers, which still owns the patent on the Ouija board, ceased production. But talking boards continue to be made. Recent boards include: A-51 Alien Contact Boards; a board with Aleister Crowley's leering face hand-painted on it; boards dedicated to the dark Greek goddess Circe; Gypsy Ouija featuring Pre-Raphaelite artist Frederick Sandy's painting of Medea; and the Creepy Necronomicon talking board with the history of H.P. Lovecraft's *Necronomicon* on the back.

Since 1994, Robert L. Murch has been collecting antique Ouija/talking/spirit boards, and has amassed over 300. "These boards," he says, "reflect very different attitudes as time passed. This has always fascinated me. These mysterious 'games' are much like chameleons, shifting and adapting to their surroundings. The artwork used to decorate these boards tells us very clearly what the attitude towards them was."

Robert, with Gary Halteman, took the history of boards into account and called on Christian Day and Deborah Norris—a New England artist—to help create Cryptique, a modern talking board designed around the Salem witch trials of 1692. "The board's background replicates a piece of bark found on a tree at Old Burial Hill in Marblehead, Massachusetts, final resting place of Wilmot Redd, the only Marblehead resident put to death in the Salem witch trials." (see Chapter 13). The seer [planchette] is shaped like a headstone, decorated with a winged skull reproduced from a grave at Old Burial Point in Salem. "Seeing firsthand the steady decline in quality and inspiration in spirit boards in the twenty-first century, Cryptique was born. We found that the atmosphere the board created was essential to how well it operated. People are greatly influenced by the artwork decorating the boards. Rather than follow the New Age trend to soften the spirit boards' image, we decided to create a board that recaptured its conjuring spirit. Cryptique was designed from the grave up. . . ."

The walls of the offices of Spirited Ventures, Inc. in Salem are adorned with original antique boards, and the séance scenes that appeared on magazines, sheet music, and book covers from the late 1800s to the 1940s. "How can one work if the spirit doesn't move them?" Robert asks, and in fact that is the company's theme: "Let the Spirit Move You."

Robert says, "Fifty percent of our customers consider themselves goth. We know this from the e-mails they send to our Web site. I'd also be willing to bet a fair amount that Cryptique owners at least wear black on a regular basis!" And while Robert and Gary are not goth, like a lot of mainstream people, they both love the imagery and atmosphere goth brings to the world. "Goth creates a mood of mystery that we tried very hard to re-create in Cryptique. We got the feeling early on that the goth community often gets left out of mainstream products even though many TV shows, movies, and music generally depict it. Cryptique gives goths a link to spirit boards. With its graveyard inspiration, goths have a choice. No one should have to use a glow-in-the-dark spirit board if they don't want to!"

URLs

The Epic of Gilgamesh, in digital form
www.gilgamesh.psnc.pl/

Elizabeth Miller, president of the Transylvanian Society of Dracula, Canadian Chapter
www.ucs.mun.ca/~emiller

Vampire movie list
www.netaxs.com/~elmo/vamp-mov.html

LizVamp
www.vampira.com.br/

Shroudeater
www.shroudeater.com/

Vincent Marcone
www.mypetskeleton.com/

Johnny Hollow
www.johnnyhollow.com/

Bite Me
www.bitememagazine.com/

Wolf howls at Wolf Country
www.wolfcountry.net/WolfSounds.html

The Throne of Bones
www.amazon.com/exec/obidos/tg/detail/-/0965813509/ref=ase_
sciencefictio0be/103-0909930-5470241?v=glance&s=books

Stories from the Thousand and One Nights
www.bartleby.com/16/

The Gothic Tarot from Westgate
www.westgatenecromantic.com/tarotintro.htm

Museum of Talking Boards
www.museumoftalkingboards.com/index.html

Antique Talking Boards
www.witchboards.net/index.html

Cryptique
www.cryptique.com

ESOTERICA

The religion of heresy

nourishing the wounded soul

Being in touch with spirituality is a way to absorb the traumas of living and the foreboding of impending demise. It also allows people to live in harmony with themselves, with others, and with the biosphere that sustains us. Unfortunately for many goths, institutionalized religions no longer cut it as a path to faith, hope, and charity. Many goths have abandoned the religion they were raised in and have embraced other spiritual paths, like Wicca.

Dark Wyccan runs a "dark Pagan" forum on the internet. He is a Wiccan, and a goth. He has been Pagan since 1984, and dedicated to Wicca since 1996. He defines Wicca in this way: "Wicca is a nature-based mystery religion. As a mystery religion it is not something one can learn in books or even from teachers—its mysteries must be learned through experience. Typically deity is perceived as a male and female (God and Goddess) that are anthropomorphic manifestations of the forces of nature. As with other aspects of the Craft one does not 'believe' in deity, one *knows* them, from experience."

He says Wicca is very different from organized religions. "It offers few specifics but rather provides suggestions and encouragement expecting the individual to do the work and find the way. Because of this, Wicca is not

Excerpt from "Underwoods"

"Under the wide and starry sky,
Dig the grave and let me lie.
Glad did I live and gladly die...."

—Robert Louis Stevenson

"The chakras are power points on your body that guide health, intuition, spirituality and sense of self. If you find some part of your life lacking, put a gemstone of that color on your chakra and meditate to activity-positive energy."

Base: Black–The basic foundation of who goths are physically, mentally, and spiritually is represented by the base chakra. Vitality and self-preservation vibrate on this level. Black absorbs negativity, promotes grounding and stability, which is why it is the favored color of witches.

Sacral/sexual: White or Gold–Our sexual chakra involves all our relationships, including romantic and creative growth. White can represent our innocence, in the frills of lace and the gentle texture of antique silk. Gold represents the solidity and growth of friendships and relationships and the prosperity of following our creative instincts.

Solar plexis: Blue–That gut instinct or intuition you have about things comes from your solar plexus. Learn how to tune into your personal power and trust it. The blue of sky and water represents the healing energy we have within ourselves.

Heart: Crimson–Who we are, our passions, what drives us emotionally is represented by the heart chakra. Crimson can represent our desire as well as our passion. It is the pulse of life, our very blood.

Throat: Green–How we communicate is represented by the throat chakra. Green can represent growth and creativity. A sip of absinthe might help to open up a closed throat chakra.

for everyone, and I do not mean that to sound elitist. We all have our needs. Some need more structure and direction than others."

Wicca is a modern religion, which began in the 1940s, according to Dark Wyccan. "It is considered a revival of ancient traditions. The ancient traditions are like a creation myth. . . . People today take the myth literally. They *want* to believe Wicca is an ancient religion, so many refuse to accept it as otherwise."

Wicca is often considered synonymous with the terms Pagan, neo-Pagan, New Age, Magic, and various others. Dark Wyccan defines them in this way: "Wicca is a Pagan religion. New Age is a general movement that draws upon various spiritual practices stressing self-improvement and spiritual well-being but is not in itself a religion, even though many confuse it as such. Magic is a practice each [practitioner] may use to make changes in their lives. Many 'kids' have a hard time telling the difference and just latch on to anything they can use.

"Wicca is more specifically a term used to describe a subset of religious witchcraft. Now depending on who you talk to, this subset of religious witchcraft could consist solely of what is known as the Gardnerian Tradition (one of the first modern forms of religious witchcraft), or any variation that derived through Gardnerian influences. As I said, witches rarely agree on much of anything!"

remembering the Inquisition

To Wiccans, the word *witch*, according to Dark Wyccan, "is generic and can mean anything from someone who just works natural magic, to the religious types that center around a goddess. It is used in so many contradictory ways today it is not even worth trying to offer a definition."

For the average person, the word *witch* comes loaded with evil, unsavory connotations. Back in the twelfth century, when social change began to threaten such community staples as marriage, Pope Innocent III organized a crusade against heretics—those who spoke against the Church or God. Included were those deemed to be witches, those who consorted with the devil.

In the thirteenth century, Pope Gregory IX, fearful that the Holy Roman emperor would take control of what came to be called the Inquisition, placed the inquisitors under the special jurisdiction of the papacy.

Punishment escalated. Freethinkers in Germany and France were targeted initially, but the rest of Europe soon followed.

Inquisitors set up camp for weeks or months, bringing charges against the locals and demanding that those guilty of heresy present themselves. Those charged had a month to confess, after which a trial took place. The right to asylum in the church did not apply to heretics. Two witnesses was considered proof of guilt.

In 1252, Pope Innocent IV officially sanctioned the use of torture. Sentences were pronounced in public, creating an auto-da-fé (public judgment and instant punishment). At the start of this period, punishments ranged from a pilgrimage or a fine to a public flogging. Wearing two tongues of red cloth sewn onto a garment marked those who made a false accusation. Penalties also included confiscation of property, or imprisonment. Life imprisonment was the limit of the inquisitors' powers of sentencing, which meant that when the person sentenced was handed over to civil authorities for the sentence to be carried out, it often resulted in their execution.

Tomás de Torquemada of the Spanish Inquisition is the most notorious grand inquisitor, personally responsible for extreme torture to accused heretics and the execution of thousands. His torture methods included nail chairs, the iron seat of a chair heated from below; an oral, rectal or vaginal wooden "pear" that was twisted open after insertion; and severing the body by means of tying horses to each limb and driving them until the limbs were torn from the torso. The iron maiden—a metal sarcophagus with spikes inside—comes from the Inquisition, as does the rack, a metal bed-like frame where the limbs are tied at the head and foot and stretched by rollers until they pop out of their joints. Some historians believe the Inquisition spanned five centuries, with an estimated nine million persons executed—most of them women—often through confessions elicited by extreme torture.

The Inquisition certainly set the stage for the witch trials in and around Salem, Massachusetts.

Two friends, nine-year-old Elisabeth Parris, and eleven-year-old Abigail Williams began throwing fits, falling into trances, and spontaneously screaming blasphemes. Physicians, stymied, declared them under the influence of Satan.

Third eye: Silver–Our mind, our unconscious and our spiritual thoughts are all contained in the third eye chakra. Silver can be the glint of steel of a knife needed to cut through to the truth of the matter.

Crown: Purple - What goth doesn't aspire to royalty and all the lushness it represents? Our crown chakra is our direct link to divinity, enlightenment, angels, and the spirit world that guides us.

Burnt Book
Photo by Marianne Werier

Wiccan Magickal Associations to Goth Colors

Black: Divination, banishing, absorbing negative energy, protection, binding

Red: Sexual love, lust, passion, fire, willpowers, courage, energy, strength, anger

Silver: The Goddess, spiritual truth, intuition, receptivity, psychic ability, stability, balance

The † Section Plan Their Funerals

biogoth "I'd like my body to go for research purposes. Once it's not useful anymore, cremated. My family and close friends can have a quiet ash-scattering ceremony. Nothing fancy."

Cemetery Crow "I'd like to die at home, in bed, or in a coffin, and be transported immediately to my crypt, no side trip to a morgue, no autopsy, no embalming. I'd like people to follow the hearse to the cemetery, witness the closing of the crypt door, but mostly I'd like them to come back in summer to see my exquisite coffin through the gatedoor. I'll leave a catering fund for future goths to picnic at my crypt."

Davis "A normal funeral but I'd be mummified everywhere but my face, and be enclosed in a pure hematite casket."

Deadly "A black casket with purple satin lining. Black and blue roses. Held at night so my friends wouldn't have to endure the sunlight. I'd be buried in my favorite dress, and with my favorite stuffed animal (Frankenbunny)—I've had her since I was born so it's only appropriate for her to go with me."

Billymod

"A floating funeral pyre on an ocean voyage to Avalon."

Community prayers and fasting didn't work. Nor did the witch cake, baked by John Indian and composed of rye meal and the urine of the afflicted girls, which when eaten was supposed to reveal the source of the problem.

The girls, under pressure, identified three women as witches. Tituba, the Parris's Carib Indian slave, Sarah Good, and Sarah Osborne. Tituba, under torture, confessed a conspiracy of witches were at work in Salem, but the other two declared their innocence.

Over the next weeks, more members of the community testified they had been under a spell, and a general "witch hunt" ensued. Frequently accused and arrested were people who disturbed the social order, especially women, some with criminal records, others oddballs, or merely widows and/or property owners.

Confessions were extracted through torture. Bridget Bishop was the first to be found guilty, and hanged in Salem in 1692. Accusations of witchcraft in New England escalated, and the Andover witch hunt began. To their credit, several people signed petitions on behalf of those they believed innocent, which must have been a risky thing to do. One man, Giles Corey, was pressed to death for refusing a trial.

The Superior Court, established in 1693, ended the convictions, but not before twenty people had been executed.

Perhaps the most monstrous thing about both the Inquisition and the Salem witch trials is the silencing of women, and the feminine energy (which has always been seen as dark, mysterious, almost supernatural) that women represented. Because women were the main victims, it is easy to imagine generations of mothers instructing their daughters, and grandmothers admonishing their grandchildren, to be submissive to authority. Just keep quiet! Women who expressed themselves, who stood out, became targets. Voicing opinions led to big trouble. Until recently, women did not legally enjoy the status of human being, but were property. Just seventy-five years ago women acquired the right to vote in enlightened lands, and there are many places left on this earth where women still are not given even basic human rights. This denegation of the feminine flies in the face of what goth is about. Goth supports the feminine in both women and men.

The culmination of centuries of fear only began to shatter in the twentieth century. No one who is oppressed comes out from under it without a measure of anger at the oppressor. Todays Wiccans are attempting to re-claim and revitalize the lost natural powers of medieval wisewomen and men who believed in the healing properties of nature. They are attracted to the pre-Christian belief—a belief shared by many peoples—that spirit dwells in all nature, and the gods and goddesses reflect humanity, not deities that imitate a feudal patriarchal being intent on dominion and sub-jugation over us all.

Dark Wyccan estimates that 70 percent of the goths he knows are Wic-can. Approximately 33 percent of *The † Section* identified their religion as Wicca, or a Pagan religion. Dark Wyccan believes "goths tend to be more open-minded and exploratory and so are more likely to be attracted to such a flexible and personal path as Wicca." He also says that goths tend to associate with dark deities, such as Hecate, Morrigan, Kali, or Lilith.

One Internet shop catering to Wiccans is Morticia's Morgue Emporium, run out of Houston for the last four years by Rebecca Riggs, who says, "Too often goth and Wiccan items seem to be considered cheap head shop and teenage-type stuff, and I wanted to offer a selection of both inex-pensive fun things, and some really nice quality and unusual items."

At forty, Rebecca is a self-proclaimed "elder goth, and I've always been Wiccan. Growing up [when the word *goth* wasn't yet in use], I was known by my friends as the 'creepy girl,' or as my husband likes to call me, 'Wednes-day's Child'—I was born on a Wednesday. I stopped going out in the sun when I was twelve and have the skin to show for it now. At Halloween—my favorite holiday—I always went as a witch, vampire, or gypsy."

Morticia's Morgue Emporium carries supplies for the modern Witch: altars, divination tools, talismans, books, jewelry, candles, parchment, and more. One of her bestselling items is a sterling-silver Celtic triquetra or triscele necklace, "an ancient triple goddess symbol, and used by the witches on the TV show *Charmed*. It's one of my personal favorites to wear." Rebecca says, "The majority of my customers are honest and fair-ly easy to deal with; perhaps they're afraid I'll put a curse on them if they aren't! [grin]"

a relationship with the Grim Reaper

One reality exists for all human beings—life ends in death. Many cul-tures believe that life is a preparation for death. The French have always viewed moments in life when the ego is forced to give way as "little

Jennie "I want to donate my body to researching mixed connective tissue dis-ease. My brain to a clinic in Switzerland that studies the neurological aspects of intersexuality. They'll have to bury me in absentia."

Madame X "When the day comes that I must die, and my remains are put away somewhere, still, should there be someone who once loved me that then is gone, I would like to rest beside them. 'At last I am wrapped in your embrace. The warmth of you, the cool of me Entwined...This final union, perfect and still Quiescent quiet enshrining me.' That's an excerpt from a song I wrote in 1999 entitled 'Decompassion.' "

Mistress Hades "Delicate black-edged note cards sent out. Maidens in gray muslin scattering red and white rose pedals before the <u>shillibere</u> (horse-drawn carriage), which is drawn by six rambunctious stallions, their heads adorned with black plumes, the proces-sion from Camden High Street to Highgate Cemetery. I would be wearing a full-length black latex hobble dress, my hair swept up in Victorian style with pearls, roses, and ostrich feathers. White makeup, black lips. Black carriages and hearses behind all this for friends and family. Finally, a New Orleans funeral-procession band, headed by a voodoo priestess."

Miss Lynx "I'd rather have a wake. My friends are depressed enough and having them in some dreary chapel would just do me in completely. [grin]"

Macabre Card 5
Image by Leilah Wendell

museumbitch "I must be cremated. Many peoples believe the soul is held back from journeying to the afterlife as long as the body continues to decompose. I'd like my dog's ashes added to mine (she's in my Pre-Raphaelite box in the living room)."

Vena Cava "I'd be cremated, have my ashes taken somewhere like Canada where there is still a wild wolf population, and scattered at night when they are howling, while 'Don't Fear the Reaper' by Blue Oyster Cult plays."

deaths," a process of building up a tolerance for ego dissolution in order to better face the Big Death. Losing love, losing a job, losing health, experiencing rejection, these are all examples of "little deaths," when we feel as if some part of us is dying.

From the moment we are born, unconsciously we retain the knowledge of coming from somewhere. Miraculously we formed out of a merged egg and a sperm. We grew and altered until we could sustain life on our own two feet, and if we are lucky and circumstances, environment, and genetics work together, we live life in an increasingly less dependent state until we reach an apex of independence. Our birth experience seems to resonate throughout our life to the grave.

Some of us are required to face our own death directly, with consciousness, which can be terrifying: aware of our departure even as we are leaving the body we have come to know so well, and the concepts of life that we cling to. Acknowledging death, as goths do, is a kind of preparation. It is part of accepting that death awaits us. Familiarity helps insure we do not go out in the same way we came in, and that the events of our lives bring us to a different place and provide some existential meaning as we climb in Charon's boat to voyage over the River Styx to whatever may await beyond.

It is a given that when we squarely face the knowledge of our demise, when it is understood on a soul level that we will die, life and all that it involves can no longer be taken for granted. Our existence and the termination of it must be viewed with the respect this bizarre existential situation deserves. The fragility of humans is that we are, apparently, the only species that knows it will one day die. And while we may not be the only life-forms to feel death as it is occurring, the knowledge of our mortality throughout a lifetime—if it is not denied out of sheer terror—can only make us more generous and more accepting of human foibles while we're still here. That knowledge allows us to live, and to die well.

URLs

Dark Pagan Forum
groups.yahoo.com/group/darkpaganforum/

Goth Witch Forum
groups.yahoo.com/group/gothwitch

Morticia's Morgue Emporium
www.morticiasmorgue.com/emporium.html

Memento Morty
www.brunching.com/morty.html

Go Goth (Promoting Gothic Lifestyle since the late twentieth century)
www.deadlysins.com/gogoth/

blood-dance.net (eclectic page, some cemeteries)
www.blood-dance.net/goth/

the Crow "I'd like to be buried in an old Celtic cemetery in Ireland."

Sky Claudette "I'd want all who knew and loved me to remember me as a decadent avant-garde spiritual debauched artistic soul, and at times jovial. Incense burning, red wine, red roses and baby's breath, fruits, and somber music. Exactly the way I am."

Slavel "I'd like my body bathed in acid so the flesh will be gone and only bone remaining. I want the bones to be painted chrome with purple accents and set up in a friend's house where I will be dressed in wigs and clothes and attend all future parties!"

VampirMike "I want to die in a lonely place where nobody can find me, and nobody knows where I am."

XjUsTcRuCifyX "I wrote a will (in one of my more paranoid moods) saying how I want to be buried I want sadness! I want to know that people are depressed and crying over losing me. I want to be mourned. I want black roses. I want to be buried in my hand-carved gothic art coffin with velvet and silk interior, wearing a beautiful gothic dress, with my favorite possessions—my stuffed animal, and a suicide letter my friend wrote to me."

The X chapter
Future tense

The future isn't over . . . yet!

knowing the unknown factions

Goth has always been a local phenomenon. Goths know the goths in their town, in their city, and not much else. It is bands that have given most goths a sense of a bigger world, with goths from other cultures out there, doing gothy things.

Goth exists around the world, and has been expanding its numbers at a frightening pace over the last few years in this, the third wave of a movement that somehow appeared out of nowhere in the mid-1970s in England and Germany. Its spread to countries one would not normally associate as goth havens indicates that something in goth touches a lot of people. With this expansion, goth is changing, as it must. A more universal concept of goth is evolving, but one that still holds onto individuality, identity, and the small community with darkly creative ideas and interests that have made goth what it is.

Many other countries outside the United States and England have a goth population, and some, like Germany, have an enormous goth population—this is as it should be, since Germany and England are where goth was born.

The Internet is a major venue for meeting goths from "elsewhere." And the Internet has plenty of free translation programs, so sending an e-

The Lost Goths
Copyright X-tra-X

mail in both your native tongue and in the language of the country you are sending to helps facilitate communication.

A few goths from around the world have generously offered a crow's-eye view of what goth is like in their homeland.

Australia by SUUANNE (one of *The † Section*)

"Gothic in Australia means many things to many different people, but perhaps an important factor in most perceptions is the isolation of our country. Obviously I can only put forward my own observations, but I feel that since the Internet has been widely in use, we have gained the inspiration and input from otherwise untouchable sources.

"UK gothic and German gothic were amazing-sounding movements that we heard little about but fantasized about greatly. Everyone else seemed more 'hardcore' and innovative and we had our well-tested styles and music. Of course, our music was drawn from both local and international sounds, but pre-Internet and pre-downloading there would have been a majority of goths who may not have heard the range we have access to now. This can also be said of goth fashion, and the broad range of resources and bases this can be built from.

"Personally, I had never even listened to such huge gothic names as Apoptygma Berzerk or VNV Nation before I was able to search the Net. I had never imagined there were such mind-blowing outfits as featured by Skin Two or Cyberdog. These discoveries led me to push the boundaries of my own sewing tendencies with my label ASYLUM Seven, and open a partnership shop UltraChamber in our hometown. The opportunity to show the population something new and beyond their day-to-day choices means that we can pass on the things that excite us to the boring masses.

"It's an obvious but important factor in Australian gothic that the Internet is particularly well-used by our genre. Even as far as living in a regional country town such as Ballarat, an hour from the closest major city, there are huge differences in day-to-day life. Wearing anything out of the norm (*normal* being jeans, windcheater, and runners) asks for abuse hurled from passing cars, blatant staring and sniggering . . . compared to larger cities where there are a greater number of goths, and they are seen more regularly. Regional towns find it hard to deal with 'freaks.'

"At the same time, there are of course wonderful people who appreciate and commend the effort we go to, and they wholeheartedly agree that there is no need to follow the herd. These people are most often the last ones you would expect, such as the old conservative grandmothers who tap you on the arm and say, 'You look lovely, dear! Isn't your hair a pretty color?', or a politician on rounds looking genuinely awestruck and commenting, 'Marvelous! Are you a local?'

"Australia is not as old in its history and creativity as most other countries, so I believe we are still in our formative years. We are only two hundred years' worth of events from white settlement, compared to five hundred, six hundred, seven hundred years in European countries. Our general population is still conservative and does not deal with change or new ideas in relation to genre and style. Of course, there are exceptions to this train of thought, and we goths are certainly the ones with the opportunity to push them."

Belgium by Roxane (member of the band the Dawn Visitors)

"Goth in Belgium is a mixture of nostalgic New Wave, Dark Wave, underground people and fetishists, superficial and empty/narrow-minded teenagers, and twenty-five-year-olds.

"The goth scene is very active and present throughout this country, but the difficulty is how to collaborate between the north and the south. So there are some famous places, clubs, festivals, gigs in the north where less and less bands from the south play. The south doesn't have the same organization, because people generally listen to Star Academy or rock 'n' roll, or techno music. Brussels, in between, offers some nice places.

"In the north there is the Steeple Chase in Waregem (every third Saturday of the month). In the south, the Cabaret Voltaire in Binche (with DJ Fred, first Friday of every month). In Brussels, the biggest program belongs to Le Fantastic Night, held most of the time at Magasin Four (www.lefantastique.net), but there is another good place to dance, which is Pilgrimage parties, at les Glacières, with DJ manu Ninety-three, DJ Gore, DJ Damien (www.pilgrimage.be).

"It's really difficult to define what goth means to us. You'll find many people in Belgium dressed in black with crazy hair and makeup, but they could listen to goth metal music, medieval music, industrial, Punk, Dark Wave, electro, gothic rock, Dark Beat . . . And all of them will tell you they are gothic!"

Canada by R351570R (a Toronto band and a group of goths)

"We write from the future, where a band of Toronto-based goths are attempting to revitalize a stagnant scene by infusion of new ideas and energy from an overcommercialized rave world. We have formed an underground movement called R351570R to attempt to bring both scenes to a new level of respect. We realize that most goth/industrial bars have very set playlists, and that the scene in general is aging. We also realized that there is a generation gap and cultural void currently with the mainstreaming of rave culture, and realized that this younger crowd, pining for the 'old days' when promoters threw themed events that attempted to create community and veritable escape through the use of seldom-heard music and deco. We also saw the evolution of Industrial Electronica in the form of Psychedelic Trance, a genre that we perceived to be more 'Cyber-Trance.'

"With these influences and markets, along with an imagery from the British Cybergoth scene, R351570R was born. I can share with you stories, pictures, reviews, and our market survey within the movement's manifesto (business plan). I've also included a review of one of our parties that Analog Pussy, the Israeli trance act, sent to their sixty-thousand-person mailing list and also published in a London rave/cybergoth magazine."

Review of R351570R by Jiga + Jinno of Israel's Analog Pussy

"Arriving to Toronto we were a bit overwhelmed seeing lots of mental cases in the streets. So many loonies in Toronto, we thought, one must wonder what the party would be like . . . the promoters explained there's a mental hospital in the center of town, so it must be the reason.

"Hmmm. after playing in their party we're still in doubts! That was one crazy event.

"Almost half of the crowd at the Reverb club were dressed with black vinyl and lace, had tattoos and colored hair. Are we at the right club? Are we supposed to play a cover song for Covenant or Bauhaus, is Sid Vicious alive?? But these creatures were dancing like naturally born trancers.

"The psy-trance scene is slowly growing in Toronto, explained Hillary and Clay from Resistor—the party promoters.

"They are practically importing the sound of trance to Toronto, 'converting' people to expand to other styles of music. The new cyber-goth music demonstrates electronic motives and more people open up to trance as well. But this sound gets its own unique interpretation in Toronto.

"Onstage, just before playing, there are few seconds of silence. eternal moments that seem like forever. At this time, you can tell what your gig will be like. You see their eyes. And their eyes were wide open, thrilled, examining—innocent in a way. It was a virgin initial experience, no unwritten code yet, not a habit. Only letting themselves go. You have to be brave to do that. For us this was getting back to our roots of trance. Where our body is taking over everyday consciousness. Only then can miracles happen.

"The promoters handed little alien dolls and alien candies to everyone, and we swear we saw there real aliens, too. That tall girl was, for sure!

"We thank Toronto for bringing us back to innocence."

France by Sire Cédric (one of *The † Section*)

"As a matter of fact, the goth population has been growing quite a bit in France lately, with the commercial success of bands such as Marilyn Manson, etc. but most mainstream people still have heavy prejudices against kids dressed in black. And prejudices that are, to me, perfectly justified (we still have a lot of grave desecrations and Satanist childish acts). Yet I think all that shall evolve with time. Goth sure has a place—and a role—in society. That's what I believe, and that's the reason why I write stories.

"Goth fashion has been growing quite a lot, too, in France these past three or four years. I go to Paris as often as I get the chance; the goth activity there is really great now. There are big parties and events and gigs every week, even a goth bar, Le Katabar, and we also have a pro-gothic magazine, *Elegy* magazine.

"Of course, goth arts are not taken seriously by mainstream businesses, but I feel hopeful. Things take time, that's all, and we are getting there slowly. That's also one of the reasons why I tell people that I am not goth, when they ask me what I am. If I told them I was goth, they would think I am just a kid listening to Marilyn Manson, see my point? So I just tell them I am an artist, that I write about love, and they accept my work as a good-though-weird art form."

France by Léa Silhol, editor at Oxymore Éditions in Montpelier, France, and publisher of the vampire magazine *Requiem*

"There are no goth writers in France besides Sire Cédric and myself—we both have a large goth readership. Sire Cédric writes vampire erotica.

My focus is more like the ancient 'colds' of the eighties. There are no major goth writers in France. Well, perhaps, Carthésian Land."

Germany by DJ Caluna (one of *The † Section*)

"The goth culture in Germany is multifaceted. We have the romantic, and they are very much into medieval themes, roleplaying, and listening to metal or darkwave musik with a big amount of medieval style in it, like Qntal and In Extremo. Then we have the eighties goths, who dress like Siouxsie and the Cure when they were young, and only listen to musik older than ten years. The electro fans like EBM [electronic body music], industrial and technoid sounds, and always argue with the eighties folk about how much techno can still be considered goth.

"We have a lot of nice music festivals. The biggest is the Wave und Gothic Trefeen in Leipzig, east Germany. I'm really looking forward to that. Then we have the Zillo Festival, Mera Luna Festival, and the Sonic Seducer Festival, all organized by the big magazines. We read magazines like *Zillo, Orkus, Sonic Seducer, Neurostyle,* and *Gothic.*

"We have problems, too, within the goth scene, with groups of neo-Nazis that try to infiltrate. That's bad and leads to conflicts."

Italy by the staff at *L'Erba della Strega* (Witch Grass) (a Web community and dark magazine)

"Our first gothic bands in Italy stopped being innovative and experimental in the middle of eighties. Unfortunately, in the last ten years just a few bands have been able to achieve popularity in our country and, occasionally, in the rest of Europe. Chants of Maldoror, Frozen Autumn, Vidi Aquam, Canaan, Kirlian Camera, Ataraxia, Burning Gates, Limbo . . . and others now have a lot of fans and perform concerts. Many organizations and individuals are trying to 'do something' (in the broadest meaning of the phrase) for the Italian gothic scene, with concerts and other musical events scheduled, artistic exhibitions, Web sites (Erbadellastrega, Ver Sacrum, Slowburn, Angelic), magazines (*Ascension Magazine, Ver Sacrum, Ritual*), retrospectives, clubs (Jungle in Rome, Siddharta in Florence, Transilvania Live in Milan), etc."

Italy by Paola (one of *The † Section*)

"First of all, I find the Italians really tolerant. I hear some real horror stories of American goths being laughed at or persecuted, but in Italy they don't automatically assume that a goth is also a rabbit-slashing Satanist, or a potential new Columbine murderer. Their view is admirably serene. This may be because most Italian goths tend to be middle-upper-class, all college students or thirty somethings with brilliant jobs, so the stigma of goth as white trash does not exist. Also, Italian goths are still Italians, so they are friendly, witty and love a laugh and the good things in life; I rarely saw dismal goths here. The Catholic imagery is closely linked to being goth: churches, cathedrals, saints, martyrs, etc., are the epitome of goth. This is a subject worth many PhD sociology papers and I don't feel qualified enough to delve more into it."

Peru by Reynaldo (one of *The † Section*)

"We in Peru who love goth music are only a few. We have just cassettes and a few CDs. We would love it if goths from around the world could help us. We are poor, and the gothic scene here in Lima is a very hidden underground. We would be happy to have promotional material, CDs, maybe even videos, anything. Please ask people to contact us. We would be very glad to have goths from around the world come and visit us, and stay with us in Peru."

The Netherlands by Nimue (one of *The † Section*)

Nimue says about goth in the Netherlands (where she was born and still visits):

"The goth scene in the Netherlands is terrific. Great. Unbelievable. Maybe the best one there is. There are so many goths in the Netherlands, and the goth scene is so big, free, relaxed, and beautiful. Most people are in the category of vampire/Wicca/Wednesday Addams goths. The way I would describe the goth scene in the Netherlands is: all a goth could wish for. Maybe I'm exaggerating, but that's just what I think. In general, people in the Netherlands respect the goth scene, simply because it's so big they can't deny its existence and its greatness."

50 Ft. Queenie "I may not be going out as much, or I just might; I refuse to be told I have to 'outgrow' something that still attracts me. I will always be eccentric, stubborn and intense."

Arantèle "Probably [I'll be goth], if it still suits my soul, and I believe it will."

biogoth "The 'me' of now could probably have a conversation with the 'me' of twenty years from now and find a lot of common ground. Poppy Z. Brite says, 'goth is a good place to grow old,' and I agree."

Deacon Syth "I'll be fifty years old with the eyeliner over the wrinkles, the PVC pants holding up the beer belly, telling my kids they don't appreciate the classics like Bauhaus, Ministry or Specimen."

Decaying Ivy "I'm sure people will ask about my strangeness, acting this way in old age. And after all, I may get bored of the color black, but I will always be gothic inside."

DJ Caluna "Still wearing black and melancholically looking back on the eighties and early nineties where life as a goth was still a thrill."

Jetgirl "I'll be sixty-six with tattoos and piercings and I still see myself as the same person. I like my clothes. I'll be

Ukraine by Vitality "Stranger" Fedun

Stranger represents all Ukranian gothic bands and is the only promoter of gothic music and subculture in the Ukraine.

"Ukrainian goth style is black clothes and silver, and the symbol of our trident, which you can see as the frontpiece of our Web site. It's difficult being goth here. Our society doesn't like the unknown, and thinks goths are Satanists.

"Our most gothic book is Remarque's *L'arc de Triomph,* and all his other books. To be honest, we think gothic is more a philosophy than vampyre stuff.

"Ukranian gothic music started here around 1988 when the bands Komu, Vnyz, and Skryabin appeared, playing sad/philosophical music with deep text. They just didn't know they were goths. . . .

"I don't know if goths here are different than goths elsewhere, but maybe are smarter. In Ukraine you're supposed to be smarter if you're goth, otherwise you're pop-flooded, with the tastes of the bubblegummers. To get goth music here is difficult; it's hard to save yourself from the flood of Britney Spears and related stuff, and from stupid metal—the two main tastes of youngsters in the Ukraine. There are no goth clubs here. We listen to CDs, which can take five or six months, a whole lifetime [wink] to get. There's no music market in the Ukraine."

Ukraine by Nimue (one of *The † Section*)

"Well, Ukraine has a very, *very* small scene. Plus it's different than in any other country. Most people are used to goth girls wearing vampire dresses and all that, but the ones in Ukraine just wear plain clothes. The only reason why they call themselves goth is because they like goth music. So it is really different."

the past impregnates the present, which births the future

A reviewer in the *Daily Telegraph,* a newspaper in England, commented on the goth culture as portrayed in two small-press books published there: "One finishes reading convinced that the main reason goth subculture hasn't been coopted by mass media is that it hasn't got much to say that wasn't said better 150 years ago."

In many ways, this reviewer is correct.

The world took a wrong turn in the 1800s. In Zen thinking, it's not *what* was done, but *how* it was done. The obsession to industrialize at all costs has ended up nearly destroying the planet with pollution, created weapons of mass annihilation, and has left the average person feeling ineffective, not to mention dehumanized. Technology is industry's bastard cousin. What we have been promised has not come to pass, and computers are a perfect example. Predictions in the 1980s—that computers would reduce the workload—were dead wrong. The opposite is in effect; computers have not only doubled the workload but have left us precious little free time, combined with a deep sense of being less connected to one another by the fleshy contact of the senses that nature intended, which helps keep us grounded.

Goth is a realm devoted to the deepest yearnings of the collective unconscious. It respects what has been traditionally called feminine values in both men and women, and traditionally those values have not been heard, to the detriment of us all. Goth espouses the beliefs of the Pre-Raphaelite Brotherhood—beauty, love, refinement, creativity. At the same time, it is sophisticated enough to be able to laugh at itself in this theater of the absurd we call life.

Goth culture remains relatively small, in many ways uncharted, experimental. It is not for everyone, and being goth requires a particular set of sensibilities. Goth is about process that does not get sacrificed to product. In the 1970s the frightening phrase became popular "the end justifies the means." Goths believe in process—allowing life to happen, in waiting to see where things will lead. This is an artistic approach to living life. And while goals are important, they are not the be-all and end-all to goths, who try to live a far better balance than what the mainstream culture suggests. Goth is all about acceptance of what the world-at-large rejects, but which, ironically, human beings desperately seem to need in order to both survive, and to survive with style and grace.

To the extent that a person has difficulty accepting death, they will also have a hard time accepting anyone or anything that personifies that dark goddess who beckons and draws us relentlessly into her realm. Goths are not afraid to *Dance Macabre* with skeletons, play grim fandango for real, and tango "to the end of love," as Leonard Cohen sang so poetically. Some people are afraid, and its natural that goths make them uncomfortable.

And while the happy, wealthy, ultra-consumer modern moguls who run the day are busily building and demolishing empires and acquiring

collecting my Social Security check in yards of black chiffon and a great hat!"

Johnny Formaldehyde "I see myself as still being goth, maybe more corporate goth, but I'll still hold my views, like my music, enjoy my art, and dress how I want when I can."

Krockmitaine "I'm an old goth. Been in since 1980, so I guess I'll be here for the next twenty years."

Madame X "I wouldn't know how else to be. Granny goth: I don't think I like that. I'll make sure there's a goth club around I can dance in...even if I have to build one myself."

museumbitch "Even more so! I expect to own my own home, then I can do even more gothy-type stuff without concern for a landlord, for example."

Sally "I don't know for sure, but I think I will never be normal."

Shekinah "You can take the girl out of the black but you can't take the black out of the girl. Perhaps more toned down. A classier type of goth. [smile]"

XjUsTcRuCifyX "I see myself as still being goth, and making a name for myself, turning around the 'all goths are druggie idiots' to 'wow, these people are very kool!'"

Gifts from the Dark Side

more and more to make life easier and easier—which too often seems to result in joylessness—goths continue to quietly live in a manner that is not of the world but yet they are in it.

One image works well to show goth in comparison to the madness surrounding it. Werner Herzog's exquisitely elegant film *Nosferatu the Vampyre* portrays the idyllic town of Bremer, overrun with rats carrying the plague, brought to its shores by a vampire. In one poignant scene, the character Lucy Harker (played by Isabelle Adjani) wanders through the town square crowded with citizens who have given way to insanity brought about by knowledge of their impending demise. Goth is the Lucy of the world, still sane, viewing the madness of the collective, unable to do much about it, but unable to ignore it either. Goths hear the proverbial fiddlers play while the city burns. When the emperor decides to go naked, goths refuse to pretend he's dressed. It's no wonder some people are uncomfortable around goths.

The nature of the mainstream is a hungry monster, a blob, eating all in its path, constantly trying to expand itself. It will likely never make space for goth in a major way; it's easier to try to swallow goth whole and spit out the bones, treating what it cannot truly digest with scorn. But perhaps it is a good thing in the long run that goth cannot be co-opted. The image of the crayfish on the tarot card the Moon could represent goth. The crayfish crawls up out of the murky depths onto the shore, and in the case of the card, it symbolizes a gift from the world of darkness to the world of light. But the home of the crayfish is *not* terra firma, so it can only leave the gift from the shadowy realm, then return from whence it came. Goth offers a gift by its very existence, but it cannot live well in the light. That's not the nature of goth, anymore than it is the nature of most people to live in the dark realms, where goth flourishes.

Goth brushes the collective consciousness like a ghostly spirit, representing values of another time which, had we maintained, could have moved us all a different way. Maybe in a more humane direction. One can only hope that this spectral contact makes a difference. Sometimes it doesn't take much. The last rose petal falling could alter the balance and topple the bush. At the very least, that petal decomposes and supports new life. And it makes a great sachet!

URLs

Australia
www.asylum7.net and ultrachamber@ultrachamber.com

Belgium
www.dawnvisitors.be.tf/

Canada
www.cyborganization.org

Chili (courtesy of Raven Ozz)
www.gothic.cl and ww.elbeso.cl

France
www.sirecedric.aewd.net/

Germany
www.nightmarezone.de

Israel
www.analog-pussy.com

Italy
www.erbadellastrega.it

Norway
www.gothamnights.com/Trond/

Peru
gothicinfo@yahoo.com

Philippines
www.subkulture.info

Russia
www.dark.gothic.ru/

Sweden
www.tordsandell.tripod.com/

Switzerland
www.sanctuary.ch

Ukraine
www.gothic.com.ua

museumbitch "Balance. Not every aspect of life/culture is sticky sweet, nor should it be."

Mylucretia "Goth lends the power to stand up and be heard."

Vena Cava "[Goth gives] permission to be more of an individual and increased openness to esoteric, religious and other ideas."

Sire Cédric "Goth already is a part of society, the dark and beautiful heart of night."

Thyssen "I think the goth scene is one of the most underestimated scenes ever. Goth will always be a part of [the overground scene], without being properly credited."

XjUsTcRuCifyX "We do what we love, and however that changes the world is whatever it does. We really add that flicker of insight and beauty and darkness to a very shallow society."

Calhoun "Goth offers a sense of mystery. We're viewed as the ones who are watching from afar and keeping all the dark aspects of life where they need to be. We're feeding and tending to the beast that others are too scared to tend to."

Nancy Kilpatrick is an award-winning author, known for her very dark fiction. She has published fourteen novels, plus five collections that incorporate some of her over 150 short stories. Her most recent short story (October 2004) is "Sleepless in Manhattan" in the Dark Horse anthology *Hellboy: Odder Jobs*. Besides a CD-ROM, she has also edited or co-edited eight anthologies, the most recent with Nancy Holder for Roc/NAL, tentative title *Outsiders: An Anthology of Misfits*. Two of her popular novel series are now being re-released: *Power of the Blood* (vampire) and *The Darker Passions* (erotic horror). She has also penned a stage play, a couple of radio scripts, three issues of the *VampErotica* comic series, and has written a considerable number of nonfiction articles. Nancy lives in lovely bilingual Montréal with her exquisite Bella la chatte noire, and travels the world with her companion, photographer Hugues Leblanc, ferreting out cemeteries, ossuaries, crypts, catacombs, mummies, and Danse Macabre artwork. Feel free to contact her directly via e-mail on her Web site, where she will continue to add to the information and ideas in this book: www.nancykilpatrick.com.